U.S. Power and the
Multinational Corporation

THE POLITICAL ECONOMY
OF INTERNATIONAL RELATIONS
SERIES
Edited by Benjamin J. Cohen

THE POLITICAL ECONOMY OF IMPERIALISM
by Benjamin J. Cohen

U.S. POWER AND THE MULTINATIONAL CORPORATION
The Political Economy of Foreign Direct Investment
by Robert Gilpin

POWER AND WEALTH
The Political Economy of International Power
by Klaus Knorr

THE CHARITY OF NATIONS
The Political Economy of Foreign Aid
by David Wall

FORTHCOMING

THE POLITICAL ECONOMY OF INTERNATIONAL
COMMUNIST RELATIONS *
by Franklyn D. Holzman

* Tentative book title

U.S. POWER AND THE MULTINATIONAL CORPORATION

The Political Economy of Foreign Direct Investment

ROBERT GILPIN

Basic Books, Inc., Publishers

NEW YORK

Library of Congress Cataloging in Publication Data

Gilpin, Robert, 1930–
    U. S. power and the multinational corporation.

    (The Political economy of international relations
series)
    Includes bibliographical references and index.
    1.   United States—Foreign economic relations.
2.   International business enterprises.   3.   International
economic relations.   4.   United States—Foreign relations.
I.   Title.
HF1455.G5   382.1'0973   75–7265
ISBN 0–465–08951–8

TO MY CHILDREN

Linda, Beth, and Robby

CONTENTS

TABLES AND CHARTS

PREFACE

Several of the basic ideas contained in this book first appeared in my report to the Senate Committee on Labor and Public Welfare entitled *The Multinational Corporation and the National Interest*. Throughout the work on this report I was encouraged and stimulated by my association with Benjamin Palumbo, then an assistant to Senator Harrison Williams (D–N.J.).

My greatest intellectual debt in the research and writing of this book is to Benjamin Cohen, the editor of the series of which this volume is a part. It is difficult to convey in words my appreciation to him for the time and effort he has given at critical points in the preparation of this book. With considerable patience and superb expository skill, he led me through the relevant economic literature and concepts. Needless to say, however, the responsibility for whatever shortcomings in economic analysis and understanding remain in the pages which follow are mine alone to bear. The teacher should not be held responsible for the shortcomings of his student.

The unencumbered time required to write this book was made possible by the generous leave policy of Princeton University and the beneficence of the Lehrman Institute of New York. In addition to its financial support, the latter institution made it possible for me to try out in preliminary form many of the ideas incorporated in this book. Through my participation in a series of seminars sponsored by the Institute, I benefited greatly from the intelligent criticism of a broad range of scholars and thoughtful individuals. I want to express here my appreciation to the Institute's founder, Lewis Lehrman, and its director, Nicholas Rizopoulos, for their support and for their foresight in establishing an attractive forum where scholarship and the practical issues of the day may be joined in intelligent and lively discourse.

I am further indebted to the Woodrow Wilson School and the Center of International Studies at Princeton University. I have enjoyed the support of and benefited from the facilities of both organizations. Special thanks are due to my secretary, Barbara Grindle, for her typing and general assistance in the preparation of the manuscript.

Lastly, I want to thank my wife, Jean, for her patient editing of the manuscript. The reader is indebted to her for whatever clarity and style the manuscript may have.

U.S. Power and the Multinational Corporation

INTRODUCTION:
THE NEED FOR A POLITICAL
ECONOMY OF THE
MULTINATIONAL CORPORATION

In her excellent study, *Sterling and British Policy,* Susan Strange points out that economists and political scientists write about international relations as if they were talking about entirely different sets of actors and activities.[1] In the contemporary age, when a petroleum boycott by militarily weak Arab states can upset the foreign policy of the world's most powerful nation and when private corporations possess assets far in excess of those of the vast majority of nation-states, students of international relations can no longer afford to ignore the interaction of economics and politics. There is an overwhelming need today for an awareness of the political economy of international relations.[2]

The broad purpose of this book is to further an understanding of the relationship between international economics and international politics. Through an examination of the so-called multinational corporation (MNC) and foreign investment, I shall show the reciprocal interaction of economics and politics in today's world. My view is that a proper understanding of economic and political phenomena requires an appreciation of the way in which economic and political factors interact in shaping international relations. Thus, in order to develop a theory of political economy, I shall analyze the multinational corporation and foreign investment from the general perspective of international relations and show the significance of foreign investment in the larger context of international politics.

By virtue of its emphasis on domestic and international politics in determining the nature of international economic relations in general and in explaining the phenomenal rise of the multinational corporation in particular, this book is in sharp contrast to the prevailing literature on the multinational corporation. It challenges the orthodox liberal emphasis on the autonomous evolution of an increasingly interdependent world economy whose major manifestation today is the multinational corporation. Furthermore, my study disagrees with the Marxist notion that American foreign policy and overseas expansion are simply instruments for fulfilling the needs of American corporate enterprise.[3] Instead, the argument of the present book is that the functioning and success of the multinational corporation and other so-called transnational actors are dependent upon particular patterns of political relations. Whether one is talking about seventeenth-century merchant adventurers, nineteenth-century finance capitalists, or twentieth-century multinational corporations, transnational actors have been able to play an important role in world affairs because it has been in the interest of the predominant or hegemonic powers for them to do so. As political circumstances have changed owing to the rise and decline of hegemonies or to political realignments in the hegemonic power itself, transnational processes have also been altered or have ceased altogether.

Although both professional economists and political scientists have written on the multinational corporation from the perspective of their respective disciplines, there has been no discussion of the subject that sufficiently integrates its economic and political aspects. This dual neglect arises out of the fact that economists do not really believe in power; political scientists, for their part, do not really believe in markets. Economists have ignored the political context and the necessary political conditions underlying foreign direct investment and the rise of the multinational corporation. Political scientists, on the other hand, have generally neglected the economic theories which explain the sufficient economic conditions for foreign direct investment both by American corporations and by those of other countries. There does not really exist, in other words, a literature devoted to the *political economy* of foreign direct investment.

Economic and technical factors alone are undoubtedly sufficient to explain the level and types of foreign investment made by relatively small capitalist countries such as Switzerland and The Netherlands. But they are insufficient to explain the deep penetration of so many foreign economies by British investors in the nineteenth century and by American multinational corporations in the twentieth. Nor do these economic factors alone explain the favorable terms on which this investment has taken place. The accessibility of foreign economies to foreign investors and the distribution of benefits are highly dependent upon domestic and international political factors.

The necessary condition for the rapid growth of multinational corporations over the past several decades has been the steady emergence of the United States as the world's dominant power. This process began in the latter part of the nineteenth century, when American industry began to supercede its European rivals. As American power grew, the United States created an increasingly large sphere of influence. This expansionism reached its zenith in the decades after World War II: Following its victory in the war and in response to the Soviet challenge, the

United States created in its own security interests the pattern of relations among the non-Communist countries within which American multinational corporations have flourished.

The sufficient conditions for the rise of the multinational corporation have been economic and technical. That is to say, the reasons why American corporations took advantage of the pattern of relationships created by the United States and expanded overseas are to be found in the evolving nature of the American economy itself and in the contemporary revolution in communications and transportation. The steady growth of American industrial corporations and shrinkage of the globe underlie this process of corporate expansionism.

Although the scale of this foreign direct investment has remained relatively constant as a percentage of gross national product (about 7 percent), its geographical expansion has roughly paralleled the growth of American political influence.[4] After their initial penetration into America's adjacent sphere of influence—Mexico, Canada, and the Caribbean—in the early decades of this century, American corporations accelerated their expansion into Latin America, Asia, and the Middle East as American influence displaced that of the receding European and Japanese empires. The weakening of the Western European economies and the creation of Atlantic security ties after World War II subsequently opened up the European economies themselves to American corporate expansionism. Moreover, with the "maturing" of the American economy the composition of this investment has shifted from extractive industries to manufacturing.

This parallel political and economic expansionism on the part of American society suggests the existence of a set of common causes: the dynamism of the American people, the decline of European and Japanese influence, and the steady compression of time and distance owing to advances in communications and transportation. To these factors one must add the traumatic experience of two world wars and the external challenges first of fascism and then of Communism, which awakened American business and political leadership to their stake in the outside world. Thus, as in the case of the Middle East, perceived national and corporate interests were joined when the United States in the early postwar years displaced British influence and established control over this strategic crossroads and reservoir of petroleum. Furthermore, the re-creation by the United States and its allies after 1945 of an interdependent international economy ushered in a period of unprecedented economic growth and affluence that proved to be a fertile environment for the expansion of the MNC. In short, the dramatic overseas expansion of American corporations and of American political influence has reflected political, economic, and technological forces at work both within the United States itself and in the larger international system. The analysis of the interplay of these political and economic factors in the rise of the multinational corporation and of American hegemony is the primary purpose of this book.

The second purpose of this book is normative: It raises important questions for American domestic and foreign economic policy. Although I accept that corporate giants will continue to play an important role in the world economy, the international environment is rapidly changing in a manner that will profoundly affect their status and the implications for the United States. The relative decline of American power and the emergence of new centers of economic power in Europe, Japan, and elsewhere will increasingly alter the distribution of the costs and benefits of foreign direct investment by American corporations.

In contrast to the prevailing assumption that American corporate expansionism is in the larger national interest of the United States, I believe the United States must address itself to the question of the costs and benefits of foreign direct investment. As American influence declines and as foreign governments force American corporations to serve their interests, Americans must more critically examine whether corporate and national interests coincide. Ironically, this is an issue that has scarcely been addressed in the existing literature on American foreign investment and the multinational corporation. Organized labor, some politicians, and a few academic critics have raised questions, but in general both the advocates and the radical opponents of multinational corporations have assumed that foreign direct investment greatly benefits the American economy.

Although I am not opposed in principle to foreign investment and the multinational corporation, I have strong doubts and misgivings with respect to the wisdom of America's continuing heavy reliance upon foreign direct investment as a means of meeting foreign competition, earning foreign exchange, and solving domestic economic problems. In particular, I shall raise some questions regarding the effect of foreign direct investment on the American economy and the long-term viability of a foreign economic policy which relies heavily on foreign investment rather than on trade, questions which have not yet been carefully considered. Specifically, is the United States as a nation repeating the error committed by other, once great economic powers, such as The Netherlands in the seventeenth century and Great Britain in the nineteenth, of overinvesting abroad to the detriment of the home economy? While this question cannot be given a definite answer, it is one which Americans must begin to ask themselves. Moreover, it is one they will be increasingly forced to ponder in the face of contemporary economic and political developments. My additional purpose, therefore, is to evaluate the multinational corporation from the perspective of the American national interest.

Definition of the Multinational Corporation

The term "multinational corporation" (MNC) is used in this study to designate any business corporation in which ownership, management, production, and marketing extend over several national jurisdictions. The term is, of course, a misnomer in that these corporations are seldom multinational in either ownership or control; however, it is the one in general usage. Though there exist more technical definitions, an MNC is essentially a corporation that invests in other countries for a variety of reasons, to have access to a foreign market, to secure foreign sources of supply, or to have the benefit of lower-cost production or lower taxes, for example. Market-oriented investment accounts for nearly 90 percent of foreign direct investment in manufacturing.[5] There also are a number of American and foreign corporations that invest abroad, especially in places like Hong Kong, Taiwan, and Mexico, in order to cut costs; the destiny of the goods produced by such "offshore production" is usually the American market itself. Increasingly, however, this latter type of investment is becoming integrated into a corporate strategy of global production of components and semiprocessed goods.

Certain general characteristics of multinational corporations may be noted. In the first place, they make *direct* investments in a foreign country.[6] In contrast to portfolio investment, which involves the purchase of noncontrolling equities in a firm or debt instrumentalities of any kind, direct investment implies the establishment of a foreign branch or subsidiary or the takeover of a foreign firm. The underlying motive behind portfolio investment is largely financial; managerial control continues to rest with the borrower, and the liabilities incurred by debt borrowing can be liquidated through repayment. The motivation behind direct investment and the possession of foreign branches or subsidiaries, on the other hand, is primarily the acquisition of managerial control over a production unit in a foreign country. Direct investments are intended to establish a permanent source of income or supply in the foreign economy; consequently, they create economic and political relationships of a lasting and significant character.

Second, the MNCs of greatest interest to this study are characterized by a parent firm (usually American) and a cluster of subsidiaries or branches (owned wholly or partially by American corporations) in several countries. There is a common pool of managerial, financial, and technical resources, and, most importantly, the parent operates the whole in terms of a coordinated global strategy. Purchasing, production, marketing, research, and so forth, are organized and managed by the parent in order to achieve its long-term goal of corporate growth. Through vertical integration and centralization of decision making, the multinational corporation seeks to perpetuate its predominant position with respect to technology, access to capital, sources of supply, or whatever else gives it competitive advantage and market power.

Traditionally, British and European capitalism have practiced portfolio investment, loans, and similar forms of capital export. Although Great Britain and other countries did make direct investments in the nineteenth century, these investments were invariably infrastructure investments (utilities, port facilities, and railroads).[7] In the twentieth century, American and other direct investment has been largely in manufacturing, particularly in the growth sectors of advanced or rapidly developing economies (e.g., Europe, Canada, South Africa, Brazil). Another major area for foreign direct investment has been petroleum.

Although Table 1 undoubtedly oversimplifies the contrast between British investment in the nineteenth century and American investment today, it does serve to point out the differing emphases of these two important capital-exporting nations. The table speaks for itself, but one point ought to be made. Whereas British investment was accompanied by mass migration of labor, American investment has been accompanied by the flow of corporate management. Management, capital, and technology have gone as a package to foreign lands in search of labor, markets, and resources.[8] In the nineteenth century, at least in the so-called lands of recent settlement (Canada, Australia, the United States, and South Africa), management and operating

TABLE 1

British and American Foreign Investment

	BRITISH, NINETEENTH CENTURY	UNITED STATES, TWENTIETH CENTURY
Investors	Banks Individuals Bond Market	Corporations
Type of Investment	Portfolio Loans	Direct
Activity	Raw Materials Agriculture Utilities (railroads and seaports)	Manufacturing Raw Materials (especially petroleum) Marketing
Primary Motivation	Local opportunity for immediate profit	Global corporate strategy
Location of Investment (bulk of investment)	Europe United States Lands of recent settlement (Australia, Canada)	Europe Latin America Canada Middle East (petroleum)
Migration	Stimulated mass migration	Corporate management

control usually remained in local hands. The essence of American direct investment has been the shift of managerial control over substantial sectors of foreign economies to American nationals. In character, therefore, these direct investors in other countries are more similar to the trading companies of the mercantilistic era than to the free traders and finance capitalists that dominated Britain in the nineteenth century.[9]

Some Facts and Figures

Although the corporations of other industrial powers are among the oldest multinationals (Royal Dutch Shell, Unilever, Nestlé), the multinational corporation today is most frequently Ameri-

TABLE 2
The Top Fifteen Multinational Corporations

COMPANY	TOTAL 1971 SALES (BILLIONS OF DOLLARS)	FOREIGN SALES AS PERCENTAGE OF TOTAL	NUMBER OF COUNTRIES IN WHICH SUBSIDIARIES ARE LOCATED
General Motors	$28.3	19%	21
Exxon	18.7	50	25
Ford	16.4	26	30
Royal Dutch/Shell °	12.7	79	43
General Electric	9.4	16	32
IBM	8.3	39	80
Mobil Oil	8.2	45	62
Chrysler	8.0	24	26
Texaco	7.5	40	30
Unilever °	7.5	80	31
ITT	7.3	42	40
Gulf Oil	5.9	45	61
British Petroleum °	5.2	88	52
Philips Gloeilampenfabrieken °	5.2	NA	29
Standard Oil of California	5.1	45	26

° Non-American multinational corporations.
Source: United Nations, Department of Economic and Social Affairs, *Multinational Corporations in World Development* (New York, 1973), p. 130.

can. Eleven of the fifteen largest multinationals are American (see Table 2).

In 1971, American corporations held 52 percent of the total world stock of foreign direct investment (see Table 3). Great Britain held 14.5 percent, followed by France (5 percent) and the Federal Republic of Germany (4.4 percent). Japan held only 2.7 percent. Although European direct investment had increased substantially by the mid-1970s, American direct investment in Europe was still three times that of European direct investment in the United States in 1973. Japanese direct investment had also increased by 1973, but it still lagged far behind that of the United States and the major West European powers (Great Britain, France, and West Germany). At the end of

TABLE 3
Major Countries' Stock of Foreign Direct Investment
(Book Value), 1967, 1971
(Millions of dollars and percentage)

	1967		1971	
COUNTRY	MILLIONS OF DOLLARS	PERCENT-AGE SHARE	MILLIONS OF DOLLARS	PERCENT-AGE SHARE
United States	59,486	55.0	86,001	52.0
United Kingdom	17,521	16.2	24,019	14.5
France	6,000	5.5	9,540	5.8
Federal Republic of Germany	3,015	2.8	7,276	4.4
Switzerland	4,250	3.9	6,760	4.1
Canada	3,728	3.4	5,930	3.6
Japan	1,458	1.3	4,480	2.7
Netherlands	2,250	2.1	3,580	2.2
Sweden	1,514	1.4	3,450	2.1
Italy	2,110	1.9	3,350	2.0
Belgium	2,040	0.4	3,250	2.0
Australia	380	1.9	610	0.4
Portugal	200	0.2	320	0.2
Denmark	190	0.2	310	0.2
Norway	60	0.0	90	0.0
Austria	30	0.0	40	0.0
Other	4,000	3.7	6,000	3.6
TOTAL	108,200	100.0	165,000	100.0

Source: United Nations, Department of Economics and Social Affairs, *Multinational Corporations in World Development* (New York, 1973), p. 139.

1972, total foreign investment in the United States was $14.4 billion, or less than one-sixth of the $94 billion in direct investment abroad held by American corporations. As shall be pointed out in Chapter IX, this situation is rapidly changing. Yet, foreign direct investment in the United States remains small compared to American direct investment abroad.

Foreign corporations and investors tend to prefer portfolio to direct investment (see Chart 1). Moreover, if one examines the international production of major countries as against their exports, it is seen that foreign countries greatly prefer exporting whereas American corporations prefer foreign production (see

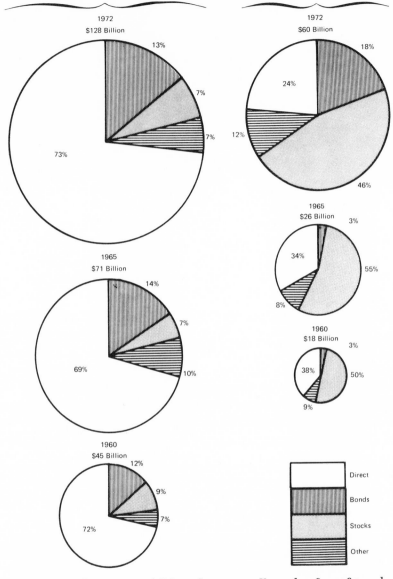

CHART 1. Composition of Private Investment, Yearend 1960, 1965, and 1972—by Type.

Source: U.S. Department of Commerce, Bureau of Economic Analysis, *Survey of Current Business* 53 (August 1973): 18–23. Reproduced from U.S. Department of State, Bureau of Public Affairs, Special Report, *The U.S. Role in International Investment*, February 1, 1974, p. 11.

TABLE 4

Major Countries' International Production and Exports, 1971
(Millions of dollars)

	STOCK OF FOREIGN DIRECT INVEST-MENT (BOOK VALUE)	ESTIMATED INTER-NATIONAL PRODUC-TION	EXPORTS	INTER-NATIONAL PRODUC-TION AS PERCENTAGE OF EXPORTS
United States	86,000	172,000	43,492	395.5
United Kingdom	24,020	48,000	22,367	214.6
France	9,540	19,100	20,420	93.5
Federal Republic of Germany	7,270	14,600	39,040	37.4
Switzerland	6,760	13,500	5,728	235.7
Canada	5,930	11,900	17,582	67.7
Japan	4,480	9,000	24,019	37.5
Netherlands	3,580	7,200	13,927	51.7
Sweden	3,450	6,900	7,465	92.4
Italy	3,350	6,700	15,111	44.3
Belgium	3,250	6,500	12,392	52.4
Australia	610	1,200	5,070	23.7
Portugal	320	600	1,052	57.0
Denmark	310	600	3,685	16.3
Norway	90	200	2,563	7.8
Austria	40	100	3,169	3.2
Total of above	159,000	318,000	237,082	133.7
Other market economies	6,000	12,000	74,818	16.0
Total	165,000	330,000	311,900	105.8

Source: United Nations, Department of Economic and Social Affairs, *Multinational Corporations in World Development* (New York, 1973), p. 159.

Table 4). For all these reasons, therefore, the term "multinational corporation" is still largely a euphemism for the outward expansion of America's giant oligopolistic corporations. Corporate control has remained in America's hands. As a British friend remarked to me, "The multinational corporation is about as 'multinational' as the Indian army was 'Indian' under the British raj. While the troops were Indian, the officers were British."

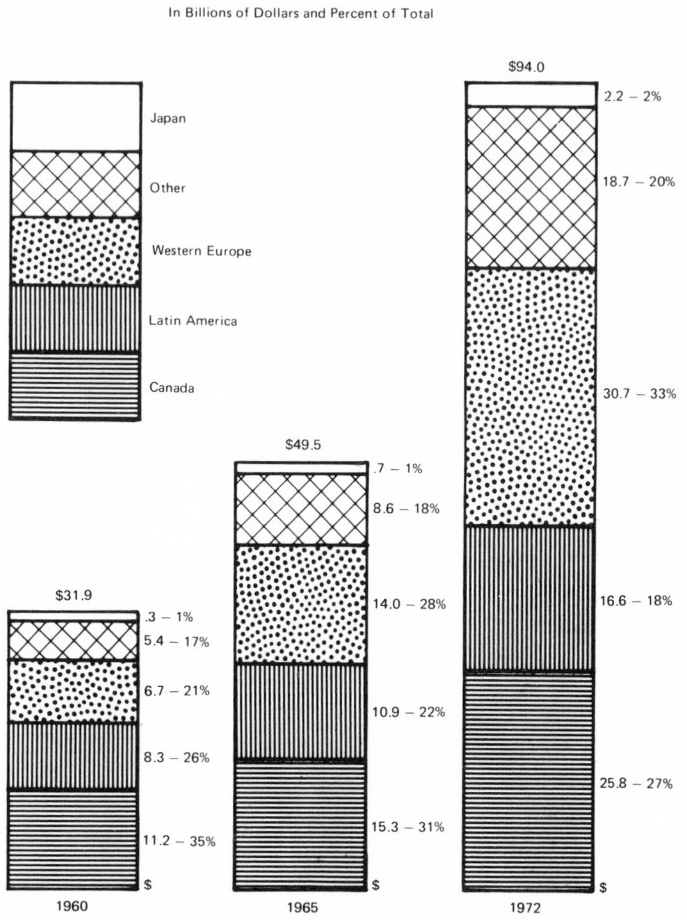
In Billions of Dollars and Percent of Total
Japan
Other
Western Europe
Latin America
Canada
$31.9
.3 – 1%
5.4 – 17%
6.7 – 21%
8.3 – 26%
11.2 – 35%
$
1960
$49.5
.7 – 1%
8.6 – 18%
14.0 – 28%
10.9 – 22%
15.3 – 31%
$
1965
$94.0
2.2 – 2%
18.7 – 20%
30.7 – 33%
16.6 – 18%
25.8 – 27%
$
1972

CHART 2. Book Value of United States Foreign Direct Investment Abroad, at Yearend 1960, 1965, and 1972—by Area.

Source: U.S. Department of Commerce, Bureau of Economic Analysis, *Survey of Current Business* 52 (November 1972): 21–34 and 53 (September 1973): 21–34. Reproduced from Department of State, Bureau of Public Affairs, Special Report *The U.S. Role in International Investment*, February 1, 1974, p. 7.

Although American firms expanded abroad as early as the 1850s, it was only after World War I that American investment abroad began to increase rapidly.[10] At the same time that Britain had to liquidate billions of dollars in overseas investment, the United States emerged from the war as a creditor nation. Throughout the inter-war period, American corporations expanded their holdings in both Latin America and Canada. Then, following World War II, and particularly after the founding of the European Economic Community or Common Market in 1958, the magnitude, direction, and character of American direct investment abroad changed rapidly.

From an initial accumulated investment of only $7 billion in 1946, by 1973 the book value of American direct investment had increased to over $100 billion, with an annual output estimated at over $200 billion.[11] Furthermore, whereas prior to World War II, Latin America accounted for most of this investment, after the war Canada, Western Europe, and other industrial areas absorbed the great bulk of it. (See Chart 2). Investment in the production of raw materials and in traditional manufacturing industries has remained strong; however, a large fraction of postwar investment (40 percent) has gone into advanced manufacturing industries, where it is heavily concentrated in the so-called commanding heights of the modern industrial economy (automobiles, chemicals, and electronics). The other large segment of U.S. foreign direct investment is in petroleum (30 percent). This $20 billion investment accounts for about 40 percent of American direct investment in the lesser developed countries (see Table 5).[12]

By the early 1970s, the United States had become more of a foreign investor than an exporter of domestically manufactured goods. International production by MNCs had surpassed trade as the main component of international economic exchange. Foreign production by the affiliates of American corporations was over four times as great as American exports abroad. Moreover, a substantial proportion of American exports of man-

TABLE 5

Sectoral Distribution of U.S. Foreign Direct Investment in Developed and Developing Countries, Yearend 1972

Developed Countries:	
Manufacturing	51.2%
Petroleum	22.1
Mining and Smelting	6.9
Other	19.8
Developing Countries:	
Manufacturing	26.4%
Petroleum	39.2
Mining and Smelting	10.8
Other	23.6

SOURCE: U.S. Department of Commerce, Bureau of Economic Analysis, *Survey of Current Business* 53 (September, 1973): 26–27. Reproduced from U.S. Department of State, Bureau of Public Affairs, Special Report, *The U.S. Role in International Investment,* February 1, 1974, p. 6.

ufactured goods were really transfers from an American branch of an MNC to an overseas branch. In 1969, the American multinationals alone produced approximately $140 billion worth of goods, more than any national economy except those of the United States and the Soviet Union, and in 1971 the MNCs accounted for 15 percent of total world output. Moreover, by the early 1970s, the financial resources held by multinational corporations were nearly $300 billion. Thus there can be little doubt of the significance of multinational corporations; they loom large as a factor in contemporary world affairs.[13]

The facts of the matter, then, are generally agreed upon; assessing the significance of these facts, however, is a matter of intense controversy. In large measure, the significance one places on these facts and on the advent of the multinational corporation is a function of one's perspective on the relationship between economics and politics, that is, on one's concept of the nature of political economy.

Conclusion

In summary, this book integrates the three types of explanations which economists and political scientists have set forth to explain the rise of an interdependent world economy and the emergence of such transnational actors as the multinational corporations. While it rejects the shared liberal and Marxist view that economic and technological factors are autonomously operating forces producing these effects, it incorporates these factors in its overall explanation. In addition, the perspective of this book incorporates the emphasis of other scholars on the importance of the domestic political order in channeling economic forces in one direction rather than another. That is to say, the emphasis on foreign investment by Great Britain and the United States is held to be a function of public policy and not, as Lenin would have it, an inevitable consequence of the inherent necessity of capitalist development. Thirdly, this book argues that the international political order created by dominant powers primarily in their security interests has provided the favorable environment for economic interdependence and corporate expansionism. In short, by integrating the relevant economic and political factors, it provides a political economy explanation of one of the most remarkable and predominant features of what future historians will undoubtedly call the American era of international relations, the domination of the world economy by gigantic American corporations.

I

THE NATURE OF POLITICAL
ECONOMY

The international corporations have evidently declared ideological war on the "antiquated" nation state. . . . The charge that materialism, modernization and internationalism is the new liberal creed of corporate capitalism is a valid one. The implication is clear: the nation state as a political unit of democratic decision-making must, in the interest of "progress," yield control to the new mercantile mini-powers.[1]

While the structure of the multinational corporation is a modern concept, designed to meet the requirements of a modern age, the nation state is a very old-fashioned idea and badly adapted to serve the needs of our present complex world.[2]

These two statements—the first by Kari Levitt, a Canadian nationalist, the second by George Ball, a former United States undersecretary of state—express a dominant theme of contemporary writings on international relations. International society, we are told, is increasingly rent between its economic and its political organization. On the one hand, powerful economic and technological forces are creating a highly interdependent world economy, thus diminishing the traditional significance of national boundaries. On the other hand, the nation-state continues to command men's loyalties and to be the basic unit of political decision making. As one writer has put the issue, "The conflict of our era is between ethnocentric nationalism and geocentric technology." [3]

Ball and Levitt represent two contending positions with respect to this conflict. Whereas Ball advocates the diminution of the power of the nation-state in order to give full rein to the productive potentialities of the multinational corporation, Levitt argues for a powerful nationalism which could counterbalance American corporate domination. What appears to one as the logical and desirable consequence of economic rationality seems to the other to be an effort on the part of American imperialism to eliminate all contending centers of power.

Although the advent of the multinational corporation has put the question of the relationship between economics and politics in a new guise, it is an old issue. In the nineteenth century, for example, it was this issue that divided classical liberals like John Stuart Mill from economic nationalists, represented by Georg Friedrich List. Whereas the former gave primacy in the organization of society to economics and the production of wealth, the latter emphasized the political determination of economic relations. As this issue is central both to the contemporary debate on the multinational corporation and to the argument of this study, this chapter analyzes the three major treatments of the relationship between economics and politics—that is, the three major ideologies of political economy.

The Meaning of Political Economy

The argument of this study is that the relationship between economics and politics, at least in the modern world, is a reciprocal one. On the one hand, politics largely determines the framework of economic activity and channels it in directions intended to serve the interests of dominant groups; the exercise of power in all its forms is a major determinant of the nature of an economic system. On the other hand, the economic process itself tends to redistribute power and wealth; it transforms the power relationships among groups. This in turn leads to a transformation of the political system, thereby giving rise to a new structure of economic relationships. Thus, the dynamics of international relations in the modern world is largely a function of the reciprocal interaction between economics and politics.

First of all, what do I mean by "politics" or "economics"? Charles Kindleberger speaks of economics and politics as two different methods of allocating scarce resources: the first through a market mechanism, the latter through a budget.[4] Robert Keohane and Joseph Nye, in an excellent analysis of international political economy, define economics and politics in terms of two levels of analysis: those of structure and of process.[5] Politics is the domain "having to do with the establishment of an order of relations, a structure. . . ."[6] Economics deals with "short-term allocative behavior (i.e., holding institutions, fundamental assumptions, and expectations constant). . . ."[7] Like Kindleberger's definition, however, this definition tends to isolate economic and political phenomena except under certain conditions, which Keohane and Nye define as the "politicization" of the economic system. Neither formulation comes to terms adequately with the dynamic and intimate nature of the relationship between the two.

In this study, the issue of the relationship between economics and politics translates into that between wealth and power. According to this statement of the problem, economics takes as its province the creation and distribution of wealth; politics is the realm of power. I shall examine their relationship from several ideological perspectives, including my own. But what is wealth? What is power?

In response to the question, What is wealth?, an economist-colleague responded, "What do you want, my thirty-second or thirty-volume answer?" Basic concepts are elusive in economics, as in any field of inquiry. No unchallengeable definitions are possible. Ask a physicist for his definition of the nature of space, time, and matter, and you will not get a very satisfying response. What you will get is an *operational* definition, one which is usable: it permits the physicist to build an intellectual edifice whose foundations would crumble under the scrutiny of the philosopher.

Similarly, the concept of wealth, upon which the science of economics ultimately rests, cannot be clarified in a definitive way. Paul Samuelson, in his textbook, doesn't even try, though he provides a clue in his definition of economics as "the study of how men and society *choose* . . . to employ *scarce* productive resources . . . to produce various commodities . . . and distribute them for consumption."[8] Following this lead, we can say that wealth is anything (capital, land, or labor) that can generate future income; it is composed of physical assets and human capital (including embodied knowledge).

The basic concept of political science is power. Most political scientists would not stop here; they would include in the definition of political science the purpose for which power is used, whether this be the advancement of the public welfare or the domination of one group over another. In any case, few would dissent from the following statement of Harold Lasswell and Abraham Kaplan:

> The concept of power is perhaps the most fundamental in the whole of political science: the political process is the shaping, distribution, and exercise of power (in a wider sense, of all the deference values, or of influence in general.)[9]

Power as such is not the sole or even the principal goal of state behavior. Other goals or values constitute the objectives pursued by nation-states: welfare, security, prestige. But power in its several forms (military, economic, psychological) is ultimately the necessary means to achieve these goals. For this reason, nation-states are intensely jealous of and sensitive to their relative power position. The distribution of power is important because it profoundly affects the ability of states to achieve what they perceive to be their interests.

The nature of power, however, is even more elusive than that of wealth. The number and variety of definitions should be an embarrassment to political scientists. Unfortunately, this study cannot bring the intradisciplinary squabble to an end. Rather, it adopts the definition used by Hans Morgenthau in his influential *Politics Among Nations*: "man's control over the minds and actions of other men." [10] Thus, power, like wealth, is the capacity to produce certain results.

Unlike wealth, however, power can not be quantified; indeed, it cannot be overemphasized that power has an important psychological dimension. Perceptions of power relations are of critical importance; as a consequence, a fundamental task of statesmen is to manipulate the perceptions of other statesmen regarding the distribution of power. Moreover, power is relative to a specific situation or set of circumstances; there is no single hierarchy of power in international relations. Power may take many forms—military, economic, or psychological—though, in the final analysis, force is the ultimate form of power. Finally, the inability to predict the behavior of others or the outcome of events is of great significance. Uncertainty regarding the distribution of power and the ability of the statesmen to control events plays an important role in international relations. Ultimately, the determination of the distribution of power can be made only in retrospect as a consequence of war. It is precisely for this reason that war has had, unfortunately, such a central place in the history of international relations. In short, power is an elusive concept indeed upon which to erect a science of politics.

Such mutually exclusive definitions of economics and politics as these run counter to much contemporary scholarship by both economists and political scientists, for both disciplines are invading the formerly exclusive jurisdictions of the other. Economists, in particular, have become intellectual imperialists; they are applying their analytical techniques to traditional issues of political science with great success. These developments, however, really reinforce the basic premise of this study, namely, the inseparability of economics and politics.

The distinction drawn above between economics as the science of wealth and politics as the science of power is essentially an analytical one. In the real world, wealth and power are ultimately joined. This, in fact, is the basic rationale for a political economy of international relations. But in order to develop the argument of this study, wealth and power will be treated, at least for the moment, as analytically distinct.

To provide a perspective on the nature of political economy, the next section of the chapter will discuss the three prevailing conceptions of political economy: liberalism, Marxism, and mercantilism. Liberalism regards politics and economics as relatively separable and autonomous spheres of activities; I associate most professional economists as well as many other academics, businessmen, and American officials with this outlook. Marxism refers to the radical critique of capitalism identified with Karl Marx and his contemporary disciples; according to this conception, economics determines politics and political structure. Mercantilism is a more questionable term because of its historical association with the desire of nation-states for a trade surplus and for treasure (money). One must distinguish, however, between the specific form mercantilism took in the seventeenth and eighteenth centuries and the general outlook of mercantilistic thought. The essence of the mercantilistic perspective, whether it is labeled economic nationalism, protectionism, or the doctrine of the German Historical School, is the subservience of the economy to the state and its interests—interests that range from matters of domestic welfare to those of international security. It is this more general meaning of mercantilism that is implied by the use of the term in this study.

Following the discussion of these three schools of thought, I shall elaborate my own, more eclectic, view of political economy and demonstrate its relevance for understanding the phenomenon of the multinational corporation.

Three Conceptions of Political Economy

The three prevailing conceptions of political economy differ on many points. Several critical differences will be examined in this brief comparison. (See Table 6.)

The Nature of Economic Relations

The basic assumption of liberalism is that the nature of international economic relations is essentially harmonious. Herein lay the great intellectual innovation of Adam Smith. Disputing his mercantilist predecessors, Smith argued that international economic relations could be made a positive-sum game; that is to say, everyone could gain, and no one need lose, from a proper ordering of economic relations, albeit the distribution of these gains may not be equal. Following Smith, liberalism assumes that there is a basic harmony between true national interest and cosmopolitan economic interest. Thus, a prominent member of this school of thought has written, in response to a radical critique, that the economic efficiency of the sterling standard in the nineteenth century and that of the dollar standard in the twentieth century serve "the cosmopolitan interest in a national form." [11] Although Great Britain and the United States gained the most from the international role of their respective currencies, everyone else gained as well.

Liberals argue that, given this underlying identity of national and cosmopolitan interests in a free market, the state should not interfere with economic transactions across national boundaries. Through free exchange of commodities, removal of restrictions on the flow of investment, and an international division of labor, everyone will benefit in the long run as a result of a more efficient utilization of the world's scarce resources. The national interest is therefore best served, liberals maintain, by a generous and cooperative attitude regarding economic relations with other countries. In essence, the pursuit of self-interest in a free, competitive economy achieves the

TABLE 6

Comparison of the Three Conceptions of Political Economy

	LIBERALISM	MARXISM	MERCANTILISM
Nature of economic relations	Harmonious	Conflictual	Conflictual
Nature of the actors	Households and firms	Economic classes	Nation-states
Goal of economic activity	Maximization of global welfare	Maximization of class interests	Maximization of national interest
Relationship between economics and politics	Economics *should* determine politics	Economics *does* determine politics	Politics determines economics
Theory of change	Dynamic equilibrium	Tendency toward disequilibrium	Shifts in the distribution of power

greatest good for the greatest number in international no less than in the national society.

Both mercantilists and Marxists, on the other hand, begin with the premise that the essence of economic relations is conflictual. There is no underlying harmony; indeed, one group's gain is another's loss. Thus, in the language of game theory, whereas liberals regard economic relations as a non-zero-sum game, Marxists and mercantilists view economic relations as essentially a zero-sum game.

The Goal of Economic Activity

For the liberal, the goal of economic activity is the optimum or efficient use of the world's scarce resources and the maximization of world welfare. While most liberals refuse to make value judgments regarding income distribution, Marxists and mercantilists stress the distributive effects of economic relations. For the Marxist the distribution of wealth among social classes is central; for the mercantilist it is the distribution of employment, industry, and military power among nation-states that is most significant. Thus, the goal of economic (and political) activity for both Marxists and mercantilists is the redistribution of wealth and power.

The State and Public Policy

These three perspectives differ decisively in their views regarding the nature of the economic actors. In Marxist analysis, the basic actors in both domestic and international relations are economic classes; the interests of the dominant class determine the foreign policy of the state. For mercantilists, the real actors in international economic relations are nation-states; national interest determines foreign policy. National interest may at times be influenced by the peculiar economic interests of classes, elites, or other subgroups of the society; but factors of geography, external configurations of power, and the exigencies of national survival are primary in determining foreign policy. Thus, whereas liberals speak of world welfare and Marxists of class interests, mercantilists recognize only the interests of particular nation-states.

Although liberal economists such as David Ricardo and Joseph Schumpeter recognized the importance of class conflict and neoclassical liberals analyze economic growth and policy in terms of national economies, the liberal emphasis is on the individual consumer, firm, or entrepreneur. The liberal ideal is summarized in the view of Harry Johnson that the nation-state has no meaning as an economic entity.[12]

Underlying these contrasting views are differing conceptions of the nature of the state and public policy. For liberals, the state represents an aggregation of private interests: public policy is but the outcome of a pluralistic struggle among interest groups. Marxists, on the other hand, regard the state as simply the "executive committee of the ruling class," and public policy reflects its interests. Mercantilists, however, regard the state as an organic unit in its own right: the whole is greater than the sum of its parts. Public policy, therefore, embodies the national interest or Rousseau's "general will" as conceived by the political elite.

The Relationship between Economics and Politics; Theories of Change

Liberalism, Marxism, and mercantilism also have differing

views on the relationship between economics and politics. And their differences on this issue are directly relevant to their contrasting theories of international political change.

Although the liberal ideal is the separation of economics from politics in the interest of maximizing world welfare, the fulfillment of this ideal would have important political implications. The classical statement of these implications was that of Adam Smith in *The Wealth of Nations*.[13] Economic growth, Smith argued, is primarily a function of the extent of the division of labor, which in turn is dependent upon the scale of the market. Thus he attacked the barriers erected by feudal principalities and mercantilistic states against the exchange of goods and the enlargement of markets. If men were to multiply their wealth, Smith argued, the contradiction between political organization and economic rationality had to be resolved in favor of the latter. That is, the pursuit of wealth should determine the nature of the political order.

Subsequently, from nineteenth-century economic liberals to twentieth-century writers on economic integration, there has existed "the dream . . . of a great republic of world commerce, in which national boundaries would cease to have any great economic importance and the web of trade would bind all the people of the world in the prosperity of peace."[14] For liberals the long-term trend is toward world integration, wherein functions, authority, and loyalties will be transferred from "smaller units to larger ones; from states to federalism; from federalism to supranational unions and from these to superstates."[15] The logic of economic and technological development, it is argued, has set mankind on an inexorable course toward global political unification and world peace.

In Marxism, the concept of the contradiction between economic and political relations was enacted into historical law. Whereas classical liberals—although Smith less than others—held that the requirements of economic rationality *ought* to determine political relations, the Marxist position was that the mode of production does in fact determine the superstructure of political relations. Therefore, it is argued, history can be understood as the product of the dialectical process—the contradiction between the evolving techniques of production and the resistant sociopolitical system.

Although Marx and Engels wrote remarkably little on international economics, Engels, in his famous polemic, *Anti-Duhring*, explicitly considers whether economics or politics is primary in determining the structure of international relations.[16] E. K. Duhring, a minor figure in the German Historical School, had argued, in contradiction to Marxism, that property and market relations resulted less from the economic logic of capitalism than from extraeconomic political factors: "The basis of the exploitation of man by man was an historical act of force which created an exploitative economic system for the benefit of the stronger man or class."[17] Since Engels, in his attack on Duhring, used the example of the unification of Germany through the Zollverein or customs union of 1833, his analysis is directly relevant to this discussion of the relationship between economics and political organization.

Engels argued that when contradictions arise between economic and political structures, political power adapts itself to the changes in the balance of economic forces; politics yields to the dictates of economic development. Thus, in the case of nineteenth-century Germany, the requirements of industrial production had become incompatible with its feudal, politically fragmented structure. "Though political reaction was victorious in 1815 and again in 1848," he argued, "it was unable to prevent the growth of large-scale industry in Germany and the growing participation of German commerce in the world market."[18] In summary, Engels wrote, "German unity had become an economic necessity."[19]

In the view of both Smith and Engels, the nation-state represented a progressive stage in human development, because it enlarged the political realm of economic activity. In each successive economic epoch, advances in technology and an increasing scale of production necessitate an enlargement of political organization. Because the city-state and feudalism restricted the scale of production and the division of labor made possible by the Industrial Revolution, they prevented the efficient utilization of resources and were, therefore, superseded by larger political units. Smith considered this to be a desirable objective; for Engels it was an historical necessity. Thus, in the opinion of liberals, the establishment of the Zollverein was a movement toward maximizing world economic welfare;[20] for Marxists it was the unavoidable triumph of the German industrialists over the feudal aristocracy.

Mercantilist writers from Alexander Hamilton to Frederich List to Charles de Gaulle, on the other hand, have emphasized the primacy of politics; politics, in this view, determines economic organization. Whereas Marxists and liberals have pointed to the production of wealth as the basic determinant of social and political organization, the mercantilists of the German Historical School, for example, stressed the primacy of national security, industrial development, and national sentiment in international political and economic dynamics.

In response to Engels's interpretation of the unification of Germany, mercantilists would no doubt agree with Jacob Viner that "Prussia engineered the customs union primarily for political reasons, in order to gain hegemony or at least influence over the lesser German states. It was largely in order to make certain that the hegemony should be Prussian and not Austrian that Prussia continually opposed Austrian entry into the Union, either openly or by pressing for a customs union tariff lower than highly protectionist Austria could stomach."[21] In pursuit of this strategic interest, it was "Prussian might, rather than a common zeal for political unification arising out of economic partnership, (that) . . . played the major role."[22]

In contrast to Marxism, neither liberalism nor mercantilism has a developed theory of dynamics. The basic assumption of orthodox economic analysis (liberalism) is the tendency toward equilibrium; liberalism takes for granted the existing social order and given institutions. Change is assumed to be gradual and adaptive—a continuous process of dynamic equilibrium. There is no necessary connection between such political phenomena as war and revolution and the evolution of the economic system, although they would not deny that misguided statesmen can blunder into war over economic issues or that revolutions are conflicts over the distribution of wealth; but neither is inevitably linked to the evolution of the productive system. As for mercantilism, it sees change as taking place owing to shifts in the balance of power; yet, mercantilist writers such as members of the German Historical School and contemporary political realists have not developed a systematic theory of how this shift occurs.

On the other hand, dynamics is central to Marxism; indeed Marxism is essentially a theory of social *change*. It emphasizes the tendency toward *dis*equilibrium owing to changes in the means of production and the consequent effects on the ever-present class conflict. When these tendencies can no longer be contained, the sociopolitical system breaks down through violent upheaval. Thus war and revolution are seen as an integral part of the economic process. Politics and economics are intimately joined.

Why an International Economy?

From these differences among the three ideologies, one can get a sense of their respective explanations for the existence and functioning of the international economy.

An interdependent world economy constitutes the normal state of affairs for most liberal economists. Responding to technological advances in transportation and communications, the scope of the market mechanism, according to this analysis, continuously expands. Thus, despite temporary setbacks, the long-term trend is toward global economic integration. The functioning of the international economy is determined primarily by considerations of efficiency. The role of the dollar as the basis of the international monetary system, for example, is explained by the preference for it among traders and nations as the vehicle of international commerce.[23] The system is maintained by the mutuality of the benefits provided by trade, monetary arrangements, and investment.

A second view—one shared by Marxists and mercantilists alike —is that every interdependent international economy is essentially an imperial or hierarchical system. The imperial or hegemonic power organizes trade, monetary, and investment relations in order to advance its own economic and political interests. In the absence of the economic and especially the political influence of the hegemonic power, the system would fragment into autarkic economies or regional blocs. Whereas for liberalism maintenance of harmonious international market relations is the norm, for Marxism and mercantilism conflicts of class or national interests are the norm.

Perspective of the Author

My own perspective on political economy rests on what I regard as a fundamental difference in emphasis between economics and politics; namely, the distinction between absolute and relative gains. The emphasis of economic science—or, at least, of liberal economics—is on *absolute* gains; the ultimate defense of liberalism is that over the long run everyone gains, albeit in varying degrees, from a liberal economic regime. Economics, according to this formulation, need not be a zero-sum game. Everyone can gain in wealth through a more efficient division of labor; moreover, everyone can lose, in absolute terms, from economic inefficiency. Herein lies the strength of liberalism.

This economic emphasis on absolute gains is in fact embodied in what one can characterize as the ultimate ideal of liberal economics: the achievement of a "Pareto optimum" world. Such a properly ordered world would be one wherein "by improving the position of one individual (by adding to his possessions) no one else's position is deteriorated." As Oskar Morgenstern has observed, "[e]conomic literature is replete with the use of the Pareto optimum thus formulated or in equivalent language." [24] It is a world freed from "interpersonal comparisons of utility," and thus a world freed from what is central to politics, i.e., ethical judgment and conflict regarding the just and relative distribution of utility. That the notion of a Pareto optimum is rife with conceptual problems and is utopian does not detract from its centrality as the implicit objective of liberal economics. And this emphasis of economics on absolute gains for all differs fundamentally from the nature of political phenomena as studied by political scientists: viz., struggles for power as a goal in itself or as a means to the achievement of other goals.

The essential fact of politics is that power is always relative; one state's gain in power is by necessity another's loss. Thus, even though two states may be gaining absolutely in wealth, in political terms it is the effect of these gains on relative power positions which is of primary importance. From this *political* perspective, therefore, the mercantilists are correct in emphasizing that in power terms, international relations is a zero-sum game.

In a brilliant analysis of international politics, the relativity of power and its profound implications were set forth by Jean-Jacques Rousseau:

> The state, being an artificial body is not limited in any way. . . . It can always increase; it always feels itself weak if there is another that is stronger. Its security and preservation demand that it make itself more powerful than its neighbors. It can increase, nourish and exercise its power only at their expense . . . while the inequality of man has natural limits that between societies can grow without cease, until one absorbs all the others. . . . Because the grandeur

of the state is purely relative it is forced to compare itself with that of the others. . . . It is in vain that it wishes to keep itself to itself; it becomes small or great, weak or strong, according to whether its neighbor expands or contracts, becomes stronger or declines. . . .

The chief thing I notice is a patent contradiction in the condition of the human race. . . . Between man and man we live in the condition of the civil state, subjected to laws; between people and people we enjoy natural liberty, which makes the situation worse. Living at the same time in the social order and in the state of nature, we suffer from the inconveniences of both without finding . . . security in either. . . . We see men united by artificial bonds, but united to destroy each other; and all the horrors of war take birth from the precautions they have taken in order to prevent them. . . . War is born of peace, or at least of the precautions which men have taken for the purpose of achieving durable peace.[25]

Because of the relativity of power, therefore, nation-states are engaged in a never-ending struggle to improve or preserve their relative power positions.

This rather stark formulation obviously draws too sharp a distinction between economics and politics. Certainly, for example, liberal economists may be interested in questions of distribution; the distributive issue was, in fact, of central concern to Ricardo and other classical writers. However, when economists stop taking the system for granted and start asking questions about distribution, they have really ventured into what I regard as the essence of politics, for distribution is really a political issue. In a world in which power rests on wealth, changes in the relative distribution of wealth imply changes in the distribution of power and in the political system itself. This, in fact, is what is meant by saying that politics is about relative gains. Politics concerns the efforts of groups to redistribute gains to their own advantage.

Similarly, to argue that politics is about relative gains is not to argue that it is a constant-sum game. On the contrary, man's power over nature and his fellow man has grown immensely in absolute terms over the past several centuries. It is certainly the case that everyone's absolute capabilities can increase due to the development of new weaponry, the expansion of productive capabilities, or changes in the political system itself. Obviously such absolute increases in power are important politically. Who can deny, for example, that the advent of nuclear weapons has profoundly altered international politics? Obviously, too, states can negotiate disarmament and other types of agreements to reduce their absolute levels of military capability.

Yet recognition of these facts does not alter the prime consideration that changes in the relative distribution of power are of fundamental significance politically. Though all may be gaining or declining in absolute capability, what will concern states principally are the effects of these absolute gains or losses on relative positions. How, for example, do changes in productive capacity or military weaponry affect the ability of one state to impose its will on another? It may very well be that in a particular situation absolute gains will not affect relative positions. But the efforts of groups to cause or prevent such shifts in the relative distribution of power constitute the critical issue of politics.

This formulation of the nature of politics obviously does not deny that nations may cooperate in order to advance their mutual interests. But even cooperative actions may have important consequences for the distribution of power in the system. For example, the Strategic Arms Limitation Talks (SALT) between the United States and the Soviet Union are obviously motivated by a common interest in preventing thermonuclear war. Other states will also benefit if the risk of war between the superpowers is reduced. Yet, SALT may also be seen as an attempt to stabilize the international distribution of power to the disadvantage of China and other third powers. In short, in terms of the system as a whole, political cooperation can have a profound effect on the relative distribution of power among nation-states.

The point may perhaps be clarified by distinguishing between two aspects of power. When one speaks of absolute gains in power, such as advances in economic capabilities or weapons development, one is referring principally to increases in physical or material capabilities. But while such capabilities are an important component of power, power, as we have seen, is more than physical capability. Power is also a psychological relationship: Who can influence whom to do what? From this perspective, what may be of most importance is how changes in capability affect this psychological relationship. Insofar as they do, they alter the relative distribution of power in the system.

In a world in which power rests increasingly on economic and industrial capabilities, one cannot really distinguish between wealth (resources, treasure, and industry) and power as national goals. In the short run there may be conflicts between the pursuit of power and the pursuit of wealth; in the long run the two pursuits are identical. Therefore, the position taken in this study is similar to Viner's interpretation of classical mercantilism:

> What then is the correct interpretation of mercantilist doctrine and practice with respect to the roles of power and plenty as ends of national policy? I believe that practically all mercantilists, whatever the period, country, or status of the particular individual, would have subscribed to all of the following propositions: (1) wealth is an absolutely essential means to power, whether for security or for aggression; (2) power is essential or valuable as a means to the acquisition or retention of wealth; (3) wealth and power are each proper ultimate ends of national policy; (4) there is long-run harmony between these ends, although in particular circumstances it may be necessary for a time to make economic sacrifices in the interest of military security and therefore also of long-run prosperity.[26]

This interpretation of the role of the economic motive in international relations is substantially different from that of Marxism. In the Marxist framework of analysis, the economic factor is reduced to the profit motive, as it affects the behavior of individuals or firms. Accordingly, the foreign policies of capitalist states are determined by the desire of capitalists for profits.

This is, in our view, far too narrow a conception of the economic aspect of international relations. Instead, in this study we label "economic" those sources of wealth upon which national power and domestic welfare are dependent.

Understood in these broader terms, the economic motive and economic activities are fundamental to the struggle for power among nation-states. The objects of contention in the struggles of the balance of power include the centers of economic power. As R. G. Hawtrey has expressed it, "the political motives at work can only be expressed in terms of the economic. Every conflict is one of power and power depends on resources." [27] In pursuit of wealth *and* power, therefore, nations (capitalist, socialist, or fascist) contend over the territorial division and exploitation of the globe.

Even at the level of peaceful economic intercourse, one cannot separate out the political element. Contrary to the attitude of liberalism, international economic relations are in reality political relations. The interdependence of national economies creates economic power, defined as the capacity of one state to damage another through the interruption of commercial and financial relations. [28] The attempts to create and to escape from such dependency relationships constitute an important aspect of international relations in the modern era.

The primary actors in the international system are nation-states in pursuit of what they define as their national interest. This is not to argue, however, that nation-states are the only actors, nor do I believe that the "national interest" is something akin to Rousseau's "general will"—the expression of an organic entity separable from its component parts. Except in the abstract models of political scientists, it has never been the case that the international system was composed solely of nation-states. In an exaggerated acknowledgment of the importance of nonstate or transnational actors at an earlier time, John A. Hobson asked rhetorically whether "a great war could be undertaken by any European state, or a great state loan subscribed, if the House of

Rothschild and its connexions set their face against it." [29] What has to be explained, however, are the economic and political circumstances that enable such transnational actors to play their semi-independent role in international affairs. The argument of this study is that the primary determinants of the role played by these non-state actors are the larger configurations of power among nation-states. What is determinant is the interplay of national interests.

As for the concept of "national interest," the national interest of a given nation-state is, of course, what its political and economic elite determines it to be. In part, as Marxists argue, this elite will define it in terms of its own group or class interests. But the national interest comprehends more than this. More general influences, such as cultural values and considerations relevant to the security of the state itself—geographical position, the evolution of military technology, and the international distribution of power—are of greater importance. There is a sense, then, in which the factors that determine the national interest are objective. A ruling elite that fails to take these factors into account does so at its peril. In short, then, there is a basis for considering the nation-state itself as an actor pursuing its own set of security, welfare, and status concerns interests in competition or cooperation with other nation-states.

Lastly, in a world of conflicting nation-states, how does one explain the existence of an interdependent international economy? Why does a liberal international economy—that is, an economy characterized by relatively free trade, currency convertibility, and freedom of capital movement—remain intact rather than fragment into autarkic national economies and regional or imperial groupings? In part, the answer is provided by liberalism: economic cooperation, interdependence, and an international division of labor enhance efficiency and the maximization of aggregate wealth. Nation-states are induced to enter the international system because of the promise of more rapid growth; greater benefits can be had than could be obtained by autarky or a fragmentation of the world economy. The historical record suggests, however, that the existence of mutual economic benefits is not always enough to induce nations to pay the costs of a market system or to forgo opportunities of advancing their own interests at the expense of others. There is always the danger that a nation may pursue certain short-range policies, such as the imposition of an optimum tariff, in order to maximize its own gains at the expense of the system as a whole.

For this reason, a liberal international economy requires a power to manage and stabilize the system. As Charles Kindleberger has convincingly shown, this governance role was performed by Great Britain throughout the nineteenth century and up to 1931, and by the United States after 1945.[30] The inability of Great Britain in 1929 to continue running the system and the unwillingness of the United States to assume this responsibility led to the collapse of the system in the "Great Depression." The result was the fragmentation of the world economy into rival economic blocs. Both dominant economic powers had failed to overcome the divisive forces of nationalism and regionalism.

The argument of this study is that the modern world economy has evolved through the emergence of great national economies that have successively become dominant. In the words of the distinguished French economist François Perroux, "the economic evolution of the world has resulted from a succession of dominant economies, each in turn taking the lead in international activity and influence. . . . Throughout the nineteenth century the British economy was the dominant economy in the world. From the [eighteen] seventies on, Germany was dominant in respect to certain other Continental countries and in certain specified fields. In the twentieth century, the United States economy has clearly been and still is the internationally dominant economy."[31]

An economic system, then, does not arise spontaneously owing to the operation of an invisible hand and in the absence of the exercise of power. Rather, every economic system rests on a particular political order; its nature cannot be understood aside from politics. This basic point was made some years ago by E. H. Carr when he wrote that "the science of economics presupposes a given political order, and cannot be profitably studied in isolation from politics." [32] Carr sought to convince his fellow Englishmen that an international economy based on free trade was not a natural and inevitable state of affairs but rather one that reflected the economic and political interests of Great Britain. The system based on free trade had come into existence through, and was maintained by, the exercise of British economic and military power. With the rise after 1880 of new industrial and military powers with contrasting economic interests—namely, Germany, Japan, and the United States—an international economy based on free trade and British power became less and less viable. Eventually this shift in the locus of industrial and military power led to the collapse of the system in World War I. Following the interwar period, a liberal international economy was revived through the exercise of power by the world's newly emergent dominant economy—the United States.

Accordingly, the regime of free investment and the preeminence of the multinational corporation in the contemporary world have reflected the economic and political interests of the United States. The multinational corporation has prospered because it has been dependent on the power of, and consistent with the political interests of, the United States. This is not to deny the analyses of economists who argue that the multinational corporation is a response to contemporary technological and economic developments. The argument is rather that these economic and technological factors have been able to exercise their profound effects because the United States—sometimes with the cooperation of other states and sometimes over their opposition—has created the necessary political framework. As former Secretary of the Treasury Henry Fowler stated several years ago, "it is . . . impossible to overestimate the extent to which the efforts and opportunities for American firms abroad depend upon the vast presence and influence and prestige that America holds in the world." [33]

By the mid-1970s, however, the international distribution of power and the world economy resting on it were far different from what they had been when Fowler's words were spoken. The rise of foreign economic competitors, America's growing dependence upon foreign sources of energy and other resources, and the expansion of Soviet military capabilities have greatly diminished America's presence and influence in the world. One must ask if, as a consequence, the reign of the American multinationals over international economic affairs will continue into the future. The last chapter of this book addresses this question.

In summary, although nation-states, as mercantilists suggest, do seek to control economic and technological forces and channel them to their own advantage, this is impossible over the long run. The spread of economic growth and industrialization cannot be prevented. In time the diffusion of industry and technology undermines the position of the dominant power. As both liberals and Marxists have emphasized, the evolution of economic relations profoundly influences the nature of the international political system. The relationship between economics and politics, to restate the theme of this volume, is a reciprocal one.

Although economic and accompanying political change may well be inevitable, it is not inevitable that the process of economic development and technological advance will produce an increasingly integrated world society. In the 1930s, Eugene Staley posed the issue which has been an underlying concern in this chapter.

A conflict rages between technology and politics. Economics, so closely linked to both, has become the major battlefield. Stability and peace will reign in the world economy only when, somehow, the forces on the side of technology and the forces on the side of politics have once more become accommodated to each other.[34]

Staley believed, as do many present-day writers, that politics and technology must ultimately adjust to one another. But he differed with contemporary writers with regard to the inevitability with which politics would adjust to technology. Reflecting the intense economic nationalism of the period in which he wrote, Staley pointed out that the adjustment may very well be the other way around. As he reminds us, in his own time and in earlier periods economics has had to adjust to political realities: "In the 'Dark Ages' following the collapse of the Roman Empire, technology adjusted itself to politics. The magnificent Roman roads fell into disrepair, the baths and aqueducts and amphitheatres and villas into ruins. Society lapsed back to localism in production and distribution, forgot much of the learning and the technology and the governmental systems of earlier days." [35]

Conclusion

The purpose of this chapter has been to set forth the analytical framework that will be employed in this study. This framework is a statement of what I mean by "political economy." In its eclecticism it has drawn upon, while differing from, the three prevailing perspectives of political economy. It has incorporated their respective strengths and has attempted to overcome their weaknesses. In brief, political economy in this study means the reciprocal and dynamic interaction in international relations of the pursuit of wealth and the pursuit of power. In the short run, the distribution of power and the nature of the political system are major determinants of the framework within which wealth is produced and distributed. In the long run, however, shifts in economic efficiency and in the location of economic activity tend to undermine and transform the existing political system. This political transformation in turn gives rise to changes in economic relations that reflect the interests of the politically ascendant state in the system.

II

THE POLITICAL ECONOMY OF
FOREIGN INVESTMENT

Foreign investment is both a cause of and a response to the historic tendency of advanced economies to decline industrially relative to their foreign competitors. Through the spread of technology and know-how, the industrial leader, over a period of time, loses more and more of its initial comparative advantages relative to its rising competitors. As a result, a gradual shift takes place in the locus of industrial and other economic activities from the core to the periphery of the international economy. While this is very much a modern phenomenon, it is also one that can be observed throughout history. As the distinguished classicist R. W. Walbank wrote, reviewing the causes of the decline of the Roman Empire, "modern investigation has revealed in the Roman Empire the operation of an economic law which finds its application equally in our society—the centrifugal tendency of an industry to export itself instead of its products and of trades to migrate from the older areas of the economy to the new."[1] The consequence of this tendency is a gradual redistribution of wealth and power within the international system.

The thesis of this chapter is that foreign investment is a strategy employed by both rising and declining dominant capitalist economies—for quite different reasons. Although a strategy of foreign investment has been central to both the British and the American experience as alternately rising and declining industrial powers, there has been no analysis of foreign investment from the perspective of its role within the dynamics of international relations. For this reason, this study will examine British portfolio investment in the nineteenth century and American direct investment (and its primary form, the multinational corporation) in the context of international political change. That is, we shall examine foreign investment from the perspective of the tendency for the locus of economic and industrial activity to diffuse within the international economy, thereby transforming the international distribution of power and political system.

This process and its consequences will be analyzed through the examination of a dynamic model of the relationship between economics and politics. While this model may provide an insight into the nature of international political change, it is not intended to be a complete model of the dynamics of the international system. For it to be so, one would have to bring into the analysis other elements, such as the role of military power; it need not be emphasized, however, that in the contemporary world industrial capability and military power are closely linked. In a subsequent study I plan to set forth a more general conception of systemic change in international relations. My more specific intention here is to further an understanding of the political economy of international relations through an analysis of foreign investment behavior.

My thesis is *not* that foreign investment is the only (or even the primary) cause of the rise and decline of industrial powers, nor does it assert that all foreign investments can be explained solely as a response to the tendency of an advanced economy to decline relative to its foreign competitors. In any economy, there are at any given time rising and declining industries and economic sectors; the foreign investment behavior of each will obviously differ. Yet, for reasons which will be developed in this and subsequent chapters, the political economy of foreign investment can be understood in large measure initially in terms of an economy's industrial expansion and subsequently as the response of an economy to its potential or actual decline relative to other economies.

In the first phase of an interdependent international economy, foreign investment is a sign of the strength of the dominant, or what I shall call the core, economy. Owing to its technological advantages and industrial efficiency, the core's income rises rapidly. There is a high level of savings, which is not absorbed domestically in consumption or investment. As the core's wealth and savings accumulate, capital is exported to the periphery of the world economy. During this phase, foreign investment in extractive industries, infrastructure, and manufacturing is primarily a function of the relative economic strength of the core.[2]

Subsequently, owing to structural changes in both core and periphery, foreign investment begins to reflect more and more the gradual shift in the locus of economic and industrial activity from core to periphery. Though the core may retain its financial and, at least in the American case, much of its technological and management predominance, extractive and manufacturing industries are increasingly located in what was formerly the periphery.

During this second phase, foreign investment becomes increasingly a response to the relative decline of the dominant industrial nation. There is an acceleration of foreign investment, reflecting one of two kinds of structural changes in the core. The first is a general decline in domestic investment opportunities in the core relative to the periphery; this was the case for Great Britain in the late nineteenth century. The second is the existence of an imperfect capital market and corporate structure, which fosters foreign, at the expense of home, investment. This has generally been the American case in the twentieth century. In either case, the core's financiers and industrialists invest abroad in order to arrest the declining profitability of their resources.

As a high rate of foreign investment can suggest either a rising or a declining core, is it possible to distinguish which is the case? In other words, are there indices that identify the point of crossover from expanding to declining core? While the dating of such a crossover cannot be precise, there are a number of structural changes in the core and periphery which indicate whether increasing foreign investment is a sign of growing strength or relative decline. Among these indices are the relative growth rates of core and peripheral economies; the changing composition of imports and exports; the shifting locus of organizational and technological innovation; and, more qualitatively, the effect of foreign investment on the exports and industrial development of the core. On the basis of these indices, the crossover for Great Britain occurred sometime after 1870; in the American case, the date is sometime after the mid-1960s.

The next part of this chapter presents a model of the world economy in which foreign investment takes place. This core–periphery model is an expansion of the argument of the previous chapter that there is a reciprocal interaction between politics and economics. The core or dominant economy organizes and manages the system in terms of its interests; over time, however, economic and political factors cause a redistribution of wealth and power toward the periphery. Following this discussion, the chapter analyzes the domestic political aspects of foreign investment and the reasons why this strategy is chosen from among several available strategies. Finally, it discusses the undesirable economic and political consequences of a foreign investment strategy.

A Model of International Change

An interdependent economic system—regional, national, or international—is an hierarchical structure composed of dominant core(s) or center(s) and a dependent periphery or hinterland.[3] The core or center constitutes the organizing and controlling component of the system. Whether it is a financial and commercial city such as London or New York or an industrial city such as Manchester or Pittsburgh, the center draws resources (food, raw materials, and manpower) from the periphery and provides goods, services, and markets in return. While the variations of the core-periphery relationships are many, the important point is the dominant role of the core in the administration and governance of the system.

The core is distinguished, and in part defined, by its size and technological superiority; the British economy in the nineteenth century and the American in the second half of the twentieth were both significantly larger and more technologically advanced than other economies. But the relationship of core to periphery is more than one of scale. It is, rather, a *functional* relationship.

The core is principally defined by its performance of certain functions in the international economy. In the first place, it performs the role of international banker. The core supplies the international currency and liquidity; in effect it establishes and manages the international monetary system. Second, it plays a critical role in creating and organizing the international trading system. Unilaterally in the case of Great Britain and the repeal of the Corn Law (1846), or multilaterally in the case of the United States and Bretton Woods (1944), the core also uses its influence and power to create a liberal trading system. Finally, through private investment or foreign aid or both, the core supplies investment capital and generates development throughout the system. In short, the core sets and enforces the rules of economic exchange and development. These rules are accepted by the periphery in part owing to the power of the core and in part because the system generates growth for both core and periphery.

These definitions of core and periphery differ from those frequently employed by Marxist and other writers. The tendency of Marxists, for example, is to regard the core as being composed of all the capitalist economies and the periphery as comprising the so-called third world. A non-Marxist economist, on the other hand, would identify several cores scattered throughout the world: viz., the great metropolitan regions of New York, Tokyo, Sao Paulo, etc. To some extent, one is dealing here with different levels of analysis. At times, these other meanings will be used. But, in general, the term "the core" refers to a particular nation-state which performs certain political and economic functions with respect to the creation and maintenance of the international economy.

In the nineteenth century, the core of the interdependent world was Great Britain; the underdeveloped periphery, until late in the century, included much of the international economy.[4] Since 1945 the core of the interdependent world economy has been the United States. Western Europe and Japan, though both are highly industrialized, have in terms of this analysis been part of the periphery. They emerged from World War II heavily dependent upon the United States and "backward" relative to the United States in technology, managerial know-how, and industrial organization. The economic history of the postwar decades can be told in terms of the diminishing industrial and technological gap between the American core and these industrialized peripheries.

Behind the phenomenon of rise and subsequent decline is the fact that a major consequence of an interdependent economic system undergoing rapid growth is its impact on the distribution of wealth and economic activity.[5] As economists have observed, economic growth does not take place evenly throughout an economic system; it is centered, at any given point in time, at particular places. These so-called growth poles become the nodal points in the system. In the words of the distinguished French economist, François Perroux, "the fact of the matter is that growth does not appear everywhere and all at once, it appears in points or growth poles with varying terminal effects for the whole of the economy." [6]

As a result, economic growth has two opposing consequences

for the distribution of wealth, power, and economic activity within an economic system. In the first place, there takes place what Gunnar Myrdal has called the backwash and Albert Hirschman has called the polarization effect; that is, wealth, industry, and economic activity tend to concentrate at the core or initial starting point. In opposition to this agglomeration process, there is an opposing tendency for a spread (Myrdal) or trickling-down (Hirschman) effect also to take place; namely, over a period of time wealth and economic activity tend to diffuse from the center into the periphery and distribute themselves at new nodal points throughout the system.[7]

In contemporary writings on international economic relations, there is perhaps no more controversial subject than the tendency of wealth to concentrate and of spread effects to be limited to certain nodal points in the system. With respect to concentration, there are essentially only two alternative explanations. One group explains the existence of great extremes of affluence and poverty by the simple fact of exploitation of the weak by the strong. According to the views of Marxists and mercantilists, over the past several centuries a transfer of wealth has taken place from the periphery of mankind to the industrial centers. The development of the latter is explained by the exploitation and underdevelopment of the former: the economic and military power of the industrial centers has enabled them to create an international division of labor which fosters accumulation of wealth in the initial centers of industrialization and produces underdevelopment elsewhere.[8]

The other major explanation of concentration in the core and limitation of spread effects to the periphery is that the rate of profit at the growth center is higher.[9] This may be due to a large number of circumstances, including the achievement of technological superiority; the availability of resources, including skilled labor; the existence of good transportation; the presence of external economies; lower transaction costs; the existing social and technical infrastructure; a high rate of savings; and economies of scale. It is this higher rate of profit in urban and industrial centers that, for example, attracts and absorbs labor, capital, and resources to the detriment of the periphery. The concentration of wealth, power, and industry in the core, then, is here explained primarily by the operation of the market and price mechanisms.

The fundamental advantage of the center over the periphery, then, is its technical and organizational superiority. It is this leadership which underlies the international division of labor between the advanced industries of the center and the lower technique, low-technology industry, or raw material producers of the periphery. However, because of its initial innovative lead and industrial superiority, the center is in a position to enjoy what may be called monopoly or "technological" rents from its economic partners. It can obtain a high rate of profit or return relative to the marginal increment of investment or effort required.

The concentration of wealth and power in industrial centers, then, is due partially to factors of market power and competitive advantage. Inequality in the modern world rests in large measure on the greater efficiency and technological supremacy of the existing industrial and urban centers. One may, if one wishes, label these advantages a form of exploitation in order to explain the phenomena of development and underdevelopment. At least it is true that economic inequalities do create the necessary conditions for exploitation, however it may be defined. Equally important, there is no doubt that industrial centers frequently seek to prevent the spread of industrialism. Certainly, the immense competitive advantages of the initial industrial centers mean that the spread of industry takes place under formidable disadvantages and usually against the resistance of the existing centers.[10]

The second, and opposed, effect of sustained economic growth is to diffuse or spread the process of growth throughout the system. With industrialism and the rise of an interdependent world economy, all the factors of production—labor, capital, technology, and even land itself (i.e., food and raw materials)—have become more or less mobile. Industry spreads from the core into what had been the periphery through the migration of skilled labor, the expansion of trade, and foreign investment. Even where the diffusion of these more tangible factors of production is not involved, the spread of scientific and technological knowledge facilitates the spread of industrialization to new industrial cores.

In the absence of countervailing political forces, such as planning, depression, or war, the tendency, at least in the short run, is for polarization effects to predominate over spread effects.[11] That is to say, the rate of growth of wealth and economic activity at the center will be greater than the spread or diffusion of wealth and economic activity into the periphery. Although economic resources or factors of production are constantly diffused from the center into the periphery, up to a point the counterflow from the periphery into the growth center or core is far greater. As one authority on economic location has written, "[t]he emergence of a polarized structure will normally be accompanied by a series of displacements, from the periphery to the center of the principal factors of production: labor, capital, entrepreneurship, foreign exchange, and raw materials in unprocessed form." [12]

Moreover, the diffusion of the growth process does not take place evenly throughout the system. The distribution of raw materials, of transportation networks, and other factors tend to favor one area over another, affecting the patterns of trade, investment, and migration. As a consequence, spread takes place in the form of new concentrations of economic power and wealth arising at particular nodal points in the periphery. In time, what was part of the periphery becomes a growth center in its own right and a center for the further diffusion of growth. While the economics of location provide few guides to forecast the new centers, the basic phenomenon has been described as follows:

> Therefore, it will be seen [that] if economic activity were left to itself to spread over the surface of the earth undisturbed by other than economic motives, it would not approximate to a condition of even distribution of marketing and manufacturing centers

throughout. On the contrary, there would be certain points of exceptional concentration of commerce or industrial activity or both.[13]

Over time, the spread of industry and economic activity does take place from the original core to points in the periphery. This process of diffusion, like that of concentration, can also be explained, at least in part, by the operation of market forces. Comparative advantage increasingly shifts to the emerging cores in the periphery. The process of economic growth brings about a variety of changes in the core—rising wage rates, diseconomies of scale, the exhaustion of resources or their rising cost, or both, the shift to a service economy, and a falling rate of profit due to capital accumulation—which encourage industry and economic activity to migrate. In sum, the differential profit rate in the periphery relative to the core encourages the export of capital and industry from the core to the periphery.[14]

In international economics this process of industrial diffusion is reflected in the so-called stages in a country's balance of payments. These stages, though imprecise, define the transformation or evolution of an economy from young debtor to mature creditor. In terms of the process being described here, however, these stages correspond to the transformation from nonindustrial periphery through industrial core to foreign investor. While this typology is generally accepted by international economists, it has not yet been analyzed, to my knowledge, in the context of the rise and relative decline of industrial economies.

During the first stage, the country is a recipient of foreign investment. Although the dependence on foreign investment has differed greatly from case to case, the young debtor or periphery economy borrows capital to develop its manufacturing or extractive industries. As its economy develops, it reaches the stage of mature debtor and begins to repay; it reduces its dependence on foreign investment. In time, it becomes a young creditor and begins to export capital in its own right. Finally, the economy becomes a mature creditor; there is a net surplus of claims over liabilities. During this last stage, which Great Britain reached in the latter part of the nineteenth century and the United States had reached by the 1970s, industry declines, and the role of merchandise exports in the country's balance of payments decreases. Instead, the country increasingly lives off its earnings from foreign investment in the periphery and in the emerging new cores. In time a gradual shift takes place in the international distribution of industry and power from the mature creditor nation to these rising industrial cores.

As Charles Kindleberger has pointed out, this evolution is not inevitable; few countries, in fact, have passed from mature debtor to young creditor.[15] Moreover, the process can be and has been cyclical: Turkey, Egypt, and India, he points out, are now young debtors, though they were once powerful imperial economies. More recently, Japan and West Germany have twice in the past century passed from mature debtor (albeit at a higher level of industrialization the second time) to young creditor. In the earlier part of this century and in the early 1970s, they challenged the declining industrial core. The possible consequences of this second challenge will be discussed in the concluding chapter.

Through their investment policies, the core's investors and frequently its political leadership seek to channel the development of the periphery to benefit their particular interests. As a consequence, foreign investment creates a division of labor between the financiers or "high-technology" industries of the core and the raw material producers or "low-technology" industries of the periphery. With British portfolio investment, this division of labor reflected primarily the desire of financiers for a higher rate of profit on their capital and of the British economy in general for improved terms of trade with respect to raw materials. American direct investment has been motivated by both of these desires as well as by the desire for managerial control over a branch-plant economy in the periphery.

In the liberal model of political economy, the opposing tendencies of concentration and spread are of relatively little political consequence. In a homogeneous culture and in the absence of political boundaries, the mobility of the factors of production tends to produce an economic and political equilibrium. Thus, the movement of industrial and economic activity to urban centers draws surplus labor from the periphery and thereby moderates the decline of wage rates in potentially overpopulated peripheral areas. As American industry moved west, for example, in response to the discovery of iron and coal, it was followed by some labor migration from the declining mill towns of New England. While this was not a painless and friction-free process, the relative mobility of all factors of production in the United States has been a major source of political stability.

In the international realm, where cultural differences and national boundaries divide core and periphery, the process of concentration and spread has profound political implications. The initial concentration of wealth, power, and industry in the core and the creation of a peculiar division of labor through foreign investment give rise to feelings of frustration and resentment in the periphery, and these feelings in turn feed the forces of economic nationalism.

The most important political consequence of the international division of labor created by foreign investment is the dependence of the periphery on the core. It is the "dependency" consequences of foreign investment which are most frustrating for important groups in the periphery and which provide the stimulus to the rise of economic nationalism, or mercantilism, in the periphery.

The concept of "dependence" has become one of the most fashionable in contemporary writings on international relations.[16] What these writings suggest is that the "dependency" relationship is an exploitative one; through trade and investment the core exploits the periphery. This is not the place to analyze this issue. As shall be argued in a subsequent chapter, however, there is a basis for arguing that, at least in the case of manufacturing investment, just the opposite is the case. The periphery is dependent precisely because it gains, or at least important elements in it gain, economically from integration with the core. The severing of ties with the core would involve an unacceptable cost to the peripheral economy. The periphery is dependent, therefore, in that it has no perceived acceptable alternatives to the economic benefits of integration with the core.

The object of economic nationalism or mercantilism is to accelerate the industrialization of the periphery and to reduce its dependence on the core. Through commercial and other public policies, mercantilism seeks to channel the forces of economic growth to the advantage of the periphery. For the peripheral nation, this means the acquisition or strengthening of an independent industrial and technological base if it is to escape its role as raw material supplier, branch-plant economy, and dependent importer of technology.

In effect, economic nationalism arises in the periphery as a protective measure against market forces which first concentrate wealth and then divide the international economy into advanced core and dependent periphery.[17] It reflects the desire of the periphery to possess and control an industrial core wherein wealth, attractive careers, and power are located. Its objective is to transform the division of labor through industrialization and to transform the peripheral nation into a relatively independent industrial core.[18]

Because of the initial industrial superiority and competitive advantages of the core, the later the industrialization of the periphery, the greater the effort must be to develop viable industries and to break into world markets, and, as a result, the greater the need for a strong national authority to offset market forces, which tend to concentrate wealth, economic activity, and power in the core.[19] For this reason, while the spread of growth, like the concentration of wealth, is to be explained in large part by market forces, a seemingly necessary condition for spread to take place at the rate desired by the periphery is the existence of some centralized political power which can counteract the economic power of existing centers and the centralizing tendency of market forces. This authority was provided in Germany (in the nineteenth century) largely by the banking institutions, in the United States by industrial corporations protected by high tariffs, and in Japan and Russia by the national government.[20]

Once set upon the course of industrialization, however, these late industrializers have enjoyed the "advantages of backwardness," which have eventually enabled them to surpass the rate of growth of the industrial leader.[21] Utilizing the most advanced, efficient industries and the lessons learned by the more advanced economies, these late starters eventually caught up with or overtook the first industrial center—Great Britain—in the latter part of the century, in time shifting the center of world industrial power and, of course, the international balance of power.

The process being described here may be characterized as follows. During the earlier phase of an interdependent world economy, such as that created by Great Britain in the nineteenth century or by the United States after World War II, polarization effects tend to predominate over spread effects. Over time, however, owing to diseconomies in the core and to the growth of the periphery, spread begins to and finally does overtake polarization. The periphery begins to grow and industrialize faster than the core. As this happens, the cost to the periphery of asserting its independence from the core begins to decrease, and the benefits of dependence on the core decline. As the economic strength of the periphery increases, more and more groups in the periphery perceive that their interests lie with a greater assertion of economic independence from the core. Then rising expectations and the appreciation of growing strength relative to the core cause these groups to swing over to disengagement from the core. Thus, as the periphery grows in strength the tendency is for it to break away from the core.

In the modern world, perhaps the first example of this phenomenon was the American Revolution. Once the American colonies had reached a certain level of development, the restrictions placed on their development by Great Britain grew intolerable. With the French defeat in Canada and the colonies' decreased dependence on Great Britain for their security, the colonies had an alternative to dependence on Great Britain. Today, the rapid industrial development of Canada has whetted the desire of Canadians to break with what they consider to be the drawbacks of economic dependence on and economic integration with the United States. And in Europe, Latin America, Japan, and elsewhere, the growing strength of these peripheral economies relative to the American core is leading to efforts to lessen dependence on the latter. In each case, economic nationalism is an expression of growing strength and rising expectations.

Underlying the growth of nationalism in the periphery today is the increasing ability of the peripheral economy to assert its independence from the core economy. In the first place, the development of the peripheral economy and particularly of its industrial sector decreases its need for foreign investment. It is increasingly able to generate its own investment capital, develop technology, and provide managerial expertise, or at least to acquire these factors of production on more favorable terms. In the area of natural resources, once the investment is in place, the advantage shifts from the supplier to the recipient of the investment. Second, as the peripheral economy advances and its attractiveness to investors increases, the resulting greater competition among foreign investors decreases the dependence of the peripheral economy on the core's investors. This is especially true in the contemporary world, where European and Japanese investors are challenging the dominant position of American multinational corporations. Finally, the relative decline of the core economy further weakens the bargaining position of the core's multinational corporations. They become increasingly dependent on foreign markets, while the peripheral economy in itself is less dependent on the core's market for its own exports. As a result of these changes the costs of a more nationalistic policy on the part of the periphery are reduced; that is, its ability to assert its independence of the core is increased. The periphery is thus both more willing and more able to change the terms on which foreign investment takes place.

The eventual consequence of the redistribution of wealth and power, then, is the undermining of the economic and political order which first benefited the core and particularly its foreign investors more than the periphery. As the peripheral nations gain industrially and their power increases, they seek to reorganize the world economy in order to advance their own economic and political interests. In time, therefore, the redistribution of wealth and power leads to a reorganization of international economic relations in a manner which reflects the power and interests of the rising states in the system. The corollary, of course, is that to the extent that the rising peripheral economies are successful and make foreign investors serve their particular interests, they cause a reassessment in the core with respect to the benefits to the core of foreign investment. Important groups in the core begin to question whether foreign investment and, in the American case, the continued overseas expansion of its corporations are in the economic and political interest of the core. Thus, the issue of foreign investment becomes increasingly politicized in both core and periphery.

Thus far, I have analyzed foreign investment, its causes, and its consequences largely in terms of the operation of market and economic forces. In the remainder of this chapter, I will analyze in more detail the political determinants of foreign investment and its effects on the core's domestic and international policies.

Domestic Politics and Foreign Investment

In domestic as in international affairs, the political order is a major determinant of the direction of economic activity. Market forces do not operate in a political vacuum; on the contrary, the domestic political order and public policies seek to channel economic forces in one direction or another. Similarly, as in international affairs, over time the evolution of economic, political, and technological forces tends to transform the configurations of domestic interests and undermine the existing political order and public policies. Economic relations become increasingly "politicized" as rising and declining economic interests clash over domestic and international economic policy. The emergent domestic political order and public policies redirect economic forces into new channels. Thus, in domestic as in international affairs, the relationship between politics and economics is a reciprocal and dynamic one.

Behind both British and American heavy reliance upon foreign investment has been the strong commitment to a liberal economic order at home and abroad. The political and economic leadership of both societies have shared this liberal perspective and have projected this vision to the international sphere. They have assumed that a liberal world of self-adjusting free trade, freedom of capital movements, and an efficient international division of labor provides the natural and best economic order, and that all reasonable men share this belief. Confident in their own economic and technological strengths, political leadership and dominant economic interests have desired an open world and asked only access (i.e., an open door) to other economies for their exporters and investors. The rationale behind the expansionism of both economies, to paraphrase an American Secretary of Defense, has been the belief that what was good for General Motors was not only good for the country but was good for the world as well, in terms of economic growth, the diffusion of productive technology, and the spread of the free enterprise doctrine itself. The economic expansion of both societies has embodied the liberal belief that underlying economic intercourse (in contrast to political relations), there is a basic harmony of interests, and that everyone can benefit through the creation of a liberal international economic order.

Specifically, the domestic political order and public policies are important in that they influence the capacity and the propensity to invest abroad. In the cases of Great Britain and the United States (and in contrast to other capitalist economies such as Germany, France, or Japan, which for political and economic reasons have been more reluctant to place their assets abroad), public policies and liberal ideology have operated to encourage massive exports of capital and the ownership of foreign assets. However, as we argue below, the consequence of this emphasis on foreign investment has been to help undermine both the domestic and international political order upon which this foreign investment strategy rested.

The capacity to invest (at home or abroad) is largely a function of the distribution of income in the core. There is a relatively high rate of savings when a large fraction of the national wealth is held by classes or groups which have a propensity to save rather than consume. In nineteenth-century Britain, with its rigid class stratification and relatively docile lower classes, a high proportion of the national wealth was held by a *rentier* class. In the United States, a large fraction of the national wealth has been held by giant corporations. In both cases, this uneven distribution of wealth to the advantage of savers and investors was a consequence of the internal politics of the society. A progressive income or corporate tax which greatly redistributed income would have significantly decreased the core's capacity to invest abroad.

Similarly, the propensity of the core to invest savings at home or abroad is influenced by public policies. Taxation and other policies determine in large measure in whose hands savings will be lodged; whether savings are held by *rentiers,* corporations, or public bodies is highly relevant for investment decisions. Furthermore, public policies profoundly affect the incentives and disincentives for investors to invest in domestic industry, foreign-government bonds, or extractive and manufacturing industries in the periphery or at home. In short, "surplus capital" and capital export are more a function of the domestic political order and public policies than an inherent feature of capitalism.

Liberal students of foreign investment tend to ignore the importance of the domestic political and social order. The reason for this neglect of domestic politics is highly significant; bringing it to light focuses attention on a critical aspect of the whole subject.

In the cases of Great Britain throughout much of the nineteenth century and the United States until the middle 1960s, foreign investment was not an issue of domestic politics. The reason, I believe, was that foreign investment was relatively costless, or perceived to be costless, to the core. To put it another way, there were no powerful groups in the core which regarded foreign investment as detrimental to their interests, or to what they held to be the "national interest." The technical superiority of the core, its high rate of savings, the international role of its currency, and liberal ideology enabled the core to export capital, technology, and other resources at what was perceived by domestic interest groups to be a low cost. With the shift in industrial power from core to periphery, however, the cost to interest groups in the core began to become apparent. Domestic labor began to see its interests adversely affected as jobs moved abroad and imports increased. Others became concerned over the fact of relative industrial decline and the shift in the locus of industrial power. In the American case, apprehension over foreign investment in extractive industries developed with the appreciation of America's growing dependence on politically vulnerable foreign sources of energy and resources. In short, foreign investment became increasingly politicized in a declining industrial power.

With respect to Great Britain, the politicization of foreign investment took place in the last decade of the nineteenth century.

For the first time, strong voices were raised which challenged the great outflow of capital. In the United States, the beginnings of this domestic challenge are to be found during the Kennedy administration. The first assault on the tax privileges of multinationals was undertaken in 1962, when the administration became concerned over the export of industry. The lowering of trade barriers proposed by the Trade Expansion Act of 1962 was partially conceived of as a means of decreasing foreign investment in, and increasing trade with, the European Common Market. By the 1970s, foreign investment had become a major issue of domestic politics.

For these reasons—the effect of domestic political factors on the capacity and propensity to export capital and the tendency, over time, for foreign investment to become politicized—the analysis of foreign investment cannot be restricted to the operation of economic and market forces. Domestic (and, as we shall see, international) politics are an important determinant of the decision of the core to emphasize a foreign investment strategy both during its rise and subsequent decline. Let us now consider the strategies available to a relatively declining core.

Industrial Decline and Domestic Response

In addition to attempting to hold its own in existing markets or to seek out new markets, there are essentially four strategies which the core can follow in response to its relative industrial decline. Certainly no country has pursued, or could be expected to pursue, one of these strategies to the exclusion of the others. But the emphasis on one strategy or another is of immense political and economic importance.

In the first place, the core can export capital in the form of loans or portfolio investments to the industrializing economies or the nonindustrial periphery. It can, in effect, become a *rentier* and increasingly live off the earnings from its investments overseas. Because the profit rates tend to be higher abroad than at home and financiers controlled her investment capital, this strategy of portfolio investment was the one chosen by Great Britain in the latter part of the nineteenth century.

An alternative strategy is the one that has been increasingly followed by the United States since the end of World War II and particularly since 1958. As we shall see, this strategy of *direct investment* is a far more complex phenomenon. It too is motivated, in part, by a differential rate of return on capital which favors foreign over domestic investment. If interest payments and capital gains were the sole motivation of American foreign investors, however, the pattern of American foreign investment would not be fundamentally different from that of Great Britain. And, in fact, a substantial amount of American foreign investment is portfolio investment.

The fundamental differences between the American strategy of direct investment and the British strategy of portfolio investment derive from the fact that the primary American investors are corporations rather than financiers or bankers. For this reason, two other critical factors are involved in their decision to go multinational and to establish branch plants or subsidiaries overseas. These American multinational corporations seek to capture or protect an additional rent on some oligopolistic advantage: a product or process innovation, a well-known trademark, or superior access to capital. The possibility of obtaining both a higher rate of profit than at home and such monopoly rents was not available to British investors, or at least to many of them. Moreover, the threatened loss of their monopolistic advantages and of market shares to foreign (or domestic) competitors is itself a further stimulus to foreign direct investment on the part of American corporations. For these several reasons, therefore, the "maturing" of the American economy has led to an immense outflow of capital in the form of direct investment.

In addition to these two strategies of foreign investment, there is, at least in theory, a third strategy available to the core in response to its threatened relative industrial decline. This is the rejuvenation of the core economy itself. In particular, this strategy implies the development of new technologies and industries and redirection of the flow of capital into neglected sectors of the core economy. Through investment in research and development, for example, capital can be employed to innovate new products and industrial processes. Government policies may also encourage greater investment in the public sector (education, transportation, urban renewal, and so forth). This strategy also implies a foreign economic policy which emphasizes trade rather than foreign investment. There is a sound basis for arguing that a greater emphasis on this strategy on the part of Great Britain in the nineteenth century would have served her national advantage. A similar argument can be made with respect to the United States today.

In terms of short-run economic benefits, there is, at least in principle, justification for foreign investment; the higher rate of profit which attracts capital abroad suggests that the capital is being more efficiently employed. As a result, total world economic welfare is advanced. On the assumption that this is indeed the case, liberalism's perspective toward foreign investment would appear to be in order. The arguments *against* foreign investment are primarily political and long-term economic ones.

From a domestic political perspective, the case against foreign investment, at least in manufacturing, is that it tends to benefit the owners of capital more than it benefits labor. Others would go further and argue that foreign investment is actually harmful to labor. While this is debatable, foreign investment does mean that labor is probably less well off than it would have been if the investment were placed in industry at home. As a consequence of foreign investment, labor's relative share of national income declines. Labor therefore regards itself as harmed by foreign investment. This, at least, has been the recent American experience, in which organized labor has turned increasingly against foreign investment and the multinational corporation.

But other domestic political consequences of a foreign economic policy which stresses investment abroad, rather than investment at home along with trade, are far more pernicious. The apparent loss of jobs due to foreign investment and the declining interest in export on the part of corporations turns labor against the very idea of a liberal international economy. Labor becomes protectionist in order to protect itself against "runaway" plants, "exported" jobs, and "cheap" imports. Moreover, this loss of labor support for free trade is not fully compensated for by industry. As most large corporations can reach foreign markets through foreign investment, they are less interested in negotiating the removal of trade barriers. Thus, the ironic effect of foreign investment may be that it undermines the domestic political base of support for a liberal international economy. I shall return to this topic in Chapter VII.

This analysis suggests that there is yet a fourth possible strategy in response to relative decline; "reaction" rather than "strategy" is perhaps the more appropriate characterization. That is, the core may withdraw into itself. As the periphery advances, as it frees itself from dependence on the core and the terms of investment shift to its advantage, the core retreats into protectionism or some sort of preference system. It throws up barriers both to the export of capital and to the import of foreign goods. It favors preferential commercial arrangements. Little is done to reinvigorate its domestic industrial base. This tendency is certainly one that has long been at work in the case of Great Britain; it is increasingly finding a responsive chord in the United States.

I have already hinted that a strategy of portfolio or direct investment may not be viable over the long run. Or, to put it another way, such a strategy harbors the inherent danger that as the periphery advances and the core declines, economic nationalism in the former and politicization in the latter will undermine the political base which has supported a policy of foreign investment. Groups in both periphery and core turn against foreign investment, with the result that the core is both pushed and pulled back into itself. Unfortunately, this withdrawal does not in itself give rise to a technological and industrial rejuvenation of the core's industrial economy. To appreciate why, one must study the nature of technological advance and its impact on the economy.

As Joseph Schumpeter and others have emphasized, the most important technical and organizational innovations which underlie the evolution of the capitalist world economy tend to cluster in time and space.[22] Major advances in industrial methods and technological products have constituted a discontinuous process, characterized by sudden clusterings or jumps such as those identified with the several phases of the continuing industrial revolution and the emergence of successive dominant cores.

The first phase of the Industrial Revolution and the rise of Great Britain as the core of the world economy were dependent upon a cluster of technical breakthroughs in steam power, iron metallurgy, and textiles. Subsequently, the railroad and the opening of new lands were the great stimuli to investment at home and abroad. In the latter part of the nineteenth century, new methods of industrial organization, the advent of new industries (electrical, steel, and chemical), and the application of scientific theory to industry led to the industrial and political rise of Germany on the European continent. In the twentieth century, the industrial and economic hegemony of the United States has rested in large measure on the cluster of innovations in managerial know-how and advanced technologies (automobile, electronics, petrochemicals) that have constituted the fundamental factors in economic and industrial growth over the past half-century.

In the Schumpeterian system, the evolution of capitalism is characterized by a process of creative destruction. This process, wherein radical new industries and technologies are created and replace older industries, is held to be responsible both for the great waves of investment and technological advance over the past two centuries and for the intermittent periods of depressions as investment opportunities have been successively exhausted. The rise and decline of innovation and of investment opportunities in Schumpeter's model account for the long, fifty-year (or Kontratieff) waves of the business cycle, which he believed were inherent in the evolution of capitalism.

Underlying the process of creative destruction there operates what Simon Kuznets has identified as the Law of Industrial Growth.[23] According to this empirical observation, the tendency for the output of any given product is to describe an S-shaped curve over time, with the percentage rate of growth generally declining throughout. This pattern reflects the retardation in the rate of technical progress as the industry exhausts its inventive potential. What the Schumpeterian model suggests, however, is that the Law of Industrial Growth is applicable to an industrial economy as a whole. Over time, unless a profound rejuvenation of the economy takes place, there is an overall decline in the rate of technical progress.

This Schumpeterian model of capitalism raises a number of critical issues. Are Kontratieff waves, for example, an inherent feature of capitalistic development? What is the underlying mechanism that explains these alleged long-waves? If it is innovative activity, what accounts for increases or decreases in the rate of such activity? These larger issues, however, fall outside the concern of this study. The important and relevant point is, rather, the empirical observation of Schumpeter and others that the industrial development of the modern world economy has been discontinuous and has passed through successive phases.

The technologies and industries identified with each of these phases have stimulated great demand for investment capital first in the core economy and, subsequently and in part through foreign investment, throughout the world economy. As each of these investment phases has run its course, crisis has ensued until new innovations or equivalent developments (e.g., war, the opening of new lands, construction booms) have provided a sufficient stimulus for massive capital investment and economic growth.

This conception of technological and industrial advance contrasts with the view that technology advances incremently and that there is a continuous introduction of novelty into the economy. As old industries decline and cease to attract investment capital, this view argues, new industries and investment opportunities constantly arise to take their place.[24] The implication of the Schumpeterian model that one can speak of the relative decline of an entire industrial economy as opposed to the decline of particular industries is rejected. As we shall see in a subsequent chapter, this conception of a constant rate of incremental innovation is a basic premise of the so-called product-cycle theory of foreign direct investment.

One need not have to choose, however, between these two views of technological change. If one distinguishes between "revolutionary" and "normal" technological innovation, as does Thomas Kuhn with respect to scientific discovery, the Schumpeterian and product-cycle conceptions are quite compatible.[25] During each phase of the evolution of capitalistic development, there has been a constant, continuous advance in technology. Yet, these incremental advances do not account for the great surges of investment in history and the highly progressive nature of capitalism. Over and above this continuous process, and accounting for the phases themselves, have been the revolutionary technological breakthroughs, which are our primary concern in explaining the rise and decline of successive capitalistic core economies.

These technological revolutions have been confined to particular core economies, such as the British in the early nineteenth and the American in the twentieth century, and have been the primary focus of investment activity. They have been a major factor in the core's rapid growth and rise relative to other societies. Subsequently, the new technologies and industries have diffused to peripheral economies. This process of diffusion has frequently been accompanied and stimulated by foreign investment on the part of the core economy. Thus, initially in the core economy, and subsequently, partially through foreign investment, in peripheral economies, successive major technological breakthroughs have stimulated a high rate of investment and growth throughout the world economy.

From this perspective, a crisis arises when these major technological innovations have run their course and the industries they have created have ceased to be the critical areas of innovation and growth. For Schumpeter, the trough between the decline of a dominant industrial sector and the emergence of new leading sectors explained the long-waves in the business cycle. One need not accept this aspect of his model, however, to appreciate that the exploitation and subsequent exhaustion of major technological breakthroughs are primary determinants of the rise of the core, its investment activity, and the subsequent rise of peripheral economies.

On the basis of this conception of the nature and importance of technological innovation, let us return to the primary issue with which we have been concerned: the strategies available to a declining core economy. Specifically, if the United States has largely exhausted the potential inherent in existing technology, much as Great Britain did in the latter part of the nineteenth century, what are the prospects that it will pursue a rejuvention rather than a protectionist strategy? The reasons for concern in this regard are very real.

Industrial economies tend to be highly conservative and to resist change. Schumpeter's process of creative destruction is an expensive one for industrial firms with heavy investment in existing plants; labor can be equally resistant. The propensity of corporations is to invest in particular industrial sectors or product lines even though these areas may be declining. That is to say, the sectors are declining as theaters of innovation; they are no longer the leading sectors of industrial society. In response to rising foreign competition and relative decline, the tendency of corporations is to seek protection of their home market or new markets abroad for old products. Behind this structural rigidity is the fact that for any firm, its experience, existing real assets, and know-how dictate a relatively limited range of investment opportunities. Its instinctive reaction, therefore, is to protect what it has. As a result, there may be no powerful interests in the economy favoring a major shift of energy and resources into new industries and economic activities. In short, an economy's capacity to transform itself is increasingly limited as it advances in age.

The rejuvenation of an economy and the shift of resources to new leading sectors would appear to result only from catastrophe, such as defeat in war, political revolution, or other major economic dislocation, such as shortages in energy and raw materials. It took near-defeat in World War I for Great Britain to begin to restructure her economy, though even then she did not go far enough. Russia's collapse and the Bolshevik Revolution accelerated her industrialization. It is not surprising today that the three most dynamic industrial powers—Japan, West Germany, and East Germany—were the defeated nations in the last world war. Nor is it surprising that outside the military realm, the two victors—the United States and the Soviet Union—are falling behind industrially. Whether the current economic dislocation (inflation, shortages of resources, and declining profitability) will trigger a rejuvenation of the declining American economy is an issue that will be discussed in a subsequent chapter.

In conclusion, the only time when there are sufficient forces in a declining economy to regenerate it may be when it is too late. If so, then the only two realistic strategies may be those of foreign investment (direct or portfolio) and some form of economic autarky. In both the cases of Great Britain and the United States, the holders of capital preferred to send it abroad. In the short run, this capital export made good sense. In the long run, however, it decreased the probability that the home economy would be reinvigorated; furthermore, it generated protectionist and autarkic attitudes in labor and other sectors of the society. For these reasons, the long-term benefit to the core of a foreign investment strategy is open to question.

The Spread of Industry and International Conflict

As the original core declines and as new cores in the periphery "catch up" industrially, the old core and the new cores increasingly come into conflict over markets, raw materials, and investment outlets. The rising industrial powers cut into the profit margins that the original core has enjoyed. The outbreak of economic conflicts at the end of the nineteenth century (and again in the 1970s) would appear to be correlated with the core's loss of industrial leadership.

In this situation, there are three possibilities. The first is that the original core somehow manages to retain or reassert its dominant position relative to the emergent cores; it continues to set the rules. Great Britain was able to do this at least with respect to the international monetary system and foreign investment long after she ceased to be the dominant industrial power, though eventually the system collapsed with the Great Depression. The second possibility is a shift from a hierarchically organized international economic system to one composed of relatively equal cores; the several cores together negotiate the rules governing trade, money, and investment. In the mid-1970s, this is essentially what the industrial powers are seeking to accomplish.

Finally, the system can break down and fragment into conflicting imperial systems or regional blocs. This tendency was a major aspect of the latter part of the nineteenth century and became the dominant feature of the world economy during the period between the two world wars. With the relative decline of American power, it has reasserted itself in the 1970s.

Although none of these three possibilities is inevitable, the argument of this study is that the third possibility is most likely.

At least, the tendency toward breakdown or fragmentation of the system greatly increases with the relative decline of the original core. As the core declines, there is likely to be an outbreak of economic and mercantilistic conflict.[26] This conflict is endemic in the system until one nation establishes itself as the new dominant core. To prevent this, one can only hope that the strongest economic powers will exercise self-restraint and negotiate a new set of effective rules reflecting the new international balance of economic and military power.

If one goes no further than this, he has the essence of Lenin's theory of capitalist imperialism. In his *Imperialism: The Highest Stage of Capitalism,* Lenin analyzed the economic and imperial clashes that preceded World War I. He regarded the conflict as arising inevitably out of the challenge of growing and expanding capitalist societies (America, Germany, France, and Russia) to the dominant capitalist power (Great Britain). On the basis of his analysis of the imperial conflicts among capitalist societies over the economic and territorial division of the global periphery, he formulated his famous "law of uneven development":

> . . . the only conceivable basis under capitalism for the division of spheres of influence, interests, colonies, etc., is a calculation of the *strength* of those participating, their general economic, financial, military strength, etc. And the strength of these participants in the division does not change to an equal degree, for the *even* development of different undertakings, trusts, branches of industry, or countries is impossible under capitalism. Half a century ago Germany was a miserable, insignificant country, if her capital strength is compared with that of the Britain of that time; Japan compared with Russia in the same way. Is it "conceivable" that in ten or twenty years' time the relative strength of the imperialist powers will have remained *un*changed? It is out of the question.[27]

Thus, the clash between declining and rising capitalist cores explains, according to Lenin, both imperialism and wars in the capitalist eras.

A critique of Lenin's theory is not in order here.[28] Yet, several points might help clarify the argument of the present study. In the first place, there was little relationship between British foreign investment and the colonial empire Britain acquired in the era prior to World War I. As shall be shown in greater detail in the next chapter, the great bulk of this investment went elsewhere, particularly to the white dominions, the United States, and Latin America. The major exception to this generalization was India, which did attract much British investment. India, however, was acquired by the British long before the events occurred which Lenin was seeking to explain by his theory. Marxists might very well retort that subsequent colonial acquisitions were necessary in order to protect the lifeline to India. While this is no doubt true, it overlooks British motivation. In part, there was a desire to protect British investors; but the real value of India (and the rest of the colonial empire) was the strategic position it conferred on Great Britain in world politics over her rising American, French, and German rivals.

Lenin's theory does help to explain some things. It accounts in part for much of the commercial and perhaps even the colonial conflict of the prewar period. But it certainly doesn't explain what he thought he was explaining: World War I. With the exception of the Boer War, all the colonial conflicts were settled through diplomacy. Two of Great Britain's fiercest commercial and imperialist competitors—the United States and France—were her allies in the war. In short, Lenin's "law of uneven development" may explain elements of what took place owing to the spread of industry and the relative decline of the British core. It does not explain, however, the dynamics which eventually led to World War I. For such an explanation one must take a closer look at the effects of the spread of industry on international economic and political relations.

The early-nineteenth-century British critics of free trade and liberalism had argued that as other nations industrialized, they would close off their markets to British goods and would become Britain's competitors in world markets. The spread of industrialism would mean the inevitable decline of British industry and power; in their opinion, therefore, it should be prevented. This argument, labeled the Torrens thesis after its foremost proponent, Robert Torrens, held that "as the several nations of the world advance in wealth and population, the commercial intercourse between them must gradually become less important and beneficial." [29] The official acceptance of this view well into the nineteenth century led to various efforts to prevent the export of machinery and the migration of skilled labor. Its repudiation in the 1820s grew out of the confidence that British technological and industrial supremacy was so great that she need fear no rivals.

From the perspective of economics, the weakness of Torrens's thesis is that it takes into account only the negative consequences for trade of the spread of industrialism. It neglects the fact that the diffusion of industry has two opposed effects.[30] On the one hand, the spread of industry is market-destroying in that newly industrializing countries become able to meet their own needs for manufactured goods. On the other hand, it is market-creating, for a number of reasons. The newly industrializing country imports capital goods and other advanced-technology goods from the older industrialized countries. Additionally, as incomes in the newly industrializing country rise, there is a greater demand for imported as well as domestically produced goods.[31]

Whether the market-creating or the market-destroying tendencies will predominate depends upon a number of factors: the flexibility of the older industrial core and its capacity to adjust the content of its exports; the nature and extent of foreign protectionism; and the rates of growth prevailing among the industrial and nonindustrial economies. While Britain tended to suffer as a result of the inflexibility of her industrial structure and the rise of protectionism, the high growth rates of the industrializing and nonindustrial countries ensured that British trade continued to grow absolutely although her relative share of exports declined.[32]

With growing markets throughout the world, Great Britain and the other industrial countries expanded into each other's home markets as well as into the lesser-developed economies. This created an ever-evolving division of labor with respect to industrial goods between the older and the newer industrial cores. More importantly, as other countries industrialized and began to meet their own needs for manufactured goods, British trade shifted to new markets in the underdeveloped periphery, especially in Latin America and the Far East. Thus, even though industrialization and protectionism did destroy some trade and did intensify commercial conflict, the market-creating effect of a so-called multilateral world economy offset somewhat the trade-destroying effects.

In overall economic terms, therefore, Great Britain may be said to have gained from the spread of industrialism. She continued to grow in wealth. She enjoyed a favorable rate of growth as well as a favorable balance-of-payments situation. Although she lost markets and fell behind in the newer areas of industrial technology, this was partly compensated for by a great increase in the volume of multilateral trade. Additionally, the overall effect on Great Britain of the rise of a multilateral network of trade, payments, and investments was to enable her to maintain a favorable balance of payments. As she fell behind her industrial rivals, Great Britain became more dependent on her huge surplus of capital. Through the export of capital and earnings from foreign investment and other invisibles, Great Britain continued to be prosperous.

But to focus solely on the economic consequences of the spread of economic growth and industrialism is to overlook what is politically the most significant fact for international relations. This was the effect of the diffusion of industry on the relative distribution of power in the international system.

By the last two decades of the nineteenth century, the spread of industry had profoundly reshaped the international balance of power. On the one hand, there were the rising industrial powers on the continent and overseas: Germany, the United States, Japan, France, and, further behind, Russia. On the other, there was the decline of the reigning hegemonic power, Great Britain, and the decaying power of the Austrian and Ottoman empires. Although everyone was gaining absolutely in economic terms, it was the effects of the uneven growth of industry on the relative distribution of power in the system that were most important politically. The outbreak of World War I was ultimately due to the consequences of this profound shift in the international balance of power. In short, the breakdown of the international economy and the outbreak of the war were the results of political rivalries among nation-states and not of economic conflicts among capitalists and foreign investors.[33]

Conclusions

Although foreign investment is not the primary cause of the shift in the locus of industrial power from core to periphery, it both accelerates this tendency and tends to abort any effort to reinvigorate the core's industrial base. Foreign investment benefits the owners of capital (*rentiers* and multinational corporations), but it does so at a cost to labor and the industrial position of the core. Thus, foreign investment may, in the short run, add strength to the core, but at the risk of preventing a long-term solution to the core's relative decline. From the point of view of the industrial and political strength of the core, then, there is reason to question a foreign investment strategy.

In a world of competing nation-states, wherein power rests ultimately on an industrial base, foreign investment contributes to an international redistribution of power to the disadvantage of the core. Of equal importance, the investor becomes increasingly dependent on host governments for foreign earnings, resources, and other benefits. This dependence of the declining core on the rising periphery becomes a source of political vulnerability. Foreign investment can also exacerbate international tensions. This was the experience of Great Britain in the nineteenth century, and as American investment in oil-producing countries as well as manufacturing investment elsewhere suggest, there is sufficient cause to believe that it may be the American experience in the mid-1970s.

The preceding elucidation of the several criticisms of foreign investment as practiced by the British at the height of their reign over the international economy or by the United States today should not be misconstrued. To repeat an earlier disclaimer, this volume is not a tract against foreign investment as such and for economic isolation. There are, as shall be subsequently argued, sound reasons for foreign investment. Our argument is rather that there is an inherent danger in an overemphasis on foreign investment to the neglect of the rejuvenation of the domestic economy and of foreign trade. This certainly is the lesson that can be drawn from the British experience in the nineteenth century, to which we now turn.

III

THE BRITISH STRATEGY OF
PORTFOLIO INVESTMENT

The British strategy of portfolio investment in the nineteenth century illustrates the several themes that have been stated in the previous chapters. In the first place, British investment was dependent upon the peculiar political and economic order created by Great Britain following its emergence as the world's leading industrial power. Secondly, the acceleration of British overseas investment in the latter part of the century was both a partial cause of and a response to the global shift in the locus of industrial power. Finally, the British experience reveals the danger inherent in overinvestment abroad at the expense of the domestic economy.

The Political Order Behind British Foreign Investment

Throughout the late seventeenth and eighteenth centuries, the five littoral states of Western Europe—Portugal, Spain, the Netherlands, France, and Britain—fought over the economic exploitation of Asia and America. One by one, these contenders for control of overseas mercantilistic empires and for European hegemony were eliminated until only France and England remained. The former, supreme on the continent of Europe, was the dominant power at that time. The latter, dominant on the high seas, was the rising challenger.[1]

Although both powers were growing in wealth and power, after 1750 British power had begun a more rapid advance due to the accelerating pace of the Industrial Revolution and to British control of access to America and Asia. Favored by rich veins of coal, deposits of iron, and an enterprising population, Britain began to take the lead in the technologies of the first phase of the Industrial Revolution—textiles, iron, and steam power. The growth of the British economy and the relative decline of French power caused increasing disequilibrium between France's dominant position and her capacity to maintain it. Eventually this struggle between a declining France and a rising Great Britain gave rise to the wars during the period of the French Revolution and Napoleonic era.

At issue in the clash between industrial Great Britain and Napoleonic France were two fundamentally opposed systems for organizing the world's economy—and ultimately, of course, for dominating the globe. Whereas the ideal of the older mercantilism had been the integration of national economies with colonial dependencies, the struggle between England and France reflected the commercial and productive potentialities of the Industrial Revolution. Great Britain, in command of the sea and leading in the productive technologies of the Industrial Revolution, desired the creation of a world economy centered on her industrial and financial core.

The objective of Napoleon, on the other hand, through the instrumentality of the Continental System, was to develop the economy of Continental Europe, with France as its main center.[2] As the dominant power of an integrated regional economy, France would be able to arrest her own decline and destroy

England's lucrative commerce with the continent; eventually a unified Europe under French leadership could itself take to the sea. This regionalization of the world economy under France would destroy the economic basis of British power and restore French grandeur. But with the final defeat of Napoleon at Waterloo, the last French effort to challenge British economic and political predominance came to an end. From then until the latter part of the nineteenth century, no nation would have the economic and territorial base to challenge British world hegemony.

The *Pax Britannica*, which determined the general structure of international relations until the collapse of the system under the impact of World War I, transformed the conduct and general features of international economic relations. At its height (1849–80), the *Pax Britannica* emphasized an open, interdependent world economy based on free trade, nondiscrimination, and equal treatment rather than one based on the control and possession of colonies. Although Great Britain and several other European powers retained the remnants of colonial empires, the conquest of territory and colonies declined in importance. Behind the shield of British command of the seas, British trade and investment had relatively free access to the world's markets and sources of raw materials.

The political order identified with the *Pax Britannica*, which constituted the necessary condition for the British strategy of portfolio investment, had two critical elements. The first was the redistribution of territory following the Napoleonic wars. The territorial settlement reached at the Congress of Vienna and the related negotiations may be divided into two parts. First, the redistribution of territory on the continent of Europe checked the ambitions of Russia in the east and France in the west. Second, the overseas conquests of the continental powers were reduced and Great Britain acquired a number of important strategic bases abroad. As a consequence, the four major powers on the continent were kept in check by their own rivalries and by

Britain, which, having no direct interests at stake on the continent, could play a balancing and mediating role.

The second major element of the *Pax Britannica* was British naval supremacy. It was able to exercise a powerful and pervasive influence over global politics owing to a fortuitous juncture of other circumstances. Britain's geographic position directly off the coast of continental Europe and her possession of naval bases strategically located throughout the world enabled her to control continental Europe's access to the outside world and to deny overseas colonies to her European rivals. Among these strategic control points were what Admiral Lord Fisher called "the five keys" which "lock up the world": Gibraltar, Singapore, Dover, the Cape of Good Hope, and Alexandria.[3] As a consequence, from 1825, when Great Britain warned France not to take advantage of the revolt of Spanish America, until the latter part of the century, the greater part of the non-European world was either largely independent (at least, politically) of European rule or else under British rule. It was in the British interest and was within British power to prevent both the reemergence of mercantilism and the struggle on the part of the European powers for exclusive overseas empires. Controlling the seas and access to the globe, the British had little need for the possession of overseas colonies in order to exploit the world's markets and riches.

In effect, as noted above, two complementary subsystems emerged from the Napoleonic wars and the subsequent peace treaties. Outside Europe there was the maritime realm, governed by British naval power. On the continent, the status quo was preserved partially by the British in their role as balancer, but principally by the distribution of power among the major states. The central features of this continental equilibrium were: the fragmentation of German power among scores of minor principalities, a growing but still relatively small Prussia, and a conservative, multi-ethnic Austro–Hungarian Empire. Thus, politically fragmented, largely agrarian, and lacking good land transportation, continental Europe was relatively stable until the unification of Germany under Prussian hegemony by the force of arms and the railroad.

The British possessed the further advantage of being able to preserve their global hegemony and the status quo at a minimal cost. Given their geographical position, they could bottle up the continent with relatively few ships; only with the re-emergence of the French navy and, more importantly, with the German navy in the latter part of the century could a continental naval power threaten British supremacy. Outside the continent there were really no challenging states until late in the century when the United States and Japan became important naval powers. With the rise of these challenging naval powers, maintaining hegemony would become a heavy economic burden for the British.[4] But until then, as Susan Strange has put it, the British empire was like a Model-T Ford: "It was comparatively easy to assemble and comparatively cheap to run." [5]

In addition to these political and strategic factors, another necessary condition for the British strategy of portfolio investment was a technological revolution in transportation. Communications and transportation by land and by sea were revolutionized with the invention of cheap steel and the application of steam power to sea and land transport. The steamship decreased the time, cost, and risk of marine transportation, thereby having a profound effect on economic relations as well as on the exercise of military power. It made possible specialization and an international division of labor on an unprecedented global scale.

To understand why Great Britain took advantage of this strategic and technological situation so as to create an interdependent world economy, one must appreciate the revolution which took place in British economic thought, namely, the triumph of liberalism.

The essence of the teaching of Adam Smith and of later free traders was that wealth from trade was due to the exchange of goods, not to territorial possession. Smith and other liberals argued that the costs and disadvantages of empire and territorial control outweighed the benefits; that imperial self-sufficiency and exclusive economic spheres impeded the natural flow of trade and handicapped growth; and that British supremacy rested on manufacturing, not on empire. They pointed out that England, with only half the population of France, was turning out two-thirds of the world's coal and half of its iron and cloth. Technologically more advanced than her competitors, the liberals argued, Britain could capture world markets with cheaper goods. Why, then, they inquired, should Britain restrict her trade to a closed empire when the whole world lay open and desired her goods? Britain's interest lay in universal free trade and the removal of all barriers to the exchange of goods. Through concentration on industrial efficiency, Great Britain could create an empire of trade rather than one of colonies.

The objective of British foreign economic policy became the creation of complementary economic relations between the British industrial core and an overseas periphery which would supply cheap food, raw materials, and markets. Through the migration of labor and the export of capital to developing lands (the United States, Canada, Australia, and so forth) Britain could acquire cheap imports and also develop a market for her growing industrial exports. She could sell her textiles, invest her capital, and purchase necessities nearly wherever she pleased. In the words of the distinguished economist Stanley Jevons, "Unfettered commerce . . . has made the several quarters of the globe our willing tributaries." [6]

Prior to leaving this discussion, a general comment needs to be made. As the proponents of the doctrine of the "imperialism of free trade" have correctly argued, the regime of free trade and investment was one that advanced British interests; free trade is the policy of the strong.[7] The conversion of the British from colonialism and formal imperialism to free trade and the Open Door did not reflect a shift in British ultimate objectives;

it represented only a change in methods. The objectives of British policy remained the expansion of British wealth and power.

These critics of liberalism, however, make one important false assumption, namely, that a liberal system operates necessarily and exclusively for the benefit of the dominant industrial power. On the contrary, while Britain was the main beneficiary of the system it created, much of the world enjoyed an unprecedented era of peace, prosperity, and development. As economic liberals are wont to point out, this British-centered, interdependent world economy generated benefits for all; international economics was not a zero-sum game.

Nevertheless, in a world of competing states, nations seek to change rules which seem to benefit the dominant power(s) more than others and create dependency relationships. In fact, owing to the mercantilist spirit, which is never far from the surface, a liberal international economy cannot come into existence and be maintained unless it has behind it the most powerful state(s) in the system. As Simon Kuznets has wryly commented, "The greater power of the developed nations imposed upon the reluctant partners the opportunities of international trade and division of labor." [8] A liberal economic system is not self-sustaining, but is maintained only through the actions—initiatives, bargaining, and sanctions—of the dominant power(s). In the words of J. B. Condliffe, "leadership in establishing the rule of law lay . . . as it always lies, in the hands of the great trading nations. . . ." [9]

The Nature of British Foreign Investment

Prior to 1870, almost all of Britain's rapidly accumulating savings went into the building of Britain's domestic economy and technical infrastructure, principally railways and towns. [10] The small amount of capital exported went into railway building, commercial and banking ventures, and loans to foreign governments. The greater part of this capital went to European governments. After 1870, the character and magnitude of British investment changed dramatically. Large quantities were exported toward the less-developed, primary producing countries of North and South America, India, Australia, and South Africa. By the eve of World War I the great bulk of investment went to Canada, Argentina, and South Africa. Nearly three-fourths of this investment was concentrated in Brazil, Argentina, the United States, the white dominions, and India.[11] The greater part of such investment went into public utilities, the development of natural resources, and especially the building of railroads.[12] The infrastructure required to populate and exploit the so-called lands of recent settlement was the great capital-absorbing enterprise of the nineteenth century.

The magnitude of this outflow was enormous. Between 1870 and 1913, Britain's foreign investment increased approximately 250 percent. In 1913, it amounted to £4 billion; it absorbed more than half of the total of British savings. Between 4 and 9 percent of Britain's net national income was going abroad.[13] Nearly one-half of British assets, other than land, were overseas at the beginning of World War I. The return on such investment was equally impressive. During this period, about 10 percent of Britain's national income came from interest on foreign investments.[14]

Many factors were responsible for the immense outward flow of investment: domestic demand for food and raw materials, the discovery of valuable sources of raw materials and the opening of the Great Plains, and the security afforded by the *Pax Britannica*. But an indispensable factor was that foreign investment had become more profitable than home investment; this was especially true of investment in raw materials.[15] Though British control and management frequently accompanied this outflow of essentially portfolio investment, what British *rentiers* and financiers desired was a good return on their investment.

The whole capital market of the City of London was in fact oriented toward the export of capital and not toward financing industrial development at home.

For a great variety of reasons, some of which will be discussed below, foreign investment had become more profitable than domestic investment. The impact of the depression of 1873, declining investment opportunities due to technological retardation and lack of entrepreneurship, and the deterioration of Britain's trading position were among the most important factors underlying this decline in the profitability of domestic investment. The result was that accumulated capital was exported abroad. In short, foreign investment after 1873 was initially the result rather than the cause of a declining British core. Subsequently, it accentuated this relative decline.

The classical liberal economists themselves were the first to point out that with the accumulation of capital there exists a tendency for the rate of return (profit) on capital to fall; or, as John Stuart Mill described it, owing to the accumulation of capital there is a "tendency of profits to fall as society advances. . . ." [16] With radical and Marxist critics of capitalism this tendency was enacted into the *law of the falling rate of profit*. This law constitutes the cornerstone of the classical theories of economic imperialism identified with John Hobson, Lenin, and Rosa Luxemburg. Unable to find profitable employment at home, the center acquires by force colonies which will absorb surplus capital and thereby salvages the capitalistic system.[17] (See Chapter II for my critique of this thesis.)

Classical liberal economists also recognized the existence of several alternative measures to counter the tendency for profits to fall; the two most important were those of foreign trade and foreign investment.[18] Through trade with other countries, the core could absorb capital in the manufacture of exports. Foreign investment would also siphon off capital and thereby keep the domestic return relatively profitable.

Prior to 1870, the British followed essentially a trade strategy.

The development of British industry and investment in domestic industry were directed largely at foreign export markets. After that date, however, British exports were increasingly noncompetitive. As the United States, Germany, and other European countries industrialized, they shut out British goods. Their status as Britain's best customers was transformed into that of her chief competitors. They invaded not only third markets but the British market as well. As a consequence, commercial conflict became intense; the profitability of British industry declined. In response, British capital increasingly shifted from domestic export industries to foreign investment. This transformation of Great Britain from trader to investor represented a profound structural change in the British core and its place in the world.

The British Climacteric

In terms of the model developed in Chapter II, throughout the middle decades of the nineteenth century, British foreign investment may be said to have reflected the economic and industrial strength of Great Britain. After 1870, British foreign investment was increasingly a response to the relative industrial decline of Great Britain. While no precise date for this crossover from increasing strength to relative decline can be set, it took place somewhere between 1870 and 1900. This maturing or climacteric of the British economy was made evident by important changes in a number of areas.[19]

In the first place, the period from 1873 to 1913 saw a deceleration of British growth. While real output and national income continued to grow, industrial production grew at a decreasing rate. Although the evidence is debatable, the rate of British industrial output began to decline in the 1870s and declined still more rapidly after 1890.[20] While the reasons for this relative decline are a matter of controversy, the fact is that

British production grew slowly between 1870 and World War I, especially in comparison with Germany and the United States.

A second indication was the changing international distribution of manufacturing. In critical industrial areas such as coal, iron, and steel, Great Britain was falling rapidly behind.[21] As shown in Table 7, by the middle of the 1880s the United States had a greater share of the world's manufacturing production than did Great Britain. The American rise was especially rapid after 1900; by 1906–10, the United States had 35 percent of world manufacturing. Germany's advance was equally spectacular; by 1906–10, it had surpassed Great Britain as a manufacturing center. Japan, too, was rising fast as a major industrial power; Russia's industrialization was slower and would not reach full stride until the interwar period (1919–39), yet her industrial output was also advancing. As a consequence, whereas Britain's share of world manufacturing was 32 percent in 1870, by 1913 it had dropped to 14 percent.

This relative industrial decline was reflected in and caused by the changing status and composition of British exports and imports. In 1870, Britain's share of world trade in manufacturing had been 40 percent; by 1913, it had declined to 27 percent.[22] Not only was Britain falling behind in those industrial areas

TABLE 7

Percentage Distribution of the World's Manufacturing Production by Country, 1870–1938

IOD	WORLD	U.S.A.	GREAT BRITAIN	GERMANY	FRANCE	RUSSIA	OTHERS
	100.0	23.3	31.8	13.2	10.3	3.7	17.7
1885	100.0	28.6	26.6	13.9	8.6	3.4	18.9
1900	100.0	30.1	19.5	16.6	7.1	5.0	21.7
1910	100.0	35.3	14.7	15.9	6.4	5.0	22.7
	100.0	35.8	14.0	15.7	6.4	5.5	22.6
1929	100.0	42.2	9.4	11.6	6.6	4.3	25.9
1938	100.0	32.2	9.2	10.7	4.5	18.5	24.9

: League of Nations, *Industrialization and Foreign Trade* (Geneva, 1945), p. 13.

of increasing importance in world trade, but she was even failing to maintain her relative share of world trade in the older industries upon which her industrial strength continued to rest. Nevertheless, the composition of her exports changed very little. In 1913, textile exports particularly to new markets in underdeveloped countries (Latin American and Asian) represented 34 percent of British exports.[23] In short, rather than developing new exports for old markets, Britain searched for new markets for old exports.[24]

A further indication of Britain's decline as a trading nation and her transformation into a *rentier* economy was the increasing separation of British exports and foreign investment. In the early and middle decades of the century, British foreign investment had been accompanied by the export of steel rails, rolling stock, and other goods associated with the development of railroads. As the century advanced, there was a decline in such exports. Britain continued to export capital for railroad and other public utilities, but the borrowers tended to purchase the goods elsewhere. Thus, foreign investment was decreasingly significant as a stimulus to her industrial development.[25]

Throughout the nineteenth century, Great Britain had a trade deficit which was financed by the sale of services and investment earnings. In the latter part of the nineteenth century, however, the nature of this deficit and the composition of British imports changed significantly. In 1850, Britain's imports were primarily raw materials and food. By 1900, food imports had risen to 42 percent of the total.[26] Between 1850 and 1913, however, manufactured imports had grown from 7 to 20 percent.[27] This dramatic decline in raw materials imports and growth in manufactured goods reflected Britain's relative deterioration as an industrial power.[28]

Behind this weakening industrial position lay two fundamental problems. In the first place, Great Britain in the late Victorian era had reached what W. W. Rostow has identified as "the age of high mass consumption." [29] Both public and private consumption were rising at a rapid rate.[30] This was placing ever greater demands on national resources. Between 1870 and 1914, especially in the last quarter of the century, private consumption increased nearly 50 percent per capita; [31] public consumption was similarly on the increase. Thus, at a moment in her history when Britain was pressed by commercial and naval rivalries, an increasing proportion of her resources was absorbed by private and public consumption.[32]

In an arena of rapidly industrializing competitors, Great Britain had become the world's first service economy.[33] Between 1871 and 1911, the number of persons in commercial occupations rose by 313 percent.[34] Reflecting Britain's rising standard of living, this development was also indicative of Britain's declining strength as an industrial power. As services have a low potential of productivity growth, the fact that nearly half the working population was engaged in services meant a decline in national productivity.[35]

The second critical problem was Britain's increasing technological backwardness. Deficient in technical education, the application of science to industry, and entrepreneurship, Great Britain was falling rapidly behind in the technologies of the second Industrial Revolution, which were based on steel, chemicals, and electricity.[36] The clustering of innovations in these technologies which were becoming the basis of industrial development took place in Germany and the United States. British entrepreneurs failed to take advantage of the technological opportunities then opening up. The heart of British industrial life continued to be the great industries of the Industrial Revolution of the late eighteenth and early nineteenth centuries: iron, textiles, and coal. Although these industries remained strong and generated exports, they had ceased to be the theaters of innovation in technique and organization. The "growth curves" for these industries had flattened; they were growing at a declining rate. At a time when the British economy should have been undergoing a reinvigoration and developing new industrial specializations, it emphasized traditional industries and the export of capital. Great Britain was suffering the consequences of having been the first industrial nation. Its leading sectors were no longer at the forefront of economic growth.[37]

As Britain's relative decline became more apparent, foreign investment became increasingly politicized. Questions were raised about possible new strategies. Most of the aspects of the succeeding debate over "national efficiency," [38] foreign policy, and imperialism cannot be explored here.[39] The one dispute which concerns us is that between the advocates of continued emphasis on foreign investment and those who argued for a reinvigoration of the British economy.

On the side of reinvigoration and domestic investment were individuals like Halford MacKinder, the Webbs, and Joseph Chamberlain. For differing reasons these individuals desired a greater emphasis on domestic investment and a dramatic slowing down of the outflow of capital. Socialists and spokesmen for labor and domestic industry wanted controls on the export of capital and the stimulation of the domestic economy. What concerned MacKinder, for example, was the industrial and technological decline of Great Britain relative to Germany and the implications of this shift in industrial strength for the European balance of power. Furthermore, he and other critics argued that the export of capital promoted industrialization and raised up foreign competitors. In his *Money-Power and Man-Power,* MacKinder argued that Great Britain, under the leadership of financiers and the City of London, was forsaking industrial and military power in order to accumulate financial wealth and foreign investment.

In contrast to MacKinder's and others' concern with national power and industrial productivity was the course followed by the controllers of British capital and finance. During the period between 1865 and 1905, the amount of physical capital invested in domestic industry per capita declined per decade as follows: [40]

1865–75	39 percent
1875–85	14
1885–95	6
1895–1905	7

From a short-term perspective, it is difficult to fault Britain's heavy reliance upon foreign investment. The heavy overseas flow of capital encouraged British exports, albeit, as we have already seen, in traditional industrial sectors and at a declining rate. It furthermore increased supplies of food and raw materials, thereby improving Britain's terms of trade. Additionally, foreign investment was more lucrative than domestic; these earnings, along with the selling of services, enabled Great Britain to have an accelerating current account surplus despite a growing deficit in commodity trade (see Table 8). Moreover, this investment played a vital role in British diplomatic competition with her European rivals.[41]

From a longer-term perspective, however, Britain's over-emphasis on foreign investment was a cardinal error. The diversion of capital and entrepreneurial energies certainly was a major factor in weakening Britain's industrial base. The attention of the British financial and political elite was focused on the safeguarding of these investments. Though the role of these investments in British foreign policy and imperialism has been misconstrued by Marxists, they were certainly a major factor in diverting British attention away from European affairs, where her vital interests lay, and in encouraging interventionist policies, especially the highly divisive Boer War.[42] In effect, foreign investment both encouraged and helped finance Britain's world position, but at the price of her domestic industrial development and primary security concerns. Her foreign investment strategy thus ill-prepared Great Britain for the emerging international challenges of the late nineteenth and early twentieth centuries.

TABLE 8

Balance of Britain's Foreign Payments in the Nineteenth Century
(Annual Averages for Five-Year Periods)

	BALANCE ON GOODS, I.E. MERCHANDISE TRADE (£ M.)	BALANCE ON SERVICES (£ M.)	BALANCE ON GOODS AND SERVICES (£ M.)	NET INTEREST AND DIVIDENDS (£ M.)	OVERALL BALANCE OF CURRENT ACCOUNT (£ M.)	ACCUMULATED BALANCE OF CREDIT ABROAD BY END OF 5-YEAR PERIODS (£ M.)
1815–20	−9	+14	+5	+2	+7	46
1821–25	−8	+14	+6	+4	+10	98
1826–30	−13	+11	−2	+5	+3	111
1831–35	−13	+14	+1	+5	+6	143
1836–40	−24	+19	−5	+8	+3	156
1841–45	−17	+15	−2	+7	+6	185
1846–50	−27	+22	−5	+9	+5	209
1851–55	−27	+23	−4	+12	+8	249
1856–60	−34	+43	+9	+16	+26	380
1861–65	−57	+57	0	+22	+22	490
1866–70	−58	+68	+10	+31	+40	692
1871–75	−62	+87	+25	+50	+75	1,065
1876–80	−125	+94	−31	+56	+25	1,189
1881–85	−104	+101	−3	+65	+62	1,497
1886–90	−91	+94	+3	+84	+88	1,935

	BALANCE ON GOODS, I.E. MERCHANDISE TRADE (£ M.)	BALANCE ON SERVICES (£ M.)	BALANCE ON GOODS AND SERVICES (£ M.)	NET INTEREST AND DIVIDENDS (£ M.)	OVERALL BALANCE OF CURRENT ACCOUNT (£ M.)	ACCUMULATED BALANCE OF CREDIT ABROAD BY END OF 5-YEAR PERIODS (£ M.)
1891–95	−130	+88	−42	+94	+52	2,195
1896–1900	−161	+100	−50	+100	+40	2,397
1901–05	−175	+111	−64	+113	+49	2,642
1906–10	−142	+136	−6	+151	+146	3,371
1911–13	−134	+152	+18	+188	+206	3,990

Note: Services include ship sales and bullion.

Source: Michael B. Brown, *After Imperialism* (Atlantic Highlands, N.J.: Humanities Press, 1970), p. 75. Reprinted by permission of Humanities Press, Inc.

The emergence of industrial rivals in the periphery had undermined Britain's economic and political position. Even where British investment played a small role, as in the case of German industrialism, the diffusion of scientific and technical knowledge from Britain was an important factor. The entry of the United States, Germany, and later Japan into world markets intensified economic competition. The struggle for markets and resources drove down profits on manufactures and was a factor in the conflict among the several European empires. This neo-mercantilist conflict and imperial rivalry contributed in no small measure to the eventual outbreak of World War I.

The relative decline of the British industrial economy was undoubtedly inevitable. The spread of British technology and industrial know-how could not have been prevented, nor, from a cosmopolitan point of view, should it have been. Though British foreign investment certainly expedited the shift in the locus of world industrial power, it was by no means the fundamental cause. The relative decline of the British economy and the advance of her competitors were due to many factors. But one may inquire whether it was inevitable that British industry should have atrophied. Was it beyond her control to develop new industries and specializations? While it would have been a difficult undertaking, there can be little doubt that actions could have been taken that would have reinvigorated British industry.[43]

As John Strachey has summarized the situation, in the face of a declining rate of profit at home and rising competition abroad, Great Britain had essentially two choices.[44] In the first place, she could have exported her vast accumulation of capital and supported herself through her foreign earnings. Or, alternatively, Great Britain could have reinvigorated the British economy and redistributed income at home. As the interests both of the financiers who dominated the British economy and of the dominant political elite favored the former course of action, it was this one that was followed. There was, in economic and diplomatic matters, a natural "harmony of action" between the City and Whitehall.[45]

Conclusion

One may reasonably argue, I believe, that in certain respects the regime of the *Pax Britannica* was the Golden Age of transnationalism. The activities of private financiers and capitalists enmeshed the nations in a web of interdependencies which certainly influenced the course of international relations. In our own era, the role of the multinational corporation in international economic relations is unprecedented, yet the private institutions of the City of London, under the gold standard and the regime of free trade, had a strategic and central place in world affairs unmatched by any transnational organization today. Prior to 1914 the focus of international economic relations was the City of London and the private individuals who managed the world's gold, traded in commodities, and floated foreign loans. Though this interdependence differs radically in kind from that which characterizes our own more industrialized world economy, this earlier great age of transnationalism—and its demise due to changes in world politics—should not be forgotten in our enthusiasm for the multinational corporation and world economic interdependence today.

In this seemingly secure and prosperous environment, Britain's heavy reliance on a foreign investment strategy appeared to be the wisest course of action. But it made sense only if a favorable political order continued to exist. This international order comprised several conditions. In the first place, Britain's emphasis on financial rather than industrial power was dependent upon the maintenance of the European equilibrium. If any European power were to succeed where Napoleon had failed in unifying continental Europe, Great Britain would have to meet that challenge with a weakened industrial base. Secondly, the reliance upon investment income necessitated command of the seas, or at least the existence of friendly relations with those rising naval powers which could threaten British access to foreign markets, investment outlets, and sources of raw materials. Finally, it required a relatively docile periphery, free from notions of nationalism and independence.

As we know, all these favorable economic and political factors were to change dramatically in the twentieth century. The shift in world industrial and military power turned British dependence on her overseas investments into a liability. As a consequence, Great Britain was to be confronted with the task of rebuilding her industrial base. Great Britain still was faced with this immense task a quarter-century after the end of World War II.

Ironically, the person who sounded a warning to his countrymen of the dangers of overdependence upon foreign investment was John Hobson. Imperialism, he argued, strengthened the periphery at the expense of the core; through the transfer of capital and technology from the core to the periphery, the core was undermining its own viability. Once industrialized, he held, the periphery would turn against the core:

> Thus fully equipped for future international development in all the necessary productive powers, such a nation may turn upon her civilizer, untrammelled by need of further industrial aid, undersell him in his own market, take away his other foreign markets and secure for herself what further developing work remains to be done in other undeveloped parts of the earth.[46]

Whether or not this warning has relevance for the United States is an underlying concern of subsequent chapters.

IV

THE POLITICAL ORDER OF
AMERICAN DIRECT INVESTMENT

In order to understand the political order which constituted the necessary condition for the American emphasis on direct investment and the multinational corporation, one must go back at least to the interwar period (1919–1939). Events during that period shaped American attitudes and provided the basis for America's policies at the end of World War II.

The Transition to the *Pax Americana*

The international economy failed to revive after World War I. This was due to many causes: the policies of economic revenge against Germany, the ill-conceived attempt to reestablish the gold standard, the nationalistic "beggar-thy-neighbor" policies pursued by most states, and so forth. In terms of our primary concern in this study, one set of factors in particular needs to be stressed; namely, the weakness of the British core and the failure of the United States to assume leadership of the world economy. Whereas before the war the British core had provided order and coordinated international economic activities, in the 1920s and

1930s Great Britain was unable and the United States was un-
willing to restructure the international economy disrupted by
World War I. The result was a leadership vacuum, which contributed in part to the onset of the Great Depression and eventually to World War II.[1]

This leadership collapse gave rise to two contradictory developments. The first was the fragmentation of the world economy into relatively isolated trading blocs centered on the several
core economies and their peripheries.[2] The United States passed
the Smoot–Hawley Tariff in 1930, and in 1933, on the eve of
the London Economic Conference, President Franklin Roose-
velt decided to take the United States off the gold standard,
thereby further isolating the United States from the world
economy. The Ottawa Agreement of 1932, which created the
sterling area of imperial preference and reversed Great Britain's
traditional commitment to multilateral free trade, was of equal
or greater importance. The purpose of the agreement between
Great Britain and the Commonwealth, an action whose intellectual roots went back to the latter part of the nineteenth
century, was to establish a regional trading bloc effectively isolated from the rest of the world economy. Germany, in central
Europe, and Japan, in Asia, went much further, organizing under
their respective hegemonies the neighboring peripheries of strategic and economic importance. This creation of exclusive economic blocs under the hegemony of the great industrial cores
was one of the most significant international developments of
the interwar period.

The other important development arising out of the lack of
international economic leadership was the passage by the United
States Congress of the Reciprocal Trade Agreements Act in
June, 1934. The purpose of this act was to enable the United
States government to negotiate reductions in tariff barriers. The
act, which was followed in 1936 by the Tripartite Monetary
Agreement, not only reflected the transformation of the United
States into a major industrial power but also represented the

first major step by the United States toward assertion of its leadership of the world economy. The determination of the United States to overcome discrimination against American exports reflected the increasing industrial strength of the American economy. The reestablishment of a liberal world economy was to become a keynote of American planning during World War II.

The importance of economic considerations in American postwar planning has led in recent years to a spate of writings by revisionist historians who interpret these efforts as part of a grand imperial design.[3] Doubtless this literature serves to correct the simple-minded orthodox position that the Cold War originated as a Communist plot to achieve world domination. It goes much too far, however, and distorts the picture in another direction. There is a certain similarity between the revisionist emphasis on the economic factor in American postwar policy and the thesis of this study. The differences between the revisionist thesis and my own, however, are crucial. A brief discussion of these differences will illuminate the present argument.

The core of most revisionist interpretations is the Marxist assumption that the causes of American postwar expansionism and of the Cold War have been the internal needs of the American capitalistic economy. Either because of the inherent contradictions of American capitalism or because of the political power of corporate and banking interests, the United States, it is argued, imposed its will on the world; it organized an imperial world economy dominated by itself. Thus, in this view, all subsequent events—the struggle over Germany, the Korean War, and of course the war in Vietnam—can be interpreted as consequences of the larger American imperial design.

If one accepts the revisionist argument that America's corporate interests were responsible for the Cold War, then the Cold War should have been between the United States and Western Europe, particularly the United Kingdom, rather than between the Union of Soviet Socialist Republics and the United States. The bête noire of American postwar planners was European discrimination, especially the British Commonwealth system of imperial preference. Indeed, American plans for the postwar era were directed against the British in particular. Beginning with the framing of the Atlantic Charter in 1941 and continuing through the negotiation of the Lend-Lease Act (1941), the Bretton Woods Agreement (1944), and the British loan (1945), the thrust of American policy was directed against Commonwealth discrimination.[4] It has, in fact, been Great Britain and the West Europeans who have been displaced in Latin America, Asia, the Middle East, and elsewhere by American expansionism.

American economic initiatives, such as the still-born International Trade Organization and the trading rules embodied in the General Agreement on Trade and Tariffs (GATT), reflected this commitment to multilateralism and opposition to European discrimination against American goods. Nondiscrimination and reciprocity were, in fact, the basic principles of American commercial policy. Beginning with the Reciprocal Trade Agreements Act of 1934, the United States sought to use its economic leverage to open foreign markets for American exporters. But, of equal importance, American statesmen were motivated by the belief that it was the collapse of the liberal world economic order that led to the Great Depression, the rise of fascism, and, ultimately, the war itself.

What is most important to appreciate, however, is that despite the intensity of American efforts to force the United Kingdom and other European countries to accept nondiscrimination and a multilateral system, such efforts were abandoned in response to the growth of Soviet–American hostility. As American leaders accepted the Soviet diplomatic and military challenge as the major postwar problem, the American attitude toward international economic relations experienced a dramatic reversal. In contrast to earlier emphases on multilateralism and nondiscrimination, the United States actually promoted discrimination against American goods in the interest of rebuilding the shattered West European economy.

In opposition to the revisionist position, the argument of this study is that the origins of the Cold War lay in the unanticipated consequences of World War II. The collapse of German power in Europe and of Japanese power in Asia created a power vacuum that both the United States and the Soviet Union sought to fill, each to its own advantage. For its own security, neither power could afford to permit the other to fill this vacuum. The efforts of each to forestall the other merely increased the insecurity of the other, causing it to redouble its own efforts. Each, in response to the other, organized its own bloc, freezing the lines of division established by the victorious armies and wartime conferences. As in the case of every great power, both the United States and the Soviet Union desired an international environment congenial to their economic and security interests.[5]

The origins of the Cold War, therefore, may indeed be said to be economic, but in the mercantilist sense of interstate competition for control of the centers of industrial power and of the economic resources that determine the international distribution of power. Both the United States and the Soviet Union coveted Europe and Japan because of their potential industrial power and their importance for the distribution of power between the two superpowers. In effect, both the Soviet Union and the United States desired an international order that was congenial to their security and to their economic and ideological interests.[6] In the long run, as has already been stressed, the economic and security interests of nation-states cannot really be separated.

The Organization of the *Pax Americana*

In terms of absolute power, the United States, in 1945, greatly surpassed the rest of the world. In addition to her vast industrial capacity, the U.S. virtually monopolized or controlled the three sources of power in the modern world: nuclear weapons, monetary reserves, and petroleum. She alone had the atomic bomb and the knowledge to produce what at the time was called the absolute weapon. American factories produced over 50 percent of the world's output, and America held approximately 50 percent of the world's monetary reserves. And with respect to petroleum—that most vital lubricant of modern industrial economies—American oil companies, in effect, controlled the non-Communist world's supply of oil. America was nearly self-sufficient in oil; American oil multinationals, along with British and Dutch companies, monopolized Middle Eastern and other sources of oil.

One vital difference between Great Britain in 1815 and the United States in 1945, however, must be appreciated. Although the United States emerged from the war as the dominant influence in the so-called rimlands of Eurasia, Western Europe, and Japan, the Soviet Union held sway from Central Europe to the Pacific. Thus, whereas Great Britain's hegemony was virtually unchallenged during most of the nineteenth century, the United States immediately after World War II faced a continental land power capable (or so it appeared) of extending its power across the entire span of the Eurasian continent from the Pacific to the Atlantic. In this emerging context, the Soviet Union enjoyed one substantial advantage: its geographical position.

The Soviet Union is a massive land power directly abutting Western Europe and the Northwest Pacific (principally Korea and Japan). As a result, it was able with relative ease to bring its military power to bear on its periphery through the possession of a large land army. The United States, on the other hand, had to organize and finance a global system of bases and alliances in order to counterbalance the Soviet Union's favorable geographical position. And whereas the Soviet Union could rely upon indigenous Communist parties and other revolutionary forces to advance its cause, the United States had to use foreign economic and military aid to maintain its influence, acquire strategic positions, and protect American overseas economic interests. In short, for military and political reasons, economic relationships provided a vital element in the organization of the *Pax Americana*.

As a result of the Soviet challenge and the geographical asymmetry of Soviet and American power, the structure of American hegemony has differed from that of Great Britain in several important particulars. These differences are significant for understanding the development of the world economy over the past several decades and the role of the multinational corporation in that economy.

First, whereas the *Pax Britannica* rested on British control of the seas, the *Pax Americana* was based on American nuclear and aerospace supremacy as well as America's command of the seas. As a result of this global strategic superiority, the United States has been able to counterbalance Soviet conventional predominance on the continent of Europe. The primary responsibility of American ground forces in Western Europe has been to assure the credibility of the nuclear deterrent. The United States has sought to maintain this credibility in response to expanding Soviet nuclear capabilities.

Secondly, for the United States and the *Pax Americana*, military alliances with the "rimlands" of Western Europe and Asia (Japan) have provided the functional equivalent of the system of naval bases upon which the *Pax Britannica* rested.[7] The American military presence in Europe, Japan, and elsewhere around the Soviet Union provided a strategic and political framework within which American hegemony was exercised. Through the instrumentalities of the North Atlantic Treaty Organization (NATO) and the Japan–United States Security Treaty, Western Europe and Japan were brought under the protection of the American nuclear umbrella.

Finally, the economic foundation of American power and American hegemony was the interdependent international economy which had been reestablished by the United States at the end of the war. The interdependent world economy created by

Great Britain had encompassed nearly the entire known world; after 1945, a large segment of the world constituted a self-contained and self-sufficient bloc, consisting of the Soviet Union, its Eastern European satellites, and, later, China. In effect, the world economy became divided into two blocs, each dominated by one of two so-called superpowers. When one speaks of the international economy after 1945, therefore, he is speaking essentially of the non-Communist world, composed principally of North America, Western Europe, and Japan as well as most of the lesser-developed countries. Pivoted upon the United States, the world economy rested upon two sets of bilateral relationships. The first was that between the United States and Western Europe; the other was that between the United States and Japan.

The American–European Relationship

Contrary to the hopes of the postwar economic planners who met at Bretton Woods in 1944, the achievement of a system of multilateral trade was soon realized to be an impossibility. The United Kingdom and the rest of Europe were simply too weak and too short of dollars to engage in a free market. A further weakening of their economies threatened to drive them into the arms of the Soviet Union. To prevent this, the United States, in cooperation with Western Europe, had to rebuild the world economy in a way never envisaged by the postwar planners.

The American policy reversal led to the Marshall Plan, through which the United States eventually financed the reconstruction of Western Europe. The Marshall Plan signaled a profound shift in American policy, away from the pursuit of global multilateralism and American commercial interests to the promotion of European regionalism.

The reconstruction of the Western European economy involved the solution of three problems. In the first place, Europe was desperately short of the dollars required to meet immediate needs and to replenish its capital stock. Secondly, the prewar European economies had been oriented toward colonial markets.

Now the colonies were in revolt, and the United States strongly opposed the revival of a world economy based on a colonial preference system. Finally, the practices of economic nationalism and colonial preference systems had completely fragmented the European economy. The legacy of imperialism, therefore, was the Balkanization of the European economy into competitive rather than complementary national economies.

The problem of Germany was particularly difficult. Her division into Soviet and Western zones as well as the Soviet occupation of the rest of Europe had cut industrial West Germany off from her natural trading partners in agricultural East Germany and Eastern Europe. West Germany was highly vulnerable unless integrated into the West economically as well as politically and militarily. The task in Germany, therefore, was to integrate the industrial Western zones into a larger Western European economy embracing agricultural France and Italy.[8]

The response that was made to this challenge is well known. Through the Marshall Plan, the Organization for European Economic Cooperation, and the European Coal and Steel Community (Schuman Plan), the European economy was revived and radically transformed. The American contribution to these efforts consisted partly in the skillful and judicious use of economic inducements to foster European cooperation and the reduction of intra-European economic barriers. Of equal importance, however, was the American provision of a sense of security, not just against the Soviet Union but also with respect to the risks inherent in dismantling protectionism and with respect to the latent fear of German domination, especially on the part of the French. Although the division of Germany had lessened French and Italian fears of economic integration with Western Europe's dominant industrial power, American political and financial backing was essential for the decision to establish a European Payments Union in 1950 and to make European currencies convertible with one another. From this daring and important initiative, it was a short step to the Rome Treaty (1957) and the European

Economic Community or Common Market. Thus, reversing its earlier commitment to global multilateralism and nondiscrimination, the United States promoted the creation of a preference area in Western Europe which discriminated against American goods.

Although the United States tolerated discrimination, it also assumed that a fast-growing Europe would eventually be more trade-creating than trade-diverting.[9] Moreover, a large and important sector of the American economy—the multinational corporations—readily appreciated that a large European market was an attractive prospect indeed. One major condition, in fact, for American support of the Rome Treaty was a European guarantee of "national treatment" for the European subsidiaries of American multinational corporations—that is, an assurance that an American-owned subsidiary would be treated equally with national firms of European countries. The importance of this policy, and of subsequently negotiated bilateral commercial treaties, for the European expansion of American corporations cannot be overemphasized.

Nevertheless, the fundamental motivation for supporting the economic unification of Western Europe was political—the security of the West against the Soviet Union. If need be, American political leadership was willing to pay an economic cost to attain this end—though not *any* economic cost, as we shall see below. American policy rested on the assumption that as Europe regained its strength, trade discrimination against the United States would cease and, further, Europe would employ its strength in the common struggle against the Soviet Union. The economic price which the United States would pay for a united Europe was thus regarded as a temporary one. The ultimate American goal remained the achievement of greater Atlantic unity and, beyond this, the existence of a global multilateral system based on free trade and nondiscrimination.

A quite different position with respect to the nature and goal of European economic integration has been taken by many of the leaders of the European movement and particularly by the French. From the very beginning, this position has viewed regional economic integration as an end in itself, not as a stepping stone to a universal or Atlantic system. Rather, the objective of economic regionalism has been seen, as it was with Napoleon, as the revival of continental European power and influence. In an age in which economic and military power rests on large markets and large concentrations of financial and industrial capability, the integration of the European economies has been regarded as necessary in order to balance Soviet—and American—power.[10]

These two conceptions of the European Common Market have been joined in uneasy alliance since its inception. For its part, the United States, supported by West Germany and later by Great Britain, has assumed the identity of American and European interests with respect to the immediacy of the Soviet threat and the ultimate goal of a greater Atlantic economic and political community. France, on the other hand, as well as powerful groups in other countries, has favored a closed and more independent Europe. As long as the Cold War maintained its fury and Europe remained economically weak, these conflicting perspectives were subordinate to the higher priority of building European strength within the framework of Atlantic unity. But with the improvement of East–West relations and the reassertion of European economic power in the late 1960s, powerful divisive forces gained strength on both sides of the Atlantic.

The American–Japanese Relationship

The other pillar of the contemporary world economy has been the American–Japanese relationship. As in the case of West Germany, with the rise of the Cold War American policy shifted from one of "reeducation" to one of integrating Japan militarily and economically into the evolving American system. In part, Japan and West Germany presented very similar problems for

American leadership. They were "two of the greatest workshops of the world," to use the phrase of Dean Acheson. Furthermore, the traditional hinterlands and economic partners of both were by 1949 firmly under Communist control. In Japan's case, with the victory of the Chinese Communists and the forming of the Sino–Soviet Alliance, the complementary economies of North China and Manchuria had fallen into unfriendly hands. China had been one of Japan's major trading partners, and there was, in fact, a strong belief that Japan could not survive without economic relations with China. To compound the problem, Japan continued to suffer from discrimination by the other industrialized states, both in their home economies and in those of their colonial empires. Thus, the United States faced the problem of making viable a highly industrialized and densely populated Japan suddenly cut off from traditional markets and essential sources of food and raw materials.

The task of American foreign policy was to integrate Japan into the larger world economy and lessen the attraction of markets controlled by the Communist bloc. To this end, the United States brought pressures to break up Dutch, French, and British colonialism in South and Southeast Asia, and encouraged the integration of these areas into a larger framework of multilateral trade. In addition, the United States, over the strong opposition of Western Europe, sponsored Japanese membership in the IMF, GATT, and other international organizations.[11] Third, and most significantly of all, following the successful conclusion of the Japanese Peace Treaty, and in marked contrast to the discriminatory policies of most European states toward Japan, the United States encouraged the export of technology to Japan, gave economic aid to that country, and lowered the barriers against Japanese exports. In effect, the United States gave Japan relatively unrestricted access to American technology and the American market.[12] As a consequence of this favored treatment, the Japanese eventually enjoyed an exceptionally favorable balance of trade with the United States. For Japan, this trade surplus with the United States paid for importing the raw materials which fueled her extraordinarily high rate of export-led economic growth.

Parallel to the American relationship with Western Europe, then, the American–Japanese alliance provided the cement which held together the world economy and provided the economic base for American global hegemony.[13] While mutual economic interest was an important factor, the primary bond was security and the balance of power in the Far East.

For the sake of rebuilding Japanese power and maintaining its strategic position in the Pacific, the United States tolerated not only Japanese restrictions on American direct investment but Japanese barriers against American exports as well, and what Americans would come to regard as Japanese "dumping" on the American market. In the larger interest of Pacific security, the United States in effect encouraged the Japanese export-led growth drive. The United States demanded no economic quid pro quo, as it did in the case of the Common Market. But, as we have already suggested, this economic relationship rested on a political and strategic perspective which considered the Soviet and Chinese as constituting a single, indivisible factor in the Pacific balance of power. When this political and strategic perspective changed, so would the economic relationship which depended on it.

Conclusion

Just as the *Pax Britannica* provided the security and political order for the expansion of transnational economic activity in the nineteenth century, so the *Pax Americana* has fulfilled a similar function in the mid-twentieth century. Under American leadership, the various rounds of GATT negotiations have enabled trade to expand at an unprecedented rate, far faster than the growth of gross national product in the United States and Western Europe. The United States dollar became the basis of the international monetary system. Finally, the multinational corporations found the global political environment a highly congenial one. As a consequence, they were able to integrate production across national boundaries. Why they chose to take advantage of this situation is the subject of the next chapter.

V

THE AMERICAN STRATEGY OF
DIRECT INVESTMENT:
WHY THE MULTINATIONAL
CORPORATION?

The *Pax Americana* provided a political and security structure which facilitated rapid expansion abroad by American corporations. Now I shall explain why American corporations took advantage of this situation and did, in fact, establish subsidiaries and branch plants overseas. At most, the creation of a favorable political environment provided the *necessary* conditions for foreign direct investment by multinational corporations; the *sufficient* conditions can be elucidated by reference to the literature of economists on the causes of foreign direct investment.

Direct Investment in Extractive Industries

In the case of extractive industries such as petroleum or minerals, the explanation of foreign direct investment is fairly straightforward. Such investment is motivated by the discovery of valuable foreign sources of supply and the decreasing cost of oceanic transportation. Beyond these basic considerations, security of supply and the preservation of monopolistic advantages are major determinants of foreign investment in minerals and petroleum.

These extractive industries are highly oligopolistic in nature. Many of them are controlled or dominated by a few large American corporations. Additionally, a few Canadian (Alcan, International Nickel) and European (Shell, Rio Tinto Zinc) corporations participate in the several oligopolies which dominate the world's sources of raw materials outside the Communist bloc. More recently, Japanese multinationals have begun to reestablish themselves in the resource picture.

These oligopolistic industries are invariably "vertically integrated." The corporation's control extends over extraction, transportation, and refining (or semiprocessing) and, in many cases such as petroleum and aluminum, over marketing as well. As a consequence, a relatively few American and foreign corporations have controlled the non-Communist industrial world's access to raw materials—and through their investment and other policies have attempted to maintain that control.

As in the case of manufacturing investment, American mining and petroleum companies first ventured overseas in the decades just prior to World War I. In petroleum particularly, American oil companies, in fierce competition with the British, sought to gain control over foreign sources of oil.[1] During and immediately following World War II, this movement was accelerated, especially in the Middle East.

In the postwar era the motivation for foreign investment by American extractive industries changed. As a consequence of the heavy drain on its resources during World War II, the United States emerged from the war a deficit nation in many important raw materials. In certain critical resources, such as iron and copper, the United States had actually exhausted its high-quality ores. Therefore, with the retreat of European influence and the discovery of high-grade ores in South America, Canada, Africa, and elsewhere, American corporations rapidly expanded their foreign operations. Thus, they further extended their domains overseas.

This overseas expansion on the part of American extractive multinationals was encouraged by the favorable provisions of American tax laws. In the wake of the outbreak of the Korean War and the fear this generated of a prolonged conflict with the Soviet Union, President Truman established a Materials Policy Commission.[2] One major set of recommendations in the commission's report (the so-called Paley Report) was that American tax laws be modified to encourage foreign investment in minerals and petroleum. As a result of the enactment of these recommendations as well as other favorable tax provisions, American extractive industries found it highly profitable to expand overseas in search of relatively cheap sources of petroleum and other raw materials and to deemphasize the development of higher-cost, lower-grade indigenous sources of energy and raw materials. In this manner the United States economy was transformed over time from one characterized by relative self-sufficiency to one overly dependent upon foreign, albeit cheaper, sources of energy and raw materials.

Direct Investment in Manufacturing

When one turns from extractive to manufacturing industries, the situation gets much more complicated. Why, for example, should a corporation choose to incur the added costs of manufacturing overseas when it could more easily, and perhaps at an even higher profit, export its products or license its patents to a foreign manufacturer? In the remainder of this chapter we shall explore the factors and theories which explain foreign direct investment in manufacturing by American multinational corporations.

In neoclassical economic theory, foreign investment is explained in very simple terms: capital tends to flow from regions where it is in surplus and has a declining rate of return to regions where it is relatively scarce and can gain a higher rate of return. With respect to portfolio, debt securities, and other forms of indirect investment, neoclassical theory, with its emphasis on short-term profit maximization, is generally adequate. But for reasons which will be discussed below, direct investment by multinational corporations requires a more complex explanation.

A number of factors which help explain the phenomenal rise of the multinational corporation and foreign direct investment over the past decade and a half come readily to mind: foreign trade barriers, American antitrust laws, local content laws, proximity to markets, and so forth. Such a listing of factors, however, does not provide a sufficient explanation. For a deeper understanding, one must turn to the theoretical work of the several economists who have written on direct investment and the multinational corporation. These theories can be grouped into three sets. In the first place, economists and other writers may be divided along normative or attitudinal lines, that is, between those writers who take a favorable attitude toward the multinational corporation and those who are essentially critical. Secondly, writers may be divided into those who consider the multinational corporation a necessary and inevitable consequence of contemporary economic developments and those who believe it is a resultant of favorable public policies, especially those bearing on the taxation of corporate earnings. For the first group, the multinational corporation is market-induced, a response to market forces; for the other, it is policy-induced. Finally, economists (especially those favoring the market-induced position) can be divided into two further groups: those who believe that the MNCs are essentially defensive or market-protecting in nature (the product-cycle and organic theories, treated below) and those who see the multinational corporation as essentially aggressive (all the other theories to be treated below, especially the oligopoly theory).

These groupings are obviously not mutually exclusive. Most

writers on the multinational corporation can be placed in two or even three of these sets or categories. Thus, to take three prominent and contrasting viewpoints, one can categorize Raymond Vernon, Stephen Hymer, and Peggy Musgrave as follows. While Vernon (a liberal) is critical of many of the practices of multinational corporations, he is essentially pro-MNC, believes they are primarily market-induced, and regards foreign direct investment as defensive. Hymer (a Marxist), on the other hand, is hostile, yet regards the multinational corporation as an inevitable consequence of modern capitalism; he believes that the MNC is aggressive in its behavior. Finally, Musgrave is closer to the mercantilist perspective in that she believes that the MNC is neither good nor inevitable, at least on its present scale, and that its behavior is primarily aggressive.

Most scholars and scientists, and this includes economists, dislike being categorized. Some may object to being labeled, for example, as pro-MNC or anti-MNC. Such objections will no doubt be warranted in certain cases. But the diametrically opposed assumptions and conclusions of different writers generally do place them in one of these camps. While the labels I have employed are perhaps not very apt ones, they do convey the tendency of a particular writer to, for example, be sympathetic to or critical of the multinational corporation.

In terms of the purpose of this study it is important to appreciate these contrasting views on the merits, the inevitability, and the behavior of the multinational corporation. The assumptions made by writers on this subject are extremely important. In fact, they determine in most cases the conclusions of scholarly and scientific research on the multinational corporation and foreign direct investment. This chapter tries to understand various arguments and conclusions in terms of the assumptions upon which they are founded.

In an attempt to develop a unified and coherent explanation of foreign direct investment, we begin with a presentation of those theories which regard the MNC as an inevitable manifestation of contemporary economic developments. We then treat those theories which focus on the role of public policy in the foreign expansion of American corporations.

The "Economic" Position

The first set of theories of foreign direct investment rests on the assumption that the multinational corporation and direct investment are the necessary consequences of contemporary economic and technological developments. Common to all the theories examined in this section is the idea that underlying the emergence of the multinational corporation is a revolution in transportation and communications. Advances in land, sea, and air transportation as well as in modern communications have made possible the global integration of manufacturing activities. The ease and decreased cost of modern transport facilitates immense economies of scale in corporate control and the location of industries in order to take advantage of the possibilities offered by various locales. At the same time, sophisticated modern communications, including the telephone and the computer, enable management to integrate the various components of a global system. As a consequence, there can take place in both manufacturing and extractive industries vertical and horizontal integration on a truly global basis.

Against this background of significant technological changes, one can identify four different yet partially complementary economic theories. The first is that of *international oligopoly*. As noted particularly by Charles Kindleberger and Stephen Hymer, the American corporations that establish subsidiaries tend to be the large oligopolies.[3] These American giants enter foreign markets because they have a monopolistic advantage which they can exploit to earn a higher rate of profit than their local competitors. The advantages over their foreign competitors may consist in technological superiority, managerial expertise, better sources of finance, or a combination of these. In general, however, the monopolistic advantage of the American firm lies in its ownership of a novel, or seemingly novel, product or production process. Thus, the firm is motivated by the opportunity to profit by the exploitation of superior commercial knowledge.

The American firms that invest abroad tend to be research-intensive industries in the most concentrated sectors of American economy. The several hundred firms that account for the great bulk of American investment are among the largest and most

TABLE 9

Comparison of Domestic and Foreign Capital Stocks of U.S. Firms, 1970

(Amounts in millions of dollars)

	U.S. DOMESTIC CAPITAL [1]		DIRECT INVESTMENT ABROAD [2]	
	AMOUNT	RANK	AMOUNT	RANK
All manufacturing	260,101	—	30,915	—
Chemicals and allied products	36,037	2	6,868	1
Transportation equipment	20,418	4	5,131	2
Nonelectrical machinery	20,367	5	3,798	3
Electrical machinery	16,107	7	2,613	5
Primary and fabricated metals	57,383	1	2,619	4
Food products	25,551	3	1,853	7
Paper and allied products	19,357	6	2,007	6
Instruments	4,084	14	1,345	8
Wood products	8,554	11	1,296	9
Rubber	7,977	12	974	11
Textiles and apparel	13,945	8	625	12
Stone, clay, and glass	13,237	9	1,046	10
Printing and publishing	10,105	10	138	14
Other	6,979	13	602	13

1. Gross book value of depreciable assets.
2. Net fixed assets of foreign affiliates of U.S. parents.
Source: United States Senate, 93d Congress, 1st session, *Implications of Multinational Firms for World Trade and Investment and for U.S. Trade and Labor.* U.S. Tariff Commission Report to the Senate Finance Committee (Washington, D.C.: Government Printing Office, February 1973), p. 407.

technologically advanced in the country (Table 9). Furthermore, their investment abroad also tends to be concentrated in sectors where there is a high degree of market concentration. Frequently, these firms are themselves the dominant producers in the foreign market. Thus, direct foreign investment, according to this theory, is "aggressive behavior." It is primarily a phenomenon associated with oligopoly and market concentration. In other words, foreign investment is a subcategory of the general phenomenon of monopolistic behavior—i.e., the suppression of competition at home and abroad through the exercise of market power.

In itself, however, the oligopolistic theory does not explain why a corporation seeks to serve a particular market or sell a particular product through the establishment of a local subsidiary rather than through licensing or exporting. One must add to the oligopolistic theory, therefore, the so-called *product-cycle* model developed by Raymond Vernon.[4] In its essentials, the product-cycle theory identifies three phases in the life history of a product: (a) the introductory phase; (b) the maturing phase; and (c) the standardized phase.

By reason of its home market (demand) and the resources available for research and development (supply), American corporations are said to have a great advantage over their foreign competitors in the introductory stage—the development and production of new products or processes. During this stage of the product cycle American corporations enjoy a monopolistic advantage on account of their technological edge and know-how. Initially, therefore, American corporations can satisfy the rising foreign demand for the product through exporting to these markets. But as the foreign market for the product grows, and especially as the technology identified with the product diffuses abroad to potential foreign competitors, the strategy of the American corporation changes. During this *maturing* phase of the product cycle an American firm begins to lose the competitive advantage accruing from its technological lead. As the relevant technology becomes available through diffusion or imitative development, the advantage shifts to foreign production, owing among other things to proximity to the local market and lower labor costs. Therefore, if the American corporation is to maintain its market share and forestall competition, it must establish foreign branches or subsidiaries. In short, the threatened loss of an export market and the rise of foreign competitors is the stimulus for the establishment of foreign subsidiaries.

Finally, in the third or standardized phase of the product cycle, production has become sufficiently routinized so that the comparative advantage shifts to relatively low-skilled, low-wage, and labor-intensive economies. This is now the case, for example, in textiles, electronic components, and footwear. It is this stage which gives rise to offshore production, particularly of components, in such places as Taiwan, Hong Kong, and other low-wage areas. During this later stage, the corporation may export components or finished products back to the United States.

Understood in these terms, direct investment and the establishment of subsidiaries abroad by American corporations is largely defensive. In order to forestall the rise of foreign competitors and to maintain its global market position, the American corporation begins to manufacture abroad itself. The following observation emphasizes the defensive nature of direct investment:

> Industries with comparatively high export sales of products involving scientific and technical aspects in their sales and servicing, *ceteris paribus,* will have a high propensity to invest in manufacturing subsidiaries in the markets they serve. . . . In these oligopoly industries, therefore, individual firms are likely to consider foreign investments as important forestalling tactics to cut off market preemption by others. And they are likely to feel obligated to counter an investment by others with an investment of their own.[5]

According to this formulation, the crux of foreign direct investment is the transference of technical and managerial knowledge.[6] In a world where technical know-how diffuses rapidly to one's potential competitors, thereby reducing the innovator's long-term profit margin, the American corporation goes abroad to protect its investment in research and development. Thus the American innovator, rather than the foreign imitator, captures the benefits from the transference of knowledge abroad. From the perspective of the corporation and the United States government, the establishment of overseas branch plants is a legitimate mechanism to encourage investment in new research and development. If foreign direct investment did not take place, American corporations might have less incentive to develop socially useful knowledge. From the perspective of the critics of the multinational corporation in host countries, however, earnings on foreign investment are pure technological rent; that is, the corporations are earning high profits abroad at a relatively low marginal cost to themselves.

In short, according to product-cycle theory, foreign direct investment by American corporations is fundamentally a method by which to eliminate potential competitors through market preemption. While this theory is primarily *descripive* of behavior, as employed by its proponents, it frequently becomes a *prescription* for behavior. The normative argument of product-cycle theorists is that an American corporation *should* invest abroad in order to preempt the rise of foreign competition.

From the perspective of the product-cycle and oligopoly theories, the massive American corporate invasion of Western Europe that began in the late 1950s resulted from a combination of short-term opportunity and long-term fear. The establishment of the European Common Market created the opportunity; the potential revival of European industry created the fear. From its very inception, the Common Market was obviously an economic development of great potential significance. If American corporations wanted access to this immense market, they had to get inside the common external tariff. Direct investment was the mechanism chosen to take advantage of this historic opportunity. Of equal importance, the diffusion of American technical and managerial knowledge to potential European competitors could mean the eventual loss of this market. Moreover, this dynamic and growing market would provide the conditions for the evolution of giant European corporations that would one day be in a position to challenge American corporations in the American market itself.[7]

If one adds to these theories the so-called *organic* theory of investment, one achieves a still more comprehensive understanding of international investment.[8] According to the organic theory, the fundamental motive of the corporation is survival. Under conditions of oligopolistic competition, the one precondition for survival is continued growth, and continued growth can be guaranteed only by a constant or increasing share of an expanding market. If an exporter or foreign investor fails to take advantage of any market opportunities and thereby foregoes the opportunity to grow, its American or foreign competitors will step in and jeopardize the future survival of the corporation. The motive, at least in the short run, is less to maximize profits than to forestall the loss of a market. In the words of Vernon, "the yield on the investment is seen largely as the avoidance of a loss of income to the system." [9] In effect, the product-cycle and the organic theories, though starting from different emphases, complement each other.

The organic theory holds that the corporation invests abroad to defend or protect the earnings capacity of its existing capital. Although this initial investment abroad may have a lower rate of return than investment at home, it protects the corporation's existing investments and also lays the basis for eventual profits from abroad. Thus, the multinational firm takes a long-term perspective with respect to the profitability of its foreign investments; it must invest continuously in order to maintain its position in the growing market. If a dominant American corporation does not keep up with the growth of the market, the expanding market provides an opportunity for a potential opponent to move into its line of production. From this base the competitor might rise to a position from which it could eventually challenge the dominant position of the American corporation. Thus, the American corporation must in effect run even faster if it is to maintain its relative position in a fast-growing market.

The so-called law of corporate survival in an oligopolistic market has been succinctly stated by Charles Kindleberger: "Direct investment is tied to markets. If markets grow, the firm must grow. If the firm stops growing, it dies. Anything that interferes with the growth of the firm, such as balance-of-payments restrictions, while the organic life of the market goes its way will kill the firm." [10]

The missing element in these explanations, according to yet another theory, is the most obvious: the fact that direct investment takes place across the boundaries of national economies and different currency areas. "The key factor in explaining the pattern of direct foreign investment involves capital market relationships, exchange risk, and the market's preferences for holding assets denominated in selected currencies." [11] What has been crucial during periods of extensive foreign investment has been the premium placed on securities denominated in a secure currency—that is, there is security of exchange value. As a consequence, entrepreneurs in the country whose currency is regarded as secure have an advantage over local enterprise abroad. The former can afford to pay more for real assets.

This *capital market view*, advanced most convincingly by Robert Aliber, rests on the fact that in the 1950s and 1960s investors preferred to hold dollar-denominated equities. [12] Because of the security of the dollar, American firms were able to borrow on more advantageous terms than their foreign competitors; they were able to borrow at lower interest rates and consequently were willing to pay more than foreign competitors for foreign assets. Where one observed the opposite tendency— European or Japanese direct investment in the United States—

it was to be explained, according to Aliber, not only by the desire to participate in the immense Amreican market but also as an attempt by the investor to secure a higher price for their own securities through higher earnings in a preferred currency.[13]

The preferred-currency status of the dollar and its role in the international monetary system suggest two related causes of the foreign expansion of American corporations. The first is that foreign investment by American corporations was stimulated in part by the overvalued exchange rate of the dollar. In fact, because of the inflated value of the dollar, foreign assets and labor were relatively cheap for American corporations. Thus, the system of fixed exchange rates which prevailed from 1945 until August 15, 1971 proved to be an inducement for American corporations to produce abroad rather than to export from the United States.

Another, related viewpoint stressing the international role of the dollar in American corporate expansion abroad was that of President Charles de Gaulle of France. Whereas Aliber is referring to the private-vehicle role of the dollar and regards foreign direct investment as a function of the market, de Gaulle emphasized the reserve role of the dollar as the major factor in American foreign investment. He certainly did not view foreign investment as an inevitable function of market forces however. On the contrary, he believed that American monetary hegemony enabled the United States simply to print dollars and to buy up foreign corporate assets. It is partially for this reason that French officials have desired a return to the gold standard. If American companies had to use neutral money, i.e., gold, to buy up European assets, de Gaulle reasoned, they would stay home. In other words, American direct investment was facilitated by the international role of the dollar. If the dollar's position in the international economy were upset, it would weaken the capacity of American corporations to pursue a strategy of foreign direct investment in order to maintain their dominant position in world markets.

In conclusion, there is a remarkable convergence between these liberal explanations of foreign direct investment—oligopoly, product cycle, organic, and capital market theories—and the Leninist argument discussed in Chapter II; namely, that capitalist expansionism is an inevitable consequence of inherent aspects of an advanced capitalist economy. Both emphasize the primacy of economic factors and the corporate necessity to expand overseas or (as Kindleberger put it) to die. The Marxists deny emphatically, and the liberals at least downplay, the alternative public policy position that foreign direct investment is a matter of policy choice and a function of the domestic political order.

The "Public Policy" Position

The second set of explanations for the development of the multinational corporation is based on a very different set of assumptions. Whereas the "economic" position sees the multinational corporation as a response to economic and technological forces, the public policy position regards the MNC as largely a product of specific public policies, particularly tax laws that encourage foreign rather than domestic investment.[14] From this perspective there is nothing inevitable or necessary about foreign investment, at least on its present scale. Rather, foreign direct investment, in large measure, is considered a mechanism through which American corporations seek to enhance their own growth and profits at the expense of the rest of the American economy. Tax avoidance and the minimization of tax liabilities are critical factors in developing corporate strategy and making the decision to invest abroad.

According to this position, then, foreign investment is to be explained by a domestic political order, liberal ideology, and public policies that encourage corporate concentration and expansionism. For example, American tax laws permitting a high rate of retained profits here and abroad fosters foreign investment at the expense of the domestic economy. While this theory accepts the argument that foreign investment has resulted from the oligopolistic structure of American industry, oligopoly itself has been permitted and even encouraged by American tax laws. Although changes in these laws would not totally eliminate foreign direct investment, they would eliminate many of the present incentives for overinvestment abroad.

Within the public policy position two different arguments may be distinguished. The first stresses the tax treatment of the foreign earnings of American subsidiaries or branch plants. The second emphasizes the effect of domestic policies on the structure of the American economy and the effects of the latter on the incentives to invest abroad. These two arguments will be treated briefly in turn.

Under the present tax laws of the United States, corporations are subject to a tax on foreign as well as domestic income. The general organizational form of foreign direct investment in extractive industries (petroleum, mining, and so forth) is in the form of foreign branches; income from such branches is included in the parent corporation's tax return and the tax on such income is paid the year it is earned. However, if the corporation operates through a subsidiary (which is the primary case in manufacturing investment), foreign earnings are subject to a tax only when they are distributed to the United States; this is called tax deferral. Moreover, a tax credit against the domestic tax is allowed for foreign taxes paid on earnings and for dividends received from abroad. There are also several other tax concessions given to so-called Western Hemisphere trade corporations, to extractive industries, and to investment in United States possessions.

The argument of the public policy position is that all these tax provisions, especially the tax credit and tax deferral provisions, violate the principle of tax neutrality. Such measures are believed to create an incentive for American corporations to overinvest abroad. The concept behind the principle of tax neutrality is that the tax system should not distort the efficiency of capital allocation; it should not influence the choice between foreign and domestic investment. That is, the decision to invest should be based on criteria other than that of tax advantage. In the words of one authority, "international tax neutrality toward investment may be defined as a situation in which the pattern of taxation does not interfere with or affect the taxpayer's choice between investing at home and investing in foreign countries." [15]

According to the proponents of foreign direct investment, a strong case exists on the grounds of tax neutrality for the granting of a tax credit for taxes paid to foreign governments. If the tax credit were eliminated and American corporations were granted a deduction only on their American tax liability, this would constitute double taxation. With such a tax burden, it is argued, American firms could not compete, as the cost to the American firm of doing business abroad would be substantially higher than that for local firms. From this perspective, the tax credit equalizes the competitive situation and makes it possible for American subsidiaries to be competitive abroad. Thus, the tax credit insures that an American firm producing in Germany and a German firm will have the same rate of taxation. Its removal therefore, would force American corporations to retrench; it would be, according to spokesmen for the multinational corporation, a violation of the principle of tax neutrality.[16]

Although the tax credit may thus be defended on the grounds of tax neutrality, according to the public policy position the tax credit as it presently operates tends to violate such neutrality by providing a positive incentive for foreign investment. In the first place, there are a variety of techniques available to the corporation which enable it to decrease its total tax liability to the United States. It may, for example, average foreign tax rates and increase the amount of foreign taxes eligible for the tax credit. Or it may carry an excess credit forward as long as five years or back two years in order to decrease its tax liability. Though in theory the tax credit is tax neutral, in practice, critics argue, it encourages foreign investment.[17] Thus, through its tax policies the United States in effect subsidizes foreign direct investment.

The other major tax provision which is believed to encourage foreign direct investment is that of tax deferral. Tax deferral is important to the corporation because it directly affects the cost of capital to the firm and therefore significantly affects its capacity to grow. While the corporation can and does borrow funds abroad to finance growth, retained earnings are cheaper than borrowing capital or selling new equities. In fact, they are so cheap as to approach a negative cost. As long as there is a reasonable basis for expansion, the corporation's incentive is to reinvest rather than repatriate earnings and pay out dividends. In effect, then, tax deferral greatly increases the firm's retained earnings and decreases the distribution of profits to the stockholders. Though it has been modified since 1960 (the most recent being the Tax Reduction Act of 1975), tax deferral has been a major factor in the growth of the firm, but in its growth *outside* the United States.

The fundamental problem according to the "public policy" position is that the multinationals tend to expand out of internal funds. Growth is achieved by depreciation and retained earnings, the cheapest and most convenient source of funds; the multinationals are frequently content with a lower rate of return in order to promote corporate growth. While this means that they may be indifferent to tax rates and do not seek out the most profitable rate of return, their behavior is profoundly affected by the possibility of tax deferral. The vast earnings they can retain and re-invest ($8 billion in 1973) in their foreign subsidiaries in order to grow outside the United States are of critical importance. In the words of one authority, "the primary objective of large firms is to maximize their own retained funds for the purpose of reinvestment in order to insure the survival and continued growth of the organization; in many ways this is equivalent to maximization of long-term profit." [18]

The full significance of the tax credit and of tax deferral cannot be fully appreciated unless one understands a major feature of modern corporate operations, namely, transfer pricing. In simplest terms, transfer pricing is the price one part of a corporation charges another for goods or services. Transfer pricing is significant because it determines the allocation of income between or among commonly owned or controlled taxpaying corporations that have commercial transactions with one another. It thus gives the corporation immense flexibility. Such transactions are internal and are not subject to the discipline of the market; the corporation can so organize its operations as to decrease considerably its total tax liability.

The corporation can arrange its transfer prices so that the parent or subsidiary shows a loss in a high tax rate country and shows its profit in a low rate area. It may also funnel its sales through a subsidiary in a low rate area such as Switzerland and carry out manufacturing elsewhere. This flexibility, and the resultant ability to minimize tax liability, affords American corporations a powerful incentive for going abroad.

This situation is best exemplified by the large oil multinationals. They have enjoyed the best of all possible worlds. In the Middle East and other producing countries they have operated through branches; this form of organization has entitled them to the oil depletion allowance and other tax benefits afforded American domestic oil producers. In Europe, Japan, and other foreign markets they have operated through subsidiaries; they have therefore been able to apply the tax credit and tax deferral to these operations. Finally, through transfer pricing and existing tax policies, they have avoided nearly all American taxation on their vast and profitable foreign operations.

The tendency of American firms to invest abroad out of internal funds leads to the second and most important aspect of the public policy position: the importance of taxation and other public policies for American economic and corporate structure. That is to say, the greatest significance of American tax law is held to be its effect on the American capital market and on the structure of the American economy. This, according to certain authorities, constitutes the crux of the problem posed for the United States by foreign direct investment.[19]

The high rate of foreign investment by American corporations is believed to result in large measure from an imperfect capital market, created in part by present tax laws. Although the American capital market is certainly superior to that of other countries, it does have built-in incentives for overinvestment abroad. As has already been discussed, American corporations with a high ratio of retained earnings, both in this country and, especially, abroad, prefer to expand abroad out of internal funds rather than invest in other sectors or industries in this country. Although the rate of earnings abroad may be the same as or lower than in this country, the objective of the company is to maintain its market position and to maximize growth; this has been easier to accomplish abroad than in the United States.

According to this position, the liberal and Marxist argument that American firms invest abroad due to the lack of domestic opportunities fails to make a critical distinction, namely, that between the lack of domestic investment opportunities for a particular firm and a lack of investment opportunities in the economy as a whole. This position argues that while it may be true that a particular firm has exhausted its domestic opportunities in its particular industrial sectors, there is certainly no lack of investment opportunities in the American economy as a whole.

The basic problem, as Richard Caves has pointed out, is that there is "low inter-industry mobility of capital" in the American economy.[20] The experience and technology of corporations creates sector-specific capital. That is to say, a corporation tends to reap diminishing returns unless it invests in areas with which it has had experience. The choice for such a firm is between investing abroad in an area they know well, and in which they therefore enjoy a relatively high rate of return, or investing at home in a new area with a relatively lower rate of return. Furthermore, increased domestic investment in their own product line might well depress their rate of profit. Through foreign investment, on the other hand, the corporation can suppress the rise of foreign competition that would depress its rate of profit in the long run. As a result, foreign investment is very attractive for these corporations even though the overall average rate of return on investment for all industries in the United States may be higher. In short, a high incidence of foreign investment is to be explained by the investment preference of corporate management, abetted by the fact that the tax system permits a high rate of retained earnings.

This argument, which was most relevant for the years that witnessed the highest rate of foreign investment (the late 1950s to the mid-1960s), in effect has two steps. First, the imperfect capital market (and the oligopolistic organization of industry, which is itself encouraged by tax laws) causes firms to have high ratios of retained earnings. Second, the firm is considered to have essentially three choices open to it, though no firm follows one course to the exclusion of the others. In the first place, the firm can make further domestic investment in the same product line; this strategy, however, would saturate the market and drive down its profit margin. Alternatively, it can grow through product diversification—that is, through the innovation of new products, initially for the American market and, subsequently through the operation of the product cycle, for foreign export markets. This, however, is a high-risk strategy for the firm to follow. Finally, the corporation can invest abroad in its experienced product line; it can follow an expansion strategy and grow through the acquisition of new foreign markets or the maintenance of old ones.

Foreign direct investment tends to be the preferred choice

because of the knowledge-specificity of the firm. Corporations prefer to reinvest their retained earnings in sectors where they have had experience and to expand their markets rather than to diversify. While there are unknowns, risks, and costs in both strategies, diversification tends to be more risky and more costly.[21]

In theory the conglomerate movement was supposed to be the answer to the conservative and sector-specific nature of American corporate investment. By replacing production-oriented managers with financiers and by making capital mobile through its retention of many product lines, the conglomerate was supposed to give a new flexibility to American investment practices. Unfortunately, it has not always worked out this way, at least not well enough to resolve the basic problem emphasized by the public policy position. In the first place, the conglomerates have not been highly profitable in the economic sense of efficiency, but only in the accounting sense. Furthermore, corporate management has proven to be nontransferable. Many American managers are engineers and are product-oriented; their expertise is sector-specific. It is precisely for this reason that American corporations prefer to "knock off" opponents here and abroad in familiar product lines rather than venture into new and uncharted areas of investment and innovation. Finally, the expansion of conglomerates through diversification into unrelated product lines has not proven to be very successful. In short, the conglomerate movement has not eliminated what the public policy position considers to be the critical problem.

In the contemporary world, the natural preference of corporations to expand the market for their existing product lines has been greatly accentuated by the ease of foreign investment. Essentially self-financing and experienced in a particular industrial sector, American corporations prefer to expand abroad rather than diversify their investments at home and develop new products or cost-reducing technologies. While diversification obviously remains an important component of corporate strategy, the emergence of large overseas markets, the existence of foreign trade barriers, and the availability of favorable tax laws (including those of host countries) have accentuated the natural preference for overseas market expansion. The incentives have practically all been in the direction of corporate expansion via the route of foreign direct investment.

Thus, the public policy position, with its emphasis on the imperfect nature of the American capital market and corporate structure, comes full circle—back to the oligopoly theory of Hymer and Kindleberger. However, the public policy position goes one step further, and argues that the structure itself and corporate investment behavior are largely the product of American tax laws, including everything from the corporate profit tax and depreciation allowances to capital gains and estate taxes. In the words of Peter Drucker, a sympathetic critic of American business, "Today's American tax laws put a tremendous premium on capital retention in the existing big and old business. In fact, the tax laws are the greatest engine for monopoly ever devised. No matter how actively the anti-trusters try to prevent concentration of economic power and to stop big business from getting even bigger, the tax laws inevitably frustrate their efforts." [22] What this means is that capital which might be distributed to stockholders or might find its way into new domestic investment opportunities is invested abroad in order to further the growth of the oligopolistic corporation.

Conclusion

What is one to conclude on the basis of this examination of the several theories which seek to explain foreign direct investment? Certainly it would be vain indeed to have expected to find one theory or set of factors which alone explain such a varied and complex phenomenon as the multinational corporation; each theory is at best a partial explanation and contains at most a grain of the whole truth. Yet, the several theories analyzed in this chapter point to one general and overriding conclusion: The primary drive behind the overseas expansion of today's giant corporations is maximization of corporate growth and the suppression of foreign as well as domestic competition.[23]

This massive corporate expansionism on an unprecedented global scale has been greatly facilitated by the contemporary revolution in communications and transportation. Other factors favoring foreign direct investment have permitted and encouraged the phenomenal growth of the multinational corporation: the dynamics of oligopolistic competition, the operation of the product cycle, the international position of the dollar, the role of taxation. These technological, economic, and public policy factors have stimulated unprecedented American corporate growth, but growth outside the borders of the United States.

Until the late 1950s or early 1960s this corporate expansion reflected the economic and industrial strength of the United States. Thereafter, however, foreign direct investment was increasingly a response to the decline of the United States relative to other industrial or industrializing economies. This change can be observed in the emergence of the concept of the *global* corporation, or George Ball's cosmocorp. This concept signaled the crossover from the strength to the relative decline of the American core as the basic factor in foreign direct investment by American corporations. With the relative decline of the American market and resources, the American multinational corporations have sought to broaden their economic and especially their political base. They have attempted to assert their independence and survive in an increasingly hostile international environment. As such, the cosmocorp concept suggests a major metamorphosis of the multinational corporation.

The several theories analyzed in this chapter treat the American multinational corporation essentially as an American corporation which for one reason or another decides to go overseas. The emphasis in the product-cycle theory, for example, is that an American corporation goes abroad in order to protect its home market position in a particular product line. Foreign operations are really peripheral, in this view, to the dominant domestic orientation of the corporation. In contrast to this perspective, which sees foreign investment as primarily defensive, the global corporation notion is that the multinational corporation is becoming a truly global entity. It has shed its national identity; it thinks of the whole world as one marketing and production system. These corporations are said to have acquired a "global scanning capacity" and a "global habit of mind." In time, so it is argued, they will become indifferent to nationality with respect to personnel, markets, money, and location of production. They will cease to be "American" oligopolies and will become autonomous international citizens.

Undoubtedly the spirit of this position has been captured best by the often quoted remark of Carl A. Gerstacker, chairman of the Dow Chemical Company:

> I have long dreamed of buying an island owned by no nation, and of establishing the world headquarters of the Dow company on the truly neutral ground of such an island, beholden to no nation or society. If we were located on such truly neutral ground we could then really operate in the United States as U.S. citizens, in Japan as Japanese citizens and in Brazil as Brazilians rather than being governed in prime by the laws of the United States. . . . We could even pay any natives handsomely to move elsewhere.[24]

While the whole world would become an integrated system of operations, according to this thesis, the basic motivations of the corporation would remain those ascribed to it by the oligopoly theory; the primary object of corporate activity is growth and market dominance. Freed from its moorings in the United States, the corporation would have a wide access to capital, labor, technology, and markets. As a consequence, the corporation would possess great flexibility and freedom in its operations and dealings with governments.

It is this model, which sees the corporation as released from the inhibiting jurisdictions of nation-states and operating as a global optimizer of resources, that has caught the imagination of certain writers. For some, the global corporation holds the promise of lifting mankind out of poverty and bringing the good life to everyone. For others, these corporations have become a law unto themselves; they are miniempires which exploit all for the benefit of a few.[25]

Insofar as this global corporation thesis is correct, it has important implications for assessing the multinational corporation from the perspective of American national interest. Under the product-cycle theory described above, for example, the American market is the principal market and foreign investment is defensive; it is a means to protect an export market and to undermine potential competitors. But this more recent tendency of looking at markets, currencies, and production from a global perspective has quite different consequences for the United States. It means, for example, that a corporation will not seek to serve a foreign market initially through export from the United States, but rather will set up production facilities abroad from the outset if cost and marketing factors are favorable. This explains, in part, the tendency to set up offshore production facilities in low-cost areas in Taiwan or Latin America in order to serve markets in advanced countries, including the United States. The implications of this trend, if it were to continue, would obviously be profound for the development of the American economy.

The exposition of this issue, however, takes us ahead of our immediate concern, namely, the relationship between the multinational corporation and American hegemony. The expansion of these corporations has extended the American presence throughout the world economy. The significance of this development for the international position of the United States is the subject of the next chapter.

VI

CORPORATE EXPANSIONISM AND AMERICAN HEGEMONY

Prior to World War I, the great network of international markets (capital, money, and commodities), whose center was the City of London, was the principal mechanism for integrating the world economy. The pivotal figures in these highly interdependent world markets were the specialized financiers and bankers whose task it was to finance world trade and investment. Although they were pursuing their private interests, these financiers and bankers constituted one of the foundations of British power and the *Pax Britannica* in the nineteenth century.

Following the weakening of this intricate mechanism due to World War I, power over international trade and investment shifted from these bankers and financiers toward industrialists and corporate executives.[1] The surge of foreign direct investment during the interwar period and especially with the victory of the United States in World War II reflected this transformation in the organization and management of the world economy. The giant modern corporations triumphed over and largely displaced the London markets as the principal mechanism for integrating the non-Communist world economy.

As a consequence of this development, American corporations also became instruments of American global hegemony. Although government officials did not foresee that American corporations would expand so as to establish a significant American presence in and impact on all the economies of the non-Communist world, American policies did encourage and protect corporate expansionism after World War II. American tax policy, the insistence that American subsidiaries in the Common Market be treated as "European" corporations, and much later, the creation of the Overseas Private Investment Corporation (1969) to insure foreign investments are but three examples of measures designed to foster corporate expansionism.[2] If British economic hegemony was based on the City of London, America's was based largely on her multinational corporations.

It would be wrong, however, to suggest that corporate expansionism abroad was planned or that the consequences of this expansion were consciously intended by American officials. Rather, officials gradually realized that the growing overseas empires of American corporations could be made to serve the larger interests of the United States. In ways frequently contrary to the wishes and interests of the corporations themselves, American officials have sought to convert the multinationals and their overseas subsidiaries into instruments of American foreign policy.

There are many examples of this tendency on the part of the American government to make the corporations serve the national interest. But the most significant illustration relates to the American balance of payments. As I shall spell out below, the geopolitical position of the United States relative to the Soviet Union and China placed a heavy balance of payments burden on the United States. By the late 1950s, the payments drain of overseas military, diplomatic, and foreign aid commitments had caused a serious balance of payments deficit for the United States. As this deficit became more severe, the multinational corporations and their rapidly growing foreign earnings were recognized as major national assets which could help finance America's global hegemonic position.

In conjunction with the international position of the dollar and with nuclear supremacy, the multinational corporation became one of the cornerstones of American hegemony. These three elements of American power interacted with and reinforced one another. As I have shown in Chapter IV, American political and military supremacy arising out of World War II was a necessary precondition for the predominant position of American multinational corporations in the world economy. But the reciprocal of this is also true: corporate expansionism in turn became a support of America's international political and military position.

This complementarity argument runs directly counter to both the prevailing liberal defense and the radical critique of the multinational corporation. In the view of its liberal proponents, corporate expansionism is largely divorced from the larger arena of world politics. The multinational corporation is regarded as an independent actor on the international scene. The relationship between American corporations and the United States government is held to be an "arm's length" one. The policies of these transnational actors are said to circumscribe the sovereignty of nation-states through an ever-widening web of economic and technological interdependence. Viewed in this way, the MNC represents the separation of economics from politics in the interest of promoting world peace and development.[3]

The neo-Marxist or radical critique of the multinational corporation and its relationship to the foreign policy of the United States is equally straightforward: (1) Owing to the internal requirements of the American capitalistic system, the large corporations are forced to expand outward in search of new markets, investment opportunities, and sources of raw materials; (2) the foreign policy of the United States reflects the expansionist interests of this dominant capitalistic class; and (3) the foremost interest of this corporate elite is to eliminate all obstacles to corporate expansionism and to protect the essentials of the capitalist system. From this set of premises, it is a short step to regarding direct investment as imperialism and considering the Cold War and the Vietnam conflict as consequences of this corporate drive for power and profits.[4]

There is, in fact, a certain parallel between the thesis advanced in the preceding chapter that foreign expansion has become an "institutional necessity"—to use the term of Theodore Moran[5]—for many American corporations and the classical socialist arguments of Hobson, Lenin, and others that capitalist expansionism or imperialism is a function of "the falling rate of profit." For individual firms, the choice is frequently between expansion abroad and a falling rate of profit on their domestic investment. It does not necessarily follow, however, that the foreign policy of the United States has become dictated by the necessity of these powerful corporations to expand overseas.[6]

On the contrary, the argument of the present study is that the corporations and the United States government have tended to share an overlapping and complementary set of interests. The relationship is not unlike that between the British government and the mercantile enterprises which dominated the world economy in the seventeenth and eighteenth centuries. There is considerable truth in the intriguing argument of Kari Levitt in her book, *Silent Surrender: The American Economic Empire in Canada*:

> The central thesis of our argument is that the subsidiaries and branch plants of large American-based multinational corporations have replaced the operations of the earlier European-based mercantile venture companies in extracting the staple and organizing the supply of manufactured goods. In the new mercantilism, as in the old, the corporation based in the metropole directly exercises the entrepreneurial function and collects a "venture profit" from its investment. It organizes the collection or extraction of the raw

material staple required in the metropolis and supplies the hinterland with manufactured goods, whether produced at home or "onsite" in the host country.[7]

The American multinational corporation, like its mercantile ancestor, has performed an important role in the maintenance and expansion of the power of the United States. American hegemony in the contemporary world has rested, in part, on the vast international operations of American corporations. In support of this thesis, the first section of this chapter analyzes the relationship between corporate interest and American foreign policy. On the basis of this discussion, I shall then examine the role of the multinational corporation in the overall foreign policy of the United States as it has evolved over the years.

Corporate Interest and National Interest

The imperative of corporate growth and expansion has, without doubt, important implications for American foreign policy. The multinationals, as we have seen, are among the largest and most powerful concentrations of economic power in the United States. That they seek to use this power to influence American foreign policy in directions which benefit them is also without doubt. But it is equally true that American foreign policy has frequently run counter to corporate interests. In general, however, corporate interest and the "national interest," as the latter has been defined by succeeding American administrations, have coincided. Corporate and political elites have shared the American vision of a liberal world economic order.

As we have seen, the political order fostered by the United States at the end of World War II was one which facilitated the overseas expansion of American corporations. The United States fostered an international milieu in which American traders and investors could expand into world markets. Just as the Open Door for British trade was the leitmotif of British foreign policy in the nineteenth century, the Open Door for American investment was a fundamental principle of American foreign policy after World War II.[8] As in the British case, there has tended to be a natural harmony of interests between American political and business leadership.[9]

On the other hand, one can cite numerous examples of corporations exercising influence over American foreign policy for their own ends. American policy toward Castro's Cuba, Allende's Chile, and other countries has been profoundly influenced by the hostile attitudes toward these nations of American business.[10] The Hickenlooper Amendment (1962) and subsequent policy statements and laws of various administrations in Washington denying financial aid to countries that confiscated the property of American corporations without "just" compensation were the outgrowth of corporate lobbying. There is a sufficient number of cases of American intervention on behalf of foreign investors to give plausibility to the leftist argument that corporate interest determines American foreign policy.

The influence of these corporations over public policy is perhaps best exemplified by the issue of corporate taxation. Not only has the favorable treatment of foreign corporate earnings encouraged foreign investment, but American tax policies are an important determinant of the corporate structure that is a major cause of foreign direct investment in the first place. The domestic power of the multinational corporations has been demonstrated by their success in defeating onslaughts against their tax subsidies.

In the late 1960s and early 1970s, foreign direct investment became increasingly politicized. Organized labor, convinced that foreign investment exported jobs, undertook a major campaign to reform the tax provisions which affected foreign direct investment. The Foreign Trade and Investment Act of 1973 (the so-called Burke–Hartke Bill) would have eliminated both the tax credit and tax deferral. The Nixon Administration, influential members of Congress of both parties, and well-financed lobbying organizations came to the defense of the multinationals. The massive counterattack of the multinationals and their allies defeated this first major challenge to their interests.

The available evidence does not, however, add up to the radical thesis that there is a systematic relationship between American policy and the multinationals. It is simply not the case that the imperative of corporate growth and expansion explains the foreign policy of the United States. On the contrary, there are many examples when corporate interest and foreign policy have sharply diverged. In such cases the tendency has been for the larger interests of foreign policy to prevail. Several examples should suffice to make the point.

Contrary to the wishes of American corporations and host governments alike, the United States government has enforced the extraterritorial application of American law. The United States has considered foreign subsidiaries of American corporations to be subject to American law even though they are legally foreign corporations. For example, America's strict antitrust laws and prohibitions against "trading with the enemy" have been thorns in the side of American companies operating abroad. Many lucrative sales have been lost to Japanese and European competitors because American subsidiaries could not sell to the Soviet Union, Cuba, or China. The removal of these export controls has long been a major goal of American corporations. In this effort, they have frequently enlisted the help of host governments against the U.S. government!

There are numerous other examples where corporate interests and American foreign policy have run counter to one another. American oil multinationals, for example, have long opposed the generally pro-Israeli stance of American foreign policy. Also, despite the contrived and highly disingenuous arguments of the Left, it is very difficult to reconcile the Vietnam War with the interests of American business. The opposition of business to the war, owing to its impact on the economy and the international position of the dollar, was in fact a major factor in the belated decision of the Johnson and Nixon administrations to seek a negotiated settlement.

Perhaps the greatest divergence between corporate interest and "national" interest can be found in the example of American policy toward Japan. American policy toward this immense market and potential outlet for surplus capital is certainly a test of the Marxist thesis. Yet, as we have seen, in the interest of national security the United States actually promoted Japanese expansion into the American market. Even more importantly, it tolerated Japanese exclusion of American investment. American corporations which desired "access" to the Japanese market were forced to license their technology to Japanese corporations. They thereby lost the technological advantages which figure so heavily in the product-cycle and other theories of foreign direct investment. How could a foreign policy be more counter to the interests of American multinational corporations than one which fostered the emergence of foreign rivals? Parenthetically, as the security concerns of the United States in the Pacific have receded in recent years, the complaints of American corporations against Japanese policies on trade and investment have been increasingly taken into account by public officials in the formulation of American policy.

There have been other occasions when corporate interests and vital interests of the United States have sharply diverged. American corporations have pursued policies which an objective outside observer might conclude were contrary to the national interest. No doubt the best example of this was the behavior of the American oil companies during the Arab oil boycott in the fall and winter of 1973. American oil companies followed the dictates of the Arab states even to the extent of refusing to supply oil to the American military, thus jeopardizing

U.S. military preparedness at a time of international crisis. Other, less dramatic examples of corporate defiance of American foreign policy objectives could easily be cited.

In general, the tendency of the corporation is to maximize its freedom from all governmental control over its activities and to employ a "divide and conquer" strategy. The corporation will pit host against home governments in order to increase its capacity to grow and to maximize profits without government interference. This, in fact, is the essence of multinationality: corporate expansion abroad in order to maximize independence and growth. There is thus a constant struggle between corporate officials and public officials with respect to whose interests the corporations will serve.

Despite the struggle of the corporations to assert their independence, the underlying assumption of American officials has been that the national interest of the United States is well served by the overseas expansion of American corporations. Corporate control by American executives and corporate dependence on the American market have encouraged public officials to believe that the corporations will on the whole behave consistently with the interests of the United States. In general, despite frequent backsliding and resistance to American government directives, this has been the case. Whether or not this assumption of the complementarity of corporate and national interests will continue to hold in the future is an issue which will be discussed in Chapter IX.

In short, corporate managers and the managers of the national interest have certain interests in common, but they also have divergent interests. At the same time, therefore, that public officials attempt to utilize the corporations to advance national objectives, corporate executives seek to maximize their freedom from *all* government restrictions; they seek to use national power for corporate advantage. Yet, in the main, the relationship between American business and government has been one wherein the activities of the corporations are seen to advance the larger foreign policy interests of the nation.

The Multinationals and American Policy

As Jacob Viner has pointed out, from the initial movement of American capital and corporations abroad the State Department and the White House have sought to channel American foreign investment in a direction that would enhance the foreign policy objectives of the United States.[11] With respect to the foreign expansion of the multinational corporation, these objectives have been seen as maintaining America's share of world markets, securing a strong position in foreign economies, spreading American economic and political values, and controlling access to vital raw materials, especially petroleum.

In the area of manufacturing, American multinationals have exercised influence over the location of economic activities, industrial production, and technological development. They have created an international division of labor between corporate centers in the home economy, where decision, finance, and research are located, and the branch-plant economies of the global periphery. In a world in which interaffiliate sales constitute a very high fraction of world trade in both manufacturing and commodities, the multinationals exercise a strong influence over the locus of manufacturing, the international balance of payments, and, in general, the nature of the international division of labor. They determine in large measure the distribution of gains in the world economy.

With respect to extractive industries, American multinationals have largely controlled the industrial world's access to petroleum and many other raw materials. Through the instrumentality of the MNC, the United States has sought to prevent its exclusion both from world markets and from sources of raw materials, to influence the policies of other states, and generally to enhance its position in the world.

The resource multinationals have been of considerable economic and political importance to the United States in a number of ways. American raw materials investments, in addition to being important earners of foreign exchange, have insured that American customers have had preference during periods of scarcity. During wartime, though with decreasing success, the United States has sought through pressures on the MNCs and host governments to keep raw material prices from rising. Thus, through encouraging and exercising influence over the natural resource multinationals, the United States government has sought to achieve security of supply and to restrain price increases. In the words of a report of the Council of the Americas, "Private foreign investment . . . assures access to supplies of raw materials." [12]

In addition to the above, three aspects of the overseas expansion of American multinational corporations have been of particular political importance. The first is the perceived role of these corporations in the creation of a liberal international economic and political order. One of the major rationales or justifications for American corporate expansionism and penetration of other economies is that they are the contemporary world's foremost instruments of economic development. Through the transfer of American technology and the free enterprise tradition, they are helping to create the democratic and pluralistic world of the American liberal vision. They are the means to fulfill the American ideological commitment to a peaceful and interdependent world in which economic cooperation and growth would supplant the clash of national rivalries.

A second aspect of the multinational corporation which has been of particular political importance has been the role of the international petroleum companies. Through their extensive development of Middle Eastern and other foreign sources of oil, these oil multinationals guaranteed the non-Communist world a secure supply of relatively cheap energy. This energy fueled Western Europe and Japan's rapid industrial growth for several decades. Relatively cheap oil from the Middle East and elsewhere facilitated the growing interdependence of the world economy. It may well be that rapid economic growth based on this oil supply was as responsible for economic cooperation and interdependence as economic interdependence was responsible for growth.

For the United States, the oil multinationals' near-monopoly of the non-Communist industrial world's supply of energy and their influence over Europe's and Japan's oil was an important source of unity. To encourage further expansion and make more secure the position of the oil companies in producing areas, particularly the Middle East, the United States, as we have seen, granted major tax concessions to the companies. This situation meant that the United States acquired leverage over policies it opposed. In 1956 the oil weapon was used with dramatic effect by the United States. To force British and French withdrawal from the ill-fated Suez invasion, the United States threatened to shut off their oil supply. This experience is one the French have not forgotten. It is an important consideration in their desire to be independent of the United States with respect to their oil supply.

The third critical impact of the multinational corporation has been on America's balance of payments. The earnings generated by corporate investment abroad have taken on a great importance for the United States government. This income has become a critical factor in America's ability to finance overseas military and diplomatic commitments. The technological and monopolistic rents extracted from abroad by American corporations are, in fact, essential to the financing of America's global hegemonic position.

Wherein lies what may be regarded as a neomercantilistic element in American foreign economic policy? It will be recalled that the essence of classical mercantilism was the desire for a trade surplus in order to acquire bullion or treasure; this treasure, in turn, was important to finance foreign military and diplomatic commitments. Similarly, the United States government has desired foreign investment earnings in part in order to finance overseas military and diplomatic commitments. The American multinational corporations have increasingly generated the foreign exchange required to finance American security interests.

How, then, have these security interests been defined? What has been the role of the multinational corporation in the larger context of American foreign policy?

The Financial Burden of Hegemony

Despite the Soviet challenge, by the mid-1950s the United States had established its hegemony over the international system through formation of the crucial triangle composed of Western Europe, Japan, and the United States itself. Inherent in this structure, however, was a fundamental conflict between American long-term economic interests and her short-term security interests. This situation constituted a major dilemma for the United States.

At the same time that American economic interests would have been best served by a liberal, multilateral world economy, the United States, for security reasons, tolerated European regionalism, discrimination against American exports, and export drives by Japan and Europe into the American economy. Thus, it sacrificed the two basic principles of American commercial policy which had been embodied in GATT: reciprocity and nondiscrimination. Additionally, in order to rebuild the economies of the non-Communist countries peripheral to the Soviet bloc, the United States fostered the diffusion of resources (especially capital and technology) and the spread of economic growth.

While the American economy benefited from the creation of strong trading and economic partners, this policy involved a real resource cost to the United States. The Marshall Plan and other American policies, for example, transferred financial and technological resources to Western Europe. Moreover, this rebuilding of foreign competition and toleration of anti-American trade discrimination was harmful to important American economic interests.

Thus, the *Pax Americana* has imposed on the United States an economic and resource burden which, throughout most of the nineteenth century, the *Pax Britannica* did not impose upon Great Britain. In the words of Harold and Margaret Sprout:

> At the peak of British power and influence, the decade of the 1860's, total expenditures for military purposes averaged less than £30 million per year. Adjusting for inflation and changes in the dollar price of sterling, this works out to something in the range of 1 to 2 percent of average U.S. military expenditures in the 1950's and early 1960's. In short, mid-nineteenth century British governments policed a worldwide empire . . . and exerted on other nations an influence as great as, if not considerably greater than, the United States can achieve today at a real cost fifty to one hundred times larger.[13]

The potential disequilibrium between America's global political commitments and the economic resource base required to sustain these commitments was masked until the early years of the Kennedy administration (1960–62). Before then the enormous extent of American economic power over the rest of the world, the so-called dollar shortage (1945–58), and America's large share of international monetary reserves had made the United States able to afford a massive transfer of money and real wealth to her European and Japanese allies.

As this relative monetary and industrial superiority diminished in the 1950s, American hegemony began to rest instead on two economic foundations. The first was the international role of the dollar as the world's reserve currency. In order to preserve this role and the system of fixed exchange rates based on the dollar, other nations were required to support the dollar and, by implication, America's global hegemony. The second basis of American hegemony was the rapid expansion overseas of American multinational corporations.

In effect, the multinational corporation enabled the United States to resolve, at least in part, the conflict between American economic and security interests. It decreased the cost to American economic interests of rebuilding the European industrial base. Through direct investment, American corporations enjoyed the benefits of growth provided by the internal lowering of European tariffs and the establishment of a common external market. As we have already seen, the guarantee of such American participation was in fact a precondition of American support for the establishment of the European Economic Community; American subsidiaries were to be treated on the same basis as European corporations.

The fundamental problem posed for the United States during this period was the asymmetry of the American and Soviet geostrategic positions. The resulting monetary burden of maintaining global hegemony and balancing Soviet power on the rimlands of Europe and Asia was (and is) substantial. Consequently, the balance of payments issue was a central one for the United States. How is it possible to pay for the maintenance of large military establishments abroad, to finance and support allies, and generally to cover the costs of far-flung overseas commitments? Such a balance of payments problem is not crucial to a strategically well-placed continental power, such as Germany prior to World War I and the Soviet Union since 1945; such continental powers are able to radiate influence from within their own boundaries. But it is of the essence for a sea power trying to balance such a land power.[14] How this problem was resolved is of critical importance for understanding American foreign economic policy in the 1960s and early 1970s.

The Role of the Dollar

Until about 1958 the United States was largely freed from balance of payments constraints on its foreign policy and overseas military commitments. Moreover, the United States could afford (from the foreign-exchange perspective) to forego potentially profitable trade with the Communist bloc, to assist the revival of Europe and Japan through aid, investment, and the provision of trade advantages, and to promote the development of the lesser-developed countries. Describing this period, Benjamin Cohen observed, "Our position as international central banker enabled us to adopt a unilateral balance of payments policy: we issued the world's principal vehicle and reserve currency in amounts presumed to be consistent with our own priorities—not with those of our depositors." [15]

Private parties and governments employed the dollar as the world's transaction, reserve, and intervention currency. In its essence, this dollar standard world had several important features: a regime of relatively fixed exchange rates between the dollar and other currencies, convertibility of the dollar into gold, and the pricing of gold at $35 an ounce. These elements provided the essentials of the international monetary system until President Richard Nixon changed the rules on August 15, 1971.

During the early years of this system (1945–58), the American balance of payments registered years of surplus and years of deficit. But as other countries desired dollars to purchase American goods and to replenish their own capital stocks, the United States felt few constraints on its printing and loss of dollars. Then, after 1958 the American balance of payments went permanently into deficit; with this continuing deterioration in the American balance of payments, the build-up of foreign dollar reserves accelerated steadily. Finally, in the mid-1960s, the American trade surplus began to disappear. Thus, after 1958 what had been a dollar shortage rapidly became a dollar glut.

While there is no simple explanation for this reversal of American economic fortunes; the fundamental change which took place in the late 1950s was the completion of postwar economic recovery in Western Europe and Japan. Both of these now rapidly growing and potentially powerful industrial centers had rebuilt their industrial and agricultural infrastructures. Less dependent now upon American exports, they recommenced their own outward expansion in search of markets. As had happened to Great Britain in the latter part of the nineteenth century, the diffusion of capital, technological know-how, and managerial skills, in addition to the stimulus of trade and governmental policies, was rapidly undermining the position of the dominant economic power. This fundamental change was concealed for a long time, however, for a very special reason.

In essence, after 1958, a bargain was struck between the three dominant poles of the international economy—the United States, Western Europe, and, to a lesser extent, Japan. Partially for economic reasons, but more importantly for political and strategic ones, Western Europe (primarily West Germany) and Japan agreed to finance the American balance of payments deficit. Commenting upon the two more important parties to the understanding, Benjamin Cohen writes that "the Europeans acquiesced in a system which accorded the United States special privileges to act abroad unilaterally to promote U.S. interests. We in turn condoned Europe's use of the system to promote its own regional economic prosperity, even if this happened to come largely at the expense of the United States." [16]

Thus, after the late 1950s the United States in effect ran its foreign policy largely on credit. The willingness of Europe and, to a lesser extent, of Japan to hold dollars helped make it possible for the United States to maintain its troop commitments in Western Europe and elsewhere around the Soviet and Chinese periphery, to finance foreign aid, and, of course, to fight the Vietnam War. For its part, the United States, as we have already pointed out, tolerated discrimination against its exports and promoted the creation of the European Economic Community even though the success of the EEC would make it a direct and significant threat to American commercial interests. Furthermore, the resulting prosperity of Europe and the relative unconcern of the United States over its balance of payments facilitated the reentry of Japan into world markets and provided the basis for the Japanese economic miracle. In short, all three parties obtained the things they wanted most, and as long as those priorities held, the system worked.

Inherent in this monetary arrangement, however, were basic asymmetries which, in the 1970s, would threaten the viability of the international monetary system. On the one hand, the role of the dollar as reserve, transaction, and intervention currency extended, as we have already seen, enormous economic and political privileges to the United States. The United States had less need than otherwise would have been the case to worry about its balance of payments in the conduct of its foreign policy or the management of its domestic economy. On the other hand, the United States, in contrast to other economies, could not devalue the dollar relative to other currencies in order to improve its trade and payments position without the acquiescence of its major trading partners; a devaluation of the dollar and an improved American competitive position would immediately have been wiped out by parallel devaluations of the pound, the mark, the yen, and other major currencies.

Whereas the United States prized the first aspect of this asymmetry, it increasingly smarted under the second. Europeans and Japanese, of course, regarded this asymmetry from the opposite perspective. But as long as the American balance-of-payments deficit was moderate and the political unity of the three centers of non-Communist industrial power held firm, the issue lay dormant. When changing economic and political conditions caused sufficient disequilibrium in the early 1970s, then the asymmetries created by the international role of the dollar would emerge as a basic issue in the reform of the international monetary system.

It is against this background that one must view that other vital expression of American presence and power in the contemporary world economy—the multinational corporation.

The Role of the Multinational Corporations

In the middle 1960s, the importance of the multinational corporation to America's place in the world began to be more fully appreciated by American political leaders. This change in attitude arose in response to growing concern over America's deteriorating trade and balance of payments position. During the first two decades after World War II (until 1958) the United States had maintained its global economic and political position primarily on the basis of its immense trade surplus. Subsequently, as we have just seen, the American international position became increasingly dependent upon the international role of the dollar. The trend was toward a growing payments constraint; there was an increasing need to worry about America's overall balance of payments. Consequently, the direction of American official thinking was toward an enhanced perception of the importance of MNC earnings as a means to finance continued hegemony.

In the late 1960s, concern over America's balance of payments situation intensified. After 1965, the American trade surplus began to dwindle. Western Europe and Japan began to accumulate more and more dollars; the international monetary system and the international position of the dollar became increasingly unstable. Faced with a deteriorating balance-of-payments situation, the United States government began to regard the multinational corporations and their growing overseas earnings as the means to finance America's hegemonic world position.

In the late 1950s and early 1960s, the capital outflow from the United States had been a major factor in America's growing balance-of-payments deficit. This fact led to successive steps being taken to stem the flow.[17] By the time these measures were taken, however, American corporations were well ensconced in Western Europe, Latin America, Canada, and elsewhere. Through reinvestment of their own earnings and through foreign borrowing, particularly in the immense Eurodollar market, the multinational corporation had become essentially self-sustaining. According to a 1968 estimate, American MNCs were financing roughly 35 percent of their overseas operations from external sources abroad; 40 percent of the expansion came from cash flows and only 25 percent through capital transfers.[18] Though not freed from dependence on capital from the United States, American subsidiaries were sufficiently well established abroad to support themselves and, more importantly, to generate a flow of earnings back to the United States.

These overseas earnings of the MNCs were increasingly promoted as a means to sustain American power and hegemony. As the so-called Peterson Report emphasized in 1971, income from foreign direct investment since the late 1960s had been greater than new capital outflows; moreover, the surplus was increasing.[19] Whereas the surplus was only $0.7 billion in 1960, by 1970 it had risen to $1.6 billion. Also, if one considers all private American investment income earnings abroad, including bonds, stocks, and short-term assets, the American gross income more than quintupled in twenty years—from $1.5 billion in 1950 to $8.7 billion in 1970; this does not include $2.5 billion earned abroad in 1970 which was reinvested. Thus, although American corporations between 1961 and 1970 invested $28.8 billion overseas and spent $1.3 billion on interest payments, this amount was more than offset by income of $41.8 billion, plus receipt of royalties and fees—a net inflow of $35.3 billion.[20] By 1980, according to *Fortune* Magazine (August 1973) the annual return on foreign investment (dividends, fees, and royalties) will be approximately $20 billion. (See Tables 10 and 11 and Chart 3.)

By far the most lucrative source of foreign investment income has been American investment in petroleum; the better part of these earnings has come from the Middle East.[21] Though the

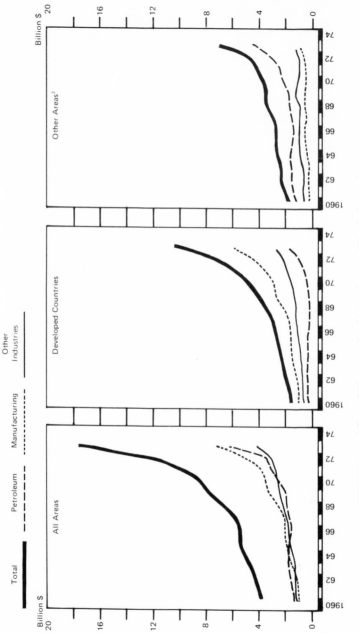

CHART 3. Adjusted Earnings by Major Area and by Industry.[1]
Source: U.S. Department of Commerce, Bureau of Economic Analysis, "Aspects of International Investment, *Survey of Current Business* 54 (August 1974): 12.

[1] Adjusted earnings data are given in Table 12.
[2] Includes developing countries, international and unallocated.

TABLE 10

Return on U.S. Direct Investment Abroad, by Area and Industry
(In millions of dollars and percentage)

	ALL AREAS				DEVELOPED COUNTRIES				OTHER AREAS [1]			
	ALL INDUSTRIES	PETROLEUM	MANUFACTURING	OTHER	ALL INDUSTRIES	PETROLEUM	MANUFACTURING	OTHER	ALL INDUSTRIES	PETROLEUM	MANUFACTURING	OTHER
Adjusted earnings: [2]												
1972p	12,526	4,613	4,969	2,939	6,959	823	4,184	1,952	5,566	3,794	785	987
1971r	10,452	3,942	3,803	2,707	5,599	576	3,184	1,799	4,893	3,366	619	908
1970	8,949	3,034	3,392	2,523	4,807	461	2,779	1,508	4,143	2,573	614	955
Adjusted earnings as a percent of direct investment position at beginning of year:												
1972p	14.5	19.1	13.9	11.1	11.9	6.4	14.1	12.2	20.1	33.9	13.1	9.5
1971r	13.4	18.2	11.8	11.2	10.5	4.9	11.9	12.3	19.5	33.7	11.3	9.5
1970	12.6	15.3	11.5	11.7	10.0	4.4	11.4	12.0	17.9	27.3	11.9	11.1

p = preliminary
r = revised
1. Includes developing countries and international unallocated.
2. Includes branch earnings, dividends, reinvested earnings, and interest.
Source: U.S. Department of Commerce, Bureau of Economic Analysis, *Survey of Current Business* 53 (1973): 34. Reprinted in U.S. Department of State, Bureau of Public Affairs, *The U.S. Role in International Investment* (Washington, January 16, 1974), p. 18.

TABLE 11

Net Effect of Capital and Services Account Flows
Associated with Direct Investment of U.S. Multinational Companies

(In billions of dollars; – denotes outflow)

CAPITAL AND SERVICES ACCOUNT FLOWS	1961	1966	1967	1968	1969	1970	CUMULATED 1961–70
United States direct investment abroad	1.6	–3.7	–3.1	–3.2	–3.3	–4.4	–28.8
Borrowing abroad by United States direct investors	*	0.7	0.5	3.4	2.4	3.9	11.2
Interest payments to for-eigners on borrowing abroad	‡	‡	–0.1	–0.2	–0.4	–0.6	–1.3
Income from direct investment abroad	2.8	4.0	4.5	5.0	5.7	6.0	41.8
Receipts of royalties and fees	0.7	1.3	1.4	1.5	1.7	1.9	12.4
Net financial flows †	1.9	2.3	3.2	6.5	6.1	6.8	35.3

* Not available.
† Estimated.
‡ Less than $50 million.
Source: Susan Foster, "Impact of Direct Investment Abroad by United States Multinational Corporations on the Balance of Payments," *Monthly Review*, July 1972, p. 172.

figures are somewhat misleading owing to transfer pricing and tax policies, Table 10 reveals the importance of this petroleum investment for America's balance of payments.

The point of this discussion is not simply that, as a mature creditor nation, the United States had to balance its current accounts through the income on foreign investments. It is, rather, that the income from foreign direct investment had an overwhelming *political* significance for the United States. Through foreign direct investment the United States desired not merely to generate sufficient foreign earnings to offset its merchandise imports and American tourism but to finance America's global political and military position. The income from foreign investment, in other words, had become an important factor in American global hegemony.

Perhaps the most explicit acknowledgment by an American official of the political importance of the MNC was that of Henry Fowler, U. S. Secretary of the Treasury. In referring to these "mighty engines of enlightened capitalism," he declared that for the United States, "They have not only a commercial importance—but a highly significant role in the United States foreign policy that has met with general approval by the Atlantic countries." He then went on to elaborate that in order to finance its military position overseas, "the United States government has consistently sought, and will continue to seek, to expand and extend the role of the multinational corporation as an essential instrument of strong and healthy economic progress through the Free World." [22]

Conclusion

Along with the international role of the dollar and America's nuclear supremacy, the multinational corporation served as one of the foundations of American global hegemony after the end of World War II. These three pillars of American power were, in fact, intimately joined. Europe and Japan acquiesced in America's role as world banker and supported the reserve role of the dollar because the United States guaranteed their security. As the world's banker, the United States was largely freed from a balance-of-payments constraint; this in turn enabled American corporations and the American military to expand abroad. Thus, since the United States could print money almost freely and other nations were willing to hold American money, it was relatively easy in the 1960s for American corporations to purchase foreign assets and expand overseas. Subsequently the earnings of these foreign assets (subsidiaries and branches) became a major positive factor in America's balance of payments. As in the case of Great Britain in the late nineteenth century, foreign investment earnings helped finance America's global hegemonic position. However, as with British portfolio investment overseas, this foreign expansionism on the part of American corporations meant a real cost to the home economy. It is to this subject that we turn in the next chapter.

VII

THE MULTINATIONAL CORPORATION AND THE AMERICAN ECONOMY: COSTS AND BENEFITS

Through following the product cycle and preempting foreign competition, American multinational corporations have sought to counter the historic tendency for the diffusion of knowledge and technique to undermine the center's industrial supremacy. The corporations have retained the ultimate source of industrial power—entrepreneurship, finance, and research and development—in the center and established production facilities throughout the periphery (including Canada, Europe, and other industrial economies). This defensive investment on the part of American corporations may be regarded as an effort to forestall the relative decline of American economic and political power.

The multinational corporation, along with the phenomenon of foreign direct investment, constitutes a major innovation in the history of international politics, in that it seeks to enable the industrial/technological leader to maintain its dominant economic position. Although technology and innovations still diffuse abroad, they do so under the control of the innovator. They are part of a package of capital, management, and technology. Foreign direct investment becomes, therefore, essentially a strategy by which to arrest relative political and economic decline.

An examination of the wisdom of this strategy is the primary concern of this chapter. In order to put the issue in sharp perspective I shall examine two contrasting positions on the wisdom and necessity of foreign direct investment by American corporations. Subsequently I shall analyze the costs and benefits of foreign direct investment to the American economy. Then, in Chapter VIII, I shall suggest an alternative strategy to what I consider the present American overemphasis on foreign direct investment.

The Service or Post-Industrial Economy Thesis

The first position, the so-called service economy thesis, is the conception of the United States as a *service-oriented island in a labor-intensive archipelago,* to use an expression coined by George Lodge, a professor at Harvard Business School. This view has been favored by economists at Harvard Business School and the Brookings Institution. It is also shared by important segments of the business community and by many public officials. Specifically, it argues that the United States must of necessity follow a foreign direct investment strategy. As Americans move into the service industries and as they export fewer and fewer products, they will export more and more technology and managerial services. These latter areas are the ones in which America's comparative advantage lies. Thus, although the United States will decline as a merchandise trading nation, it will enjoy huge earnings on foreign investment.[1] These earnings will enable the United States to pay its way in the world. According to this liberal vision, the international division of labor will be one of American brains and foreign hands.

The transformation of the United States into a service economy is reflected in employment figures. Nearly twice as many people today (46 million) are employed in the production of services (such as transport, commerce, education, health services, and government) as are employed in the production of goods (such as in manufacturing, construction, mining, and agriculture).[2] This is a remarkable shift if one compares these figures with the situation prevailing at the end of World War II. In 1947, the American labor force was divided equally between these two sectors. Between 1947 and 1969, however, while the goods-producing sector increased by only 5 percent, the services sector increased by 81 percent. Today it accounts for over 65 percent of the total labor force. And this trend is likely to continue throughout the decade. The prediction is that by 1980 only one-third of the U. S. labor force will be producing goods.

Within this larger framework of a service economy, the most important growth area in terms of employment has been governmental services, especially at the state and local levels. Other areas of growth have been education; general services, including private education and health care; and finance, insurance, and real estate business. Meanwhile, the fastest growing goods-producing industry has been contract construction, which of course makes little contribution to the competitive position of the United States. The growth of the manufacturing labor force has been considerably below the growth rate of the labor force as a whole.

According to the service economy thesis, the implications of these changes for the American economy and its place in the world are profound. Given the relative decline of industry, the export of goods will become decreasingly profitable; the export of managerial services, capital, and technology will become more important.[3] The major exceptions to this decline in trade are agriculture and certain high-technology products. In the intermediate range of products, however, the United States will serve foreign markets primarily through direct investment. The tradable goods sector of the economy is predicted to increase slowly as compared with the increase of the entire labor force. What this means is that the trading of manufactured goods will be of declining interest to Americans.

The other side of the coin, of course, is that the American demand for imports will rise. With the decline of the export sector of the American economy, the merchandise trade balance of the United States will continue to be weak. Like Great Britain, especially after 1890, the United States could well have a permanent trade deficit. Moreover, like Great Britain the United States would cover the imbalance through the income on "invisibles," such as investment earnings and the selling of licenses and services. The United States would become a high-technology core surrounded by a periphery of low-technology industrial powers and exporters of raw materials.

According to this thesis, there are three implications of these developments for the United States. In the first place, the United States has little to gain by the further liberalization of international trade in any area other than agriculture. Secondly, organized labor, which tends to represent the goods-producing industries, will be permanently hostile to the general thrust of an American economy oriented toward the export of capital and the import of goods. Finally, corporations will increasingly emphasize foreign operations at the expense of the domestic economy and exports. They will become the globalists or cosmocorps that the most visionary prophets of the multinational phenomenon envisage (see Chapter V, pp. 135–137).

This argument assumes that the modern service economy is fundamentally different from that of Great Britain in the latter part of the nineteenth century. A major transformation that is believed to have taken place is that knowledge has become the primary factor of production. As a consequence, the "knowledge industries"—education, information processing, and research and development—have become the most important sectors of advanced industrial societies. The production and utilization of new knowledge is said to have become more important than the production of goods. Thus, it is argued, it is misleading to focus attention on such indices as the output of goods or the nation's balance of trade in an emergent post-industrial society.

Underlying this position is the view that the competitive advantage of the United States lies in its technological edge. Given its high wage structure, the United States could not compete without its technological lead. But we live in a world in which technological knowledge diffuses to America's foreign competitors at a faster and faster rate. Therefore, in order to compete, the United States must go abroad to forestall the rise of foreign competitors and to maintain its relative position in world markets. In short, direct investment is a response to a world in which America's technological advantage is rapidly dissipated owing to the spread of scientific and technical knowledge. Only through direct foreign investment can the United States compete against lower-cost economies which are able, by imitation, to vitiate America's foremost competitive advantage in technological innovation and management.

In summary, this view reaches several conclusions: (a) The multinational corporation is the most dynamic, vital, and growing sector of the American economy; these corporations represent America's greatest strength and should be encouraged; (b) the MNC is an inevitable consequence of contemporary economic and technological developments; (c) given (a) and (b), the United States would suffer economic and political decline if it failed to exploit to the fullest the potential of the MNC; and (d) the multinational corporation, through the export of capital and technology, raises the standard of living elsewhere, thus creating economic partners for the United States and nations committed to the American values of free enterprise and political democracy. Thus, everyone benefits from American foreign direct investment.

The Trade Strategy or Domestic Investment Thesis

The other position on foreign direct investment is put forth by organized labor and academic critics of the multinational corporation. In this study, I shall not spend much time on the views of labor, as I have treated them in detail elsewhere.[4] In any case, the most telling of labor's criticisms of foreign direct investment are embodied in the criticisms of academics (including myself), whose reservations regarding foreign direct investment will here be juxtaposed against the views of its defenders. There is one major difference, however, between the views of organized labor and those of the academic critics which should be underscored.

Organized labor would not only greatly restrict the export of capital and technology but would also impose high tariffs on imports. Labor's position is protectionist and as such runs counter to the prevailing opinion of the academic critics, who favor a foreign economic policy that emphasizes trade rather than investment.

The academic critics of the multinational corporation take the following position: While the MNC no doubt does maintain America's position in *existing* markets, the United States must pay a real economic price in terms of lost tax revenues, impaired domestic economic development, and skewed distribution of income in the United States. This position argues that trade would be more beneficial than investment to the American economy and would not entail the political risks and costs of foreign direct investment. Whereas the pro-MNC position emphasizes the surplus of investment income over capital outflow, the anti-MNC position stresses the huge export of capital over many years that has made this surplus possible. How much more beneficial it would have been for the nation, it is argued, if this capital base had been invested at home.[5]

This position argues that supporters of the MNC incorrectly assume that there are no domestic investment opportunities and that foreign investment is therefore necessary. To the contrary, MNC critics believe, there are domestic opportunities which have been neglected because tax subsidies, the American corporate structure, and other factors created by public policies have made foreign investment more profitable than domestic investment to many American corporations.

The trade or domestic investment strategy position would concede that the imposition of restraints on foreign direct investment might mean a decline in America's position in certain world markets and perhaps even a loss of foreign exchange. This position argues, however, that a dollar earned from trade is worth more than one earned from foreign investment. The dollar earned from trade contributes more to government revenues; it generates greater domestic economic development; and it is more evenly distributed between labor and capital. Therefore, even if a decrease in direct foreign investment meant a decreased American economic presence in the world economy, the cost/benefit ratio of trade rather than investment would on the whole favor the American national interest.

In terms of world economic welfare, foreign direct investment may raise the level of income abroad by more than the loss of income in the United States. On the other hand, producing abroad by U.S. companies is not the same as selling domestically produced products abroad. A trade strategy could also raise world economic welfare, but without the unfortunate economic and political consequences for the United States economy of transferring the actual resources abroad. By investing abroad, the United States transfers part of its comparative advantage to foreign economies; inevitably, therefore, its competitive position must deteriorate. Furthermore, foreign investment provides an avenue by which the large oligopolies continue to expand; it thus contributes to further market concentration. Finally, expansion by American corporations produces unfortunate political consequences in both home and host countries. For all these reasons, the critics of the multinational corporation favor a foreign economic policy that emphasizes trade rather than foreign investment.

Evaluation of Foreign Direct Investment

A precise quantitative evaluation of these contrasting arguments is an impossible task. In the first place, even though one might be able to define the national interest in terms of employment or balance-of-payments goals, foreign investment may advance one objective at the same time that it retards another. It is necessary, therefore, to establish priorities or weigh trade-offs among such goals as international competitiveness, domestic economic development, and equitable distribution of national income. Secondly, the sad fact is that there are too few studies of the implications of direct investment for the American national interest; as noted earlier, the general assumption in the writings of liberal supporters and radical critics alike has been that foreign investment benefits the United States. Studies of the British experience as foreign investor and several important theoretical and empirical studies suggest the opposite.[6]

It must also be emphasized that the position taken with respect to the value of direct investment for the United States depends on particular assumptions that are made—for example, about what would have occurred if the direct investment had not taken place, and about the alternatives to direct investment that are available. Thus, in the analysis of foreign investment and its effects on the American economy, one must recall Charles Kindleberger's point that the answer to all the significant questions in economics is "It depends."[7]

The argument of this study in evaluating foreign direct investment and its impact on the American economy is that the fundamental economic issue is: Does foreign direct investment displace or supplement domestic investment in the United States? In other words, does foreign investment by American corporations decrease investment in this country or does it represent additional investment over and above what American corporations are investing in the United States? In short, are domestic and foreign investment competitive?

Obviously other issues are important, including the effect of foreign direct investment on labor, trade, and the balance of payments. These issues will also be analyzed. But the predominant issue from the perspective of the American economy is the effect of foreign direct investment on American economic development. From this perspective, this writer has developed strong reservations with respect to the impact of foreign direct investment on the United States. Our first concern, however, will be to evaluate the effect of foreign direct investment on American labor, trade, and balance of payments, and we shall then consider its implications for domestic economic development.

Effect on Labor

Organized labor argues that by exporting jobs foreign direct investment causes domestic unemployment. This view was embodied in the Burke–Hartke provision for the creation of an authority to regulate capital exports whenever the President determines that U.S. employment would be reduced by foreign direct investment.

It is not easy to determine whether foreign direct investment exports jobs, as labor contends, or creates them, as the proponents of the MNC maintain. The latter argue that direct investment creates jobs in this country in three ways. In the first place, it creates a market for the manufacture and export of capital goods to be used in the new plants overseas. Subsidiaries of American corporations tend to import capital goods from the United States, whereas foreign corporations might buy from other national suppliers. Secondly, there is the export of components from the United States which are further processed abroad. Unless this mixture of American and foreign components were possible, it is argued, American corporations would have no exports in the product area concerned. And thirdly, there are a number of manufactured goods which are exported because the corporation is established abroad; it has access to local markets for a broad variety of its own products which would not otherwise be exported.

On the basis of these factors and on the assumption that foreign investment is defensive, one study estimates that direct investment saves about 250,000 production jobs in the United

States. If one adds managerial, technical, and support workers, approximately 600,000 jobs in the United States are dependent upon direct investment. Furthermore, it is argued that these positions are at a higher level of wages and skills than would have prevailed in the absence of foreign investment. The contention is not only that direct investment creates jobs but also that it creates *better* jobs that otherwise would not have existed.[8]

In other words, the effect of foreign direct investment is to create managerial and white-collar positions in the United States; the obverse of this, of course, is that it shifts blue-collar positions overseas. Therefore, although foreign direct investment may not benefit the American blue-collar worker directly, it creates better positions for his son or daughter. Through social mobility, they will inherit the managerial and technical careers that are associated with the global enterprises of the multinationals.

Other studies support the argument that foreign investment is job-creating. These studies point out, for example, that over the past decade the MNCs have increased their domestic employment faster than the average for manufacturing as a whole.[9] These corporations also invest at home more rapidly than other industries. One could go on making similar comparisons between MNCs and non-MNCs, but such comparisons do not and cannot answer the most important question; namely, what would be the consequences for domestic employment if the MNCs were to invest more in this country and rely more on exporting? These corporations are among the largest and most dynamic in the economy, and they are the ones most interested in foreign markets. The appropriate comparison with regard to employment, therefore, is between a policy of foreign investment and a policy of investment at home by these same companies.

With respect to the question of whether or not the growth of employment would have been even greater in the absence of foreign investment, the pro-MNC faction falls back on the argument that American exports are not competitive; rather, foreign investment displaces import-substitution investments abroad by foreign firms. "The realistic question," so this argument goes, "is not whether foreign investment is to occur, because it will in any event, but whether its advantages will accrue to the United States or to other countries." [10] One could continue this debate almost ad infinitum.

The argument regarding the net effect of foreign direct investment as job-creating or job-destroying diverts attention from the critical fact that the primary determinant of the level of employment in the United States is total aggregate demand. This is a function of the fiscal and monetary policies of the national government and of the exchange rate. Foreign investment affects the level of employment only if the government does not pursue a compensatory full-employment policy and if the dollar is overvalued relative to other currencies. In the absence of such a full-employment policy, for example, foreign investment may or may not contribute to unemployment depending on a number of factors, such as whether foreign investment substitutes for domestic expenditures or whether it gives rise to the export of capital goods. Yet, even if the aggregate number of jobs remains the same, foreign investment destroys existing jobs and imposes upon labor the primary burden of adjustment.

The other issue directly affecting labor is the effect of foreign investment on the distribution of income between capital (including management) and labor. Labor has a strong case with respect to this issue. Yet it is one that labor has not sufficiently stressed. Both theoretical and empirical studies indicate that the export of capital has the effect of increasing capital's relative share of national income, thereby decreasing labor's relative share.[11]

The effect of foreign investment is to decrease the capital stock with which Americans work; this decreases the productivity of American labor. As a result, real wages are depressed below what they would have been if the foreign investment had not taken place. By one estimate, the annual reduction in labor's income stemming from foreign investment is around $6 billion.[12]

This is obviously a rough estimate, but it serves to indicate that the export of capital benefits management and the owners of capital more than it does labor. Moreover, in a service economy such as the United States has become, there is less productivity growth and therefore less growth of real income in the economy. Thus, there is a strong case to be made that foreign direct investment by the United States reduces national income and skews its distribution to the disadvantage of American labor.

The conclusion that foreign investment has certain disadvantages for American workers might be qualified in one important respect; namely, the export of capital may increase total national income (including all labor income and earnings on capital both in this country and abroad). As a consequence, although labor's *relative* share may decline with respect to that of capital and management, its *absolute* income may benefit. If this were the case, however—and it is difficult to prove or disprove—the proper course of action would be not to stop foreign investment, but rather to tax the extra gain to capital. This extra gain would then be redistributed to labor in order to make up for labor's loss. This can be done, of course, only if the increased earnings are returned to the United States, which has seldom been the case.

Effect on Trade and Payments

A second major issue concerning foreign investment is its effects on American exports and balance of payments. This issue is more complex than the question of its impact on labor. The assumptions one makes here are even more critical. They include consideration of such questions as: Does foreign investment displace or supplement domestic investment abroad by local investors which would be import-substituting? To what extent is foreign investment export-displacing or export-creating? What is the relative worth of a dollar earned from trade and a dollar earned from foreign investment? What is the effect of foreign investment on third markets?

The basic assumption of the proponents of foreign investment is that American direct investment "somewhat accelerated a process of [local] import substitution that would in any event have occurred." [13] According to this position, therefore, the issue is not exporting versus investing, but investing versus losing the market. The only real choice is between the establishment by an American corporation of a foreign subsidiary and the establishment by a competitor (American or foreign) of an export-displacing facility. Thus, in accordance with the product-cycle and organic theories of investment, direct investment is held to be defensive; it displaces local investment which would compete with American exports. Without direct investment American corporations would lose their position in world markets to lower-cost foreign producers.

The proponents of foreign investment do not regard exports and investments as opposed to one another; rather, they are held to be complementary. Their relationship is said to be a dynamic one. Both are growing at a rapid rate; foreign investment grows about 10 percent a year as against 6 to 7 percent for exports.[14] Although foreign investment may displace a particular export that is being lost in any case, the investment generates additional exports.

Unfortunately, economists have not disaggregated foreign investment into types and effects. One exception is Thomas Horst. After reviewing the existing literature and analyzing the available data, Horst concludes that there are both competition and complementarity between different types of American foreign investment and American exports. Direct investment, in varying degrees and with one major important exception, helps exports, albeit slightly. The complementarity results from shared information about market opportunities and shared distribution networks. Specifically, Horst concludes, "While on average subsidiary activity has tended to complement U.S. exports, the complementarity has been strongest in the consumer goods industries, somewhat weaker in the countries where most of our trade and investment goes, and offset or reversed in the high-technology industries." [15] Thus, in the important area of high-technology industries, exporting and subsidiary production are alternative means for American firms to exploit their comparative advantages.

In addition to arguing that foreign investment generates exports, its proponents emphasize that American subsidiaries abroad are largely financed by local borrowing and retained earnings. As a consequence, American corporations benefit through an increase in working capital; they are able to grow at a relatively low cost to the United States. American capital is, in effect, seed money which generates foreign capital for corporate expansion. Seen in these terms, direct investment increases the overall control of American corporations over world corporate assets and wealth. The multinational corporation is held to be a resource mobilizer; it employs local resources in order to expand its market position and generate a flow of earnings back to the United States. According to a 1968 estimate, American MNCs have financed roughly 35 percent of their overseas operations from external sources abroad; 40 percent of the expansion came from cash flows, and only 25 percent resulted from capital transfers.[16] Thus, from the perspective of its proponents, direct investment has increased the assets of American corporations and has generated the increasingly valuable flow of foreign earnings discussed in Chapter VI.

Whereas the proponents of foreign investment assume that foreign investment supplements American domestic investment and displaces local investment abroad, its opponents assume, contrariwise, that foreign investment by American firms displaces American domestic investment and supplements local investment (or consumption) abroad. They reject the assumption that foreign investment enables the United States to maintain a position in foreign markets at little cost to the domestic American economy. On the contrary, they believe, foreign investment causes a net addition to investment abroad and a net decrease in domestic American economic development. What it does is to accelerate the shift in the locus of industrial development abroad to the disadvantage of the United States. I shall return to this subject in the next section.

For the critic of the multinational corporation, trade displacement is a major consequence of the establishment of overseas production facilities. In part, this is because the multinationals tend to be America's foremost exporters; but instead of exporting, they have served overseas markets through local production by subsidiaries. The sales of these subsidiaries are at two to three times the level of United States exports of manufactured products.[17] The critics cite British and American data which suggest that foreign direct investment substitutes for exports. Detailed analyses by Hufbauer and Adler, Musgrave, and others argue that direct investment is harmful over the long run for American exports.[18]

Direct investment may displace American exports to third countries as well as to the host country. This is especially true of American investments in lesser-developed countries: A sizable fraction of the resultant output is exported, partially because of the need for a larger market. Also, many such governments will permit foreign direct investment only on condition that a fraction of the output be exported; this is the policy, for example, of Brazil. This practice of serving world markets by means of subsidiaries abroad is especially characteristic of American investment in Latin America, Canada, and Asia. As a consequence, the exports of American subsidiaries in Latin America, for example, are now substantial. By 1968, United States subsidiaries there were exporting over $750 million a year, a figure which then represented more than 40 percent of all Latin American exports of manufacturers. Moreover, between 1955 and 1964, one-third of the increase in Western Europe's research-intensive exports was accounted for by American subsidiaries.[19]

One particular type of export displacement that is destined to grow arises from so-called offshore production. Originally, this type of investment was motivated solely by cost considerations:

American corporation sought out pools of skilled, cheap labor in places like Taiwan and Hong Kong to produce goods for the American market. The subsidiaries established in such enclaves, however, have increasingly been made an integral part of the global sourcing strategies of the multinationals. They now export components and finished goods throughout the world.

The sophistication of offshore manufacture, moreover, has increased. American exports to third countries from subsidiaries in Taiwan, South Korea, and elsewhere, having begun with simple toys and plastic items, now include such items as telecommunication equipment, office machines, and motorcycles. This type of export displacement is undoubtedly destined to grow (see Chapter IX).

A third way in which American direct investment is said to have harmed American exports is through raising the productivity of European and other competitors. What American corporations have taken abroad is the comparative advantage of the United States: technology, management, and organization.[20] By example and by transfer, this has raised the competitive efficiency of European and other countries. The result, it is argued, has been to harm America's terms of trade in manufactured goods.

For its critics, two considerations are central in evaluating the impact of foreign direct investment on American exports and balance of payments. The first is whether American exports would have been larger (and how much larger) if corporations had followed a trade rather than an investment strategy. In particular, would exports to other developed countries and in high-technology industries be substantially higher? For any given corporation, obviously, investment was considered to be the more profitable policy, at least in the long run; otherwise, the corporation would not have undertaken the foreign investment. The question is, however, how much more profitable? Is it sufficiently more profitable to be justifiable in terms of the national interest? The critics' challenge to foreign direct investment, in other words, is one of opportunity cost: What are we as a nation giving up as a consequence of foreign investment?

What the anti-MNC position stresses, therefore, is the immense investment base abroad that has been required to generate the flow backwards of earnings and complementary exports emphasized by the proponents of the MNC. What, it is asked, would have been the contribution to the domestic economy and what would have been the export earnings if this $80 billion or more had been invested in the United States rather than abroad? These resources, this position argues, could have been more beneficially invested at home:

> While it is believed that U.S. investment abroad has on the whole been economically beneficial to foreign host countries, its benefits to the U.S. economy are less obvious. The accumulated capital outflows of the last 20 years have generated a return flow of income which now (at $6 billion in 1970) exceeds the continuing capital outflow (at $4.4 billion in 1970). Yet, measured as a rate of return on the $80 billion stock of capital in place abroad, such income flows compare unfavorably with earnings on domestic capital in the U.S. While such income inflows have come over time to provide a helpful credit in the balance of payments, the underlying trade effects are less obvious and more controversial." [21]

The second consideration emphasized by the critics of foreign direct investment is the relative worth of a dollar earned from trade and a dollar earned from investment. The assumption underlying foreign investment is that maintaining the shares of foreign markets held by American multinationals is a high national priority. For the corporation, it undoubtedly is. But is it a high enough national priority when evaluated in terms of the costs involved, such as lower return to labor, exported comparative advantage, and neglected domestic investment opportunities? The critics argue, in fact, that although decreased foreign investment would mean less income to American corporations, a dollar earned through export is worth more in terms of national interest than one earned by investment. This is essentially the thrust of the following argument:

> As to the export argument, it should be emphasized that sales by U.S. subsidiaries abroad do not correspond, in their effects on the U.S. economy and balance of payments, to exports by firms producing in the United States. It is surely not "share of foreign markets" by U.S. capital which is the relevant objective but "share of foreign markets" by U.S. value-added, including both that contributed by capital and labor. The former objective may have some political significance but little of an economic nature. If we are interested in the share of American value-added in world markets, then export subsidies might well be preferable to foreign investment, and combined with restraints on capital outflow.[22]

Thus, in response to the argument of the proponents of the MNC that direct investment is the only real alternative, the critic of direct investment argues that "the economic and political effects of maintaining a share of foreign markets via foreign production are very different from doing so via domestic production and export. The principal difference lies in the effects on labor productivity and shares in national income. Foreign investment may enhance the private profitability of U.S. capital but it is likely to reduce the real wage to U.S. labor as well as the government's tax share in the profits."[23] Thus, the balance-of-payments effects of maintaining a share of foreign markets via production abroad are very different from doing so via domestic American production and export. One dollar of exports, the critics of foreign investment point out, produces a one-dollar credit in the balance of payments, whereas a dollar of foreign sales by a U.S. subsidiary abroad yields only, say, six cents of foreign exchange. (Such is the case if we assume a 20 percent profit margin on sales, a 35 percent foreign profits tax, a 50 percent payout ratio, and a 15 percent withholding tax on dividends.)[24]

In terms of the American national interest, then, the pertinent question is: Which is more valuable, a larger volume of corporate earnings from investment with a smaller per-dollar contribution to the overall national welfare, or a smaller volume from export with a larger per-dollar contribution to the overall national welfare? One cannot reach any conclusions from this analysis with respect to the relative merits of a national policy biased in favor of exports as against one biased toward investment. But if one cannot conclude that exports would be better than investment, the opposite also holds. Therefore, so the critics argue, one can at least challenge the current tendency in official thinking to support policies that encourage foreign direct investment by American corporations.

From the foregoing arguments, it is clear that foreign direct investment is both export-destroying and export-creating. Whether it is more one than the other cannot really be determined; the position one takes on the matter depends on unproven and unprovable assumptions. While the evidence suggests that investment is a response to the loss of export markets and can generate exports, this does not in itself establish the case for foreign investment as the best solution to the threatened loss of foreign markets. At best, the work of Horst, reported above, suggests that from a national-interest point of view foreign direct investment is most defensible in consumer products and in non-advanced economies. It is export-substituting and least defensible in high-technology areas—those wherein America's comparative advantage lies.

The exports of any particular corporation may decline, thus making investment abroad more profitable for it than continued domestic investment and export. But from a national point of view, other exports could be generated in different and newer lines of production. This can happen, however, only if available investment capital goes into those newer areas of the domestic economy rather than into investment in existing product-lines abroad. Too often the corporations with the capital to invest find it to their particular advantage to go abroad rather than invest at home. In the words of one critic, "When a businessman claims that there is no domestic alternative to foreign investment, he means that the domestic expansion possibilities for his particular corporation are limited, not that there are no domestic investment possibilities that would absorb corporate savings." [25]

One may also ask whether defensive investment abroad by U.S. corporations is in the interest of the American consumer. Such investment, by its very nature, may decrease world competition. If the investment really does displace local investment by foreign investors, it could decrease general world welfare. Would the American consumer have benefited, for example, if Ford and General Motors had, by defensive investment, prevented the rise of the European and Japanese automotive industries? For all these reasons, the burden rests on the proponents of direct investment to make a better case for it than presently exists. In Raymond Vernon's otherwise excellent study of direct investment, for example, he devotes only 5 or so pages out of 284 to the impact of foreign direct investment on the American economy. Yet there is a basis for arguing that from the perspective of the home economy the benefits of foreign direct investment are private; the *costs* (and they are substantial) are public. Such investment benefits the owners of capital to the overall disadvantage of other groups and the economy as a whole.

This differentiation between private and public costs and benefits necessitates that in evaluating the arguments for a proinvestment as opposed to a protrade foreign economic policy, an important distinction made by Robert Aliber should be kept clearly in mind; [26] namely, that between market shares and output shares. The first refers to the share of total production of a product attributable to American firms, whether located in the United States or abroad. The second refers to the share of total production attributable to firms (domestic or foreign) located in a particular country. What is of primary concern to an individual corporation is its market share. What should be of concern to a nation, however, is its output share. It is American domestic production or value-added that is of primary importance for the long-term growth of the American economy.

It is on this basis that I have strong reservations with respect to the present American emphasis on foreign direct investment. Although foreign direct investment may be the sensible response of a particular corporation to the loss of an export market, it is not necessarily the best solution from the perspective of the American economy as a whole. Its consequence, in the long run, is overinvestment abroad at the expense of domestic economic development. It is to this issue that we now turn.

Effect on Economic Development

The most important issue with respect to foreign direct investment, and the one least discussed in the literature, is the significance of foreign investment for American economic development. From the perspective of the United States as a whole, is foreign investment the most profitable use of American resources? In particular, what are the consequences of foreign investment on the productivity of national resources, on the nature of American industrial development, and on the rate of economic growth? To what extent, for example, does the concentration of corporate energies and resources on the maintenance of a position in foreign markets detract from domestic economic development?

An excellent summary of the existing literature on direct foreign investment and the MNC makes a highly relevant observation:

> An important related question which, somewhat surprisingly, receives almost no attention in these volumes and which we mention only in passing is the relationship between foreign investment and the rate of capital formation and growth in the home country. Magdoff alludes only briefly to a severely qualified version of the Marxist surplus capital doctrine,* and all of the writers apparently assume that net advantages accrue to the investing country. This

---

* "What matters to the business community, and to the business system as a whole, is that the option of foreign investment (and foreign trade) should remain available." Magdoff, p. 20. (Italicized in original.) Is this a Marxist equivalent of Pascal's bet?

contrasts sharply with accounts of the costs to the British economy of foreign investment in the nineteenth and early twentieth century * and is no doubt attributable to the view that if foreign investment is essentially a diffusion of existing technology abroad, it may well raise the return to domestic investment in knowledge creation and therefore be complementary to domestic investment rather than competitive with it. However, in cases in which the multinational firm scans investment opportunities internationally only in its own industry (which is probably the normal case) it is perfectly possible that the result, both for the investing country and for the world as a whole, will be inferior to that produced by a well-functioning domestic capital market in which savings are retained at home.[27]

This is not to argue, however, that the export of capital has become the main determinant of American economic development. Fiscal and monetary policy are obviously of much greater significance. In terms of total capital formation in the United States, the export of capital, even at its height, was rather modest; according to Vernon, it has never represented more than 2 percent of annual gross capital formation in the United States.[28] On the other hand, this admittedly unimpressive figure applies to all American industry. If one looks at just the multinationals and the industries they represent, the percentage of their total investments that went abroad is in many cases substantial. A survey of seventy-four of the largest American multinationals conducted by the Emergency Committee for American Trade, a pro-MNC group, revealed that in industries such as chemicals, fabricated metal products, and motor vehicles, foreign direct

---

* See Leland H. Jenks, *The Migration of British Capital to 1875* (New York: Alfred A. Knopf, 1927); and Alexander K. Cairncross, *Home and Foreign Investment 1870–1913: Studies in Capital Accumulation* (Cambridge: Cambridge University Press, 1953). The question at issue is the extent to which the very slow growth of British productivity in the years prior to World War I can be attributed to insufficient capital deepening, especially in new, high productivity industries, and the relation of this to heavy investment abroad.

investment was between 10 and 60 percent of domestic investment.[29] The result has been a substantial strengthening of foreign economies.

This conclusion is reinforced by a study of the United States Tariff Commission, which found that in a seven-country survey, U.S. MNCs accounted for 13 percent of all capital spending. In the industrial "backbone" sectors—metals, machines, and transportation equipment—the proportion was 22 percent.[30] In these important growth areas, one can argue that foreign investment by American corporations has decreased domestic investment and restricted economic development in the United States to the advantage of its foreign competitors.

In terms of American national interest and the profitability of national resources, it can be argued that foreign investment is justified only if the *net* return abroad (earnings after taxes) is greater than the *gross* return in the United States. That is to say, the national interest of the United States would be served only if foreign earnings after taxes from a particular investment were greater than the combined return (corporate profits, labor's wages, and taxes paid) from a comparable investment made in the United States. Yet, on the contrary, the net return on foreign investment is in general lower than the gross on domestic investment; this is especially true in Europe and Canada.[31] It has been less true, however, with respect to the return on investment in less developed countries and in extractive industries, especially petroleum. There is little doubt that, given the effect of tax laws, trade barriers, and the threatened rise of foreign competition, foreign investment makes sense to the investor in terms of its own earnings, especially over the long run; but, one may question whether the American economy benefits in terms of national interest and economic growth.

Additionally, even if foreign and domestic investment have identical effects with respect to employment and economic growth, domestic investment has a much more beneficial effect on the industrial development of the country. Whereas foreign investment may well provide a higher rate of earnings for a particular corporation itself, domestic investment provides important benefits for the whole economy. It stimulates technological change, the development of human skills, and other so-called externalities. Foreign investment transfers abroad not only resources but the social benefits of improved technology and technical skills as well. While these structural changes and dynamic effects do not necessarily make domestic investment preferable to foreign investment, they are important. The situation has been summarized as follows:

> Investment brings two kinds of benefits: *direct* benefits in the form of profits to the investing enterprises; and *indirect* or development benefits in the form of productivity gains and higher wage rates. Conventional resource allocation precepts, in asserting that enterprises should invest in regions, domestic and foreign, that yield them the largest return, neglect the second type of benefit. If enterprises elect to invest abroad because the return to capital there is marginally higher than at home, then presumably the gains in development accrue to the foreign rather than the domestic economy. A recognition of both types of benefits leads to the conclusion that foreign investment, to be advantageous to the domestic economy, must yield a premium sufficiently in excess of what home investment would yield to compensate for the development benefits that are foregone.[32]

On the other hand, the multinational corporations do enhance the total resources or assets of American citizens. As noted earlier, these corporations have financed their expansion abroad substantially from retained earnings and foreign borrowings. What they have really exported, especially to Europe and Canada, is technology and management. These resources, along with American seed capital, have provided the nucleus for American mobilization and control of foreign capital. While this investment strategy has promoted the growth of American corporations abroad and has generated a substantial flow of income back to the United States, one can still argue that it has shifted the location of industries to other countries. In the modern economy, technology, productive know-how, and managerial skills are the critical factors of production; it is precisely these factors that the MNCs take abroad.[33]

The available evidence suggests that in the so-called commanding heights of the modern economy (high technology, chemicals, electronics, etc.), where the multinationals reign supreme, foreign investment can benefit the foreign economy to the detriment of the American economy. Technology and managerial skills are transferred abroad and facilitate foreign economic development and productivity; although the technology remains under the control of the American corporation, the technology and capital transfer do harm America's terms of trade and labor productivity. Under present circumstances—including the existence of tax laws that encourage retained earnings abroad and the oligopolistic nature of American industry—too many incentives are in the direction of foreign investment even though it may lower American industrial growth and productivity.[34]

The fundamental assumption of this criticism is that foreign direct investment in manufacturing is a substitute for domestic investment. Although foreign direct investment does maintain the American market position, it does so at a cost to the domestic economy. Contrary to the curiously Leninist argument of the defensive investment position—that there is a lack of domestic investment opportunities and that direct investment destroys foreign industry—our critique stresses the cost to the national economy in terms of the transfer abroad of real wealth. Furthermore, insofar as the export of capital is a substitute for the export of goods, the multinational corporation shifts the locus of industrial power abroad and makes the home economy dependent on income from foreign investment.

The principal argument of the proponents of the multinational corporation—that MNCs increase the wealth of the United States —forces one to inquire into the meaning of "wealth." Is wealth to be interpreted as the total assets of U.S. corporations, whether these assets are located in this country or abroad? Is it the

financial flow back to the United States and the consequent benefits to the American balance of payments? Or is it the indigenous
productive capability of the United States?

Recent government reports, such as those of the Peterson and
Williams Commissions, which defend foreign investment as a
generator of foreign earnings and as a positive factor in the
American balance of payments, suggest that "wealth" is defined
in terms of financial return (see Chapter VI). If so, there is a
classical mercantilistic element in current American economic
policy, in that real resources are being given up (as in the transfer of capital goods, for example) for a surplus in America's
balance of payments. In essence, the issue raised by the multinational corporation is that there is a cost to the country, in terms
of real resources and industrial power, in maintaining the global
position of great American corporations and of the United States
itself.

As in the case of classical mercantilism, the nation must pay a
real economic cost for political benefits derived from a mercantile
policy. In the seventeenth and eighteenth centuries, the balance-
of-payments surplus desired by national governments meant the
export of real resources. For political and military reasons, a
nation gained gold and foreign exchange through exporting real
wealth, consumer products, and capital goods. As Murray Kemp
has demonstrated, and as this study has argued with respect to
Great Britain in the nineteenth century, there is a tendency for
capital-rich countries to export too much capital and thereby
weaken their own industrial base.[35]

Similarly, the desire of the United States to maintain its share
of world markets, to gain control of production units in foreign
economies, and, for political reasons, to earn foreign exchange
has cost the nation in terms of real wealth. Through the export of
capital, technology, and managerial skills, the United States has
strengthened its industrial competitors. Although this transfer of
resources has been accompanied, except in Japan, by the extension of American control over important sectors of the foreign

economy, this does not alter the fundamental fact that a shift in the locus of industrial power has been facilitated. For the sake of a long-term favorable balance of payments and the maintenance of a world market position, the United States economy has paid a price, in terms of real resources and productive capacity.

An American Climacteric?

The conclusion that American emphasis on foreign direct investment has had a detrimental effect on the economic and industrial development of the United States takes one to the last and most critical question. Has foreign direct investment by American corporations become a response to the relative decline of the American economy? Is there evidence to suggest that a crossover has occurred from foreign investment as a sign of strength to foreign investment as a sign of a weakening industrial economy? Could one detect, in other words, an American climacteric in the second half of the twentieth century similar to that which affected Great Britain after 1870?

There is sufficient evidence to suggest that sometime in the 1950s or early 1960s American foreign direct investment became decreasingly a sign of industrial strength and increasingly one of relative industrial decline. By the time of President Nixon's announcement of his New Economic Policy in August, 1971 (see Chapter IX), a profound shift in economic power had taken place, particularly in the direction of Western Europe and Japan. Throughout the 1950s and 1960s, Western Europe (with the exception of Great Britain) and Japan enjoyed higher rates of growth of gross national product than did the United States (see Chart 4). Whereas Japan was growing at 13 percent a year and Europe at 7 percent, the United States throughout this period tended to grow at 3 to 4 percent a year. As a result, the United States's share of world GNP had fallen dramatically from nearly 40 percent in 1950 to around 30 percent in 1970, while the Common Market share had risen from 11 percent to nearly 15 percent

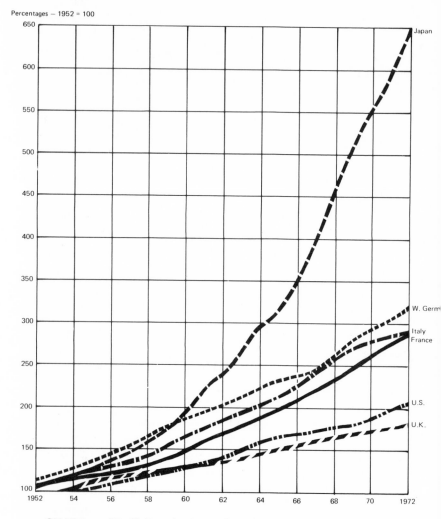

Percentages — 1952 = 100

CHART 4. "Real" Growth of GNP for Selected Countries, 1952–1972.
Source: U.S. Department of State, Bureau of Public Affairs, *Economic Growth of OECD Countries 1962–1972*, August 1973, p. 11.

in the same period. European competitiveness also improved; the American share of global exports shrunk from 16.7 percent in 1950 to 13.7 percent in 1970, while the Common Market share rose from 15.4 percent to 28.6 percent in that period, of which nearly half was in intra-EEC trade.

Additional evidence for an American climacteric comes from the area of technological innovation. National comparisons of innovativeness must be approached with care. Yet, the evidence has suggested to acute observers like Charles Kindleberger that, outside the military and aerospace spheres, American innovation in commercial technology has become sluggish.[36] In areas where the United States has formerly reigned supreme and in other areas as well—automobiles, steelmaking, shipbuilding—Japanese firms, in particular, have been taking the lead. Japanese entrepreneurship has been more dynamic. The Japanese save and invest more: 29 percent of GNP as against 14 for the United States and 20 for West Germany. As a consequence, Kindleberger observes, "the balance of payments difficulties of the United States [have been] due to a slowing down of innovative capacity relative to Europe and, above all, to Japan, and to an increase in spending, relative to income, on the part of business, households, and government." [37]

In addition to its relative rates of economic growth and innovative capacity, the composition of American imports and exports reflected its decline as an industrial economy (see Table 12). After 1967, America's trade surplus began to decline dramatically. By 1971, the United States had a trade deficit. Although American exports in technology-intensive manufactures (capital goods, transportation, scientific instruments, etc.) and agriculture continued to remain strong, the United States went into severe deficit with respect to fuels, consumer products, and other categories. But even in technology-intensive goods, the rate of export growth declined and imports increased. As Table 13 reveals, in technology-intensive goods the United States not only had a declining surplus with Western Europe, but it actually had a deficit with Japan as well.

Among American economists there have been two contrasting sets of explanations for the deterioration in America's trading position.[38] On one side of this debate were those economists, like Richard Cooper and Robert Solomon, who emphasized the factor of the American price level. American goods had become noncompetitive because of Vietnam-generated inflation and the apparent inability of the United States to devalue the dollar. This situation had also encouraged American corporations to invest abroad rather than export. According to this position, the American problem was not economic maturity but rather an overvalued dollar; it was a cyclical phenomenon. It could be reversed through devaluation and other appropriate policy changes.

On the other side of this debate were economists like Kindleberger, William Branson, Richard Nelson, and Michael Boretsky, who argued that the deterioration in America's trading position was mainly the result of longer-term trends in America's competitive position. Owing to foreign direct investment and the "catching up" of her industrial competitors, through their own efforts, the technological gap between the United States and the rest of the world had closed. In effect, the United States had lost a substantial part of its traditional technological advantages in manufacturing. The trade deficit represented a secular change in America's economic position.

In Kindleberger's view, the disturbing element was that this trade reversal was more than a normal change, i.e., of exports being displaced by earnings from foreign investment. The critical factor was that the balance of payments on current accounts had also turned adverse. The disappearance of an export surplus in merchandise trade indicated a deterioration in America's traditional dynamic competitive advantage—its ability to replace dying exports with a new wave of innovative exports. Instead, the United States not only appeared unable to main-

TABLE 12

Structural Changes in U.S. Merchandise Trade,[1] Selected Years, 1960–1971

(Dollar amounts in millions)

COMMODITY GROUP	1960	1965	1970	1971	AVERAGE ANNUAL GROWTH IN 1960–70 (PERCENT)	GROWTH IN 1971 OVER 1970 (PERCENT)
Agricultural products:						
Exports	$4,830	$6,229	$7,247	$7,695	3.3	6.1
Imports	3,824	4,082	5,767	5,768	3.9	0
Balance	1,006	2,147	1,480	1,927		
Minerals, fuels, and other raw materials:						
Exports	2,277	2,565	4,504	3,818	6.6	−18.0
Imports	3,985	5,372	7,005	7,910	6.0	12.9
Balance	−1,708	−2,807	−2,501	−4,092		
Not technology—Intensive manufactured products:						
Exports	3,573	4,409	6,778	6,262	7.1	−8.0
Imports	4,494	7,350	12,928	14,550	12.4	12.5
Balance	−921	−2,941	−6,150	−8,288		
Technology—Intensive manufactured products:						
Exports	9,010	13,030	22,565	24,187	10.0	7.2
Imports	2,369	3,895	12,978	15,898	21.7	22.5
Balance	6,641	9,135	9,587	8,289		
Commodities not classified by kind:						
Exports	718	954	1,496	1,535	7.2	2.6
Imports	401	730	1,274	1,476	14.7	15.8
Balance	317	224	222	59		
All commodities:						
Exports, including reexports	20,608	27,530	43,224	44,137	7.7	2.1
Imports	15,073	21,429	39,952	45,602	11.3	14.1
Balance	5,535	6,101	3,272	−1,465		

[1] The commodity breakdown in this table slightly differs from that presented in Secretary Stans's testimony of July 27, 1971.
Source: U.S. Congress, House, Committee on Science and Astronautics, *Science, Technology, and the Economy,* 92d Congress, 2d sess., April, 1972, p. 5.

TABLE 13

Trade [1] in Technology-Intensive Manufactured Products, by Region

(Dollar amounts in millions)

AREA	1960	1965	1970	1971	ANNUAL GROWTH IN 1960–70 (PERCENT)	GROWTH IN 1971 OVER 1970 (PERCENT)
Europe: [2]						
U.S. exports	$2,555	$3,708	$7,070	$6,965	9.5	–1.5
U.S. imports	1,363	2,067	4,701	5,373	14.6	14.3
Balance	1,192	1,641	2,369	1,592		
Japan:						
U.S. exports	378	590	1,544	1,523	11.1	–1.6
U.S. imports	196	677	2,578	3,597	26.9	39.5
Balance	182	–87	–1,034	–2,074		
Canada:						
U.S. exports	1,829	3,111	5,608	6,673	13.6	19.0
U.S. imports	339	916	4,788	5,840	29.5	21.9
Balance	1,490	2,195	820	833		
Rest of world:						
U.S. exports	3,937	5,760	7,698	8,254	7.0	7.2
U.S. imports	471	235	910	1,088	8.8	19.6
Balance	3,466	5,525	6,788	7,166		

[1] Excludes special-category shipments.
[2] 26 West European countries.
Source: U.S. Congress, House, Committee on Science and Astronautics, *Science, Technology, and the Economy.* 92d Congress, 2d sess., April, 1972, p. 8.

tain its monopoly position with respect to older products, but had not innovated new exports to take their place. The product cycle of generating new exports to replace dying ones appeared not to be working as it had in the past. Americans, Kindleberger surmised, like the British before them, had become more interested in consumption than in production.

Behind this fading trade surplus was also the fact that American productivity had not grown as rapidly as that of her competitors. As shown by Table 14, the United States during the decade from 1960 to 1970 had the lowest productivity growth of any non-Communist country. In fact, a substantial decline in productivity took place after the mid-1950s, the period when American industry accelerated its investment abroad. While some economists believe the drop to be cyclical, others believe the cause to be a secular trend toward low-productivity industries, particularly services and government.[39]

The explanation for America's declining trade position undoubtedly lies in some combination of the cyclical and climacteric positions.[40] The trade balance with other industrial countries did improve after the dollar was devalued in December, 1971, and again in February, 1973. What was significant from the perspective of the present study, however, was that price competition had become increasingly important precisely because the United States had lost much of its former technological lead in many products and industrial processes. The United States had lost many of its technological rents and had to compete with other industrial countries on the basis of price with a resulting decline in profit margins. It appeared not to be generating new exports essential to the smooth operation of the product cycle. The implications of this situation will be pursued in more detail in Chapter IX.

In addition to this transformation in the relative position of the American economy, changes in the character of the American multinational corporation itself suggested that a crossover had taken place and that American foreign investment was

TABLE 14

Comparative Growth in Output per Man-Hour in Manufacturing in the 1960s and in 1971

(In percent)

COUNTRY	AVERAGE ANNUAL GROWTH IN 1960–70	GROWTH IN 1971 OVER 1970
United States	2.8	3.6 [1]
United Kingdom	3.3	6.2
France	5.9	2.8
West Germany	5.5	5.4
Italy	7.4	0
Japan	10.8	6.6
Canada	3.7	1.5

[1] In 1969 U.S. output per man-hour increased only 1.3 percent; thus the 1971 upswing does not bring up the 3-year average to the long-term trend presumed to be about 3.29 percent.
Source: U.S. Congress, House, Committee on Science and Astronautics, *Science, Technology, and the Economy,* 92d Congress, 2d sess., April, 1972, p. 9.

increasingly a response to relative decline. In the latter part of the 1960s, the American MNC became more and more a global corporation. The motive for foreign investment was decreasingly that of following the product cycle; rather, global sourcing and dependence on foreign markets had become important aspects of corporate policy. Although the American market remained predominant, the corporation's decision making with respect to production and marketing was increasingly global. As such, there was a growing separation between the corporation's global activities and the resulting stimulus to the American domestic economy.

Conclusion

The available evidence as of the mid-1970s is inconclusive in determining how much the relative economic and industrial decline of the United States has been due to temporary cyclical factors or to a more permanent climacteric in the American economy. Yet, the evidence supporting the latter position is inescapable, and it focuses attention on the causes of America's relative industrial decline and appropriate remedial courses of action. In line with this concern, the next chapter sets forth the arguments for an alternative strategy to the one of foreign investment that has been emphasized by the United States over the past several decades.

In proposing an alternative, my argument is not that the relative decline of the American economy has been due principally to foreign direct investment; nor is it that this relative decline was somehow avoidable. Powerful economic forces beyond the control of the United States have accounted for this shift in the locus of industrial power. But certainly foreign direct investment has been a contributing factor in that it has accelerated the process and has inhibited what in the view of this study would have been a more appropriate response to relative decline: a rejuvenation of the American economy.

VIII

AN ALTERNATIVE STRATEGY
TO FOREIGN INVESTMENT

The argument of this study is that, in light of the preceding analysis, the strategy of foreign investment by American multinational corporations is, in the language of economists, only the *second-best solution* to the challenge posed by foreign competition and the relative decline of the American economy. In simplest terms, what the United States has been doing is exporting or trading away its comparative advantages (technology, technical know-how, and management) and potential productivity gains in exchange for future foreign earnings. Insofar as the United States continues to move in this direction, it is converting itself into the type of *rentier* economy, that is, one which lives off investment income, that Great Britain became in the latter part of the nineteenth century. Overall, the United States in the second half of the twentieth century may be said to be facing many of the same problems and choices that Great Britain faced in the latter half of the nineteenth.

In the United States today, the idea of living off foreign investment income has become very attractive. In fact, in the short run, the balancing of America's international accounts through the return on foreign investment has become a necessity. Though the magnitude of this American dependence on foreign investment income certainly does not match the British experience, the importance of this income should not be minimized; it has become a critical factor in America's economic welfare and global political position. Without it the United States could not finance its foreign military commitments, its escalating imports of manufactures, petroleum, and raw materials, and other expenditures abroad. The loss of this income, under present circumstances, would necessitate either a drastic lowering of the American standard of living or a major retrenchment from overseas security commitments.

Fortunately, the United States has not become as dependent upon foreign investment earnings as did Great Britain. There are, however, several considerations which support the judgment that it has become overdependent on foreign investment. In the early 1970s, foreign investment accounted for more than 20 percent of annual corporate expenditures for plant and equipment. In certain key industries, such as chemicals (30 percent), consumer goods (40 percent), and electrical goods (75 percent), a large fraction of total assets in the early 1970s was located abroad. Additionally, in 1973 foreign investment income represented over 15 percent of American foreign receipts ($18.5 billion out of $120.5 billion total foreign receipts). These percentages were certain to increase.[1] In effect, the United States has become highly dependent on the earnings of assets subject to foreign control.

This is a substantially different situation from that which obtains with respect to export earnings. Though one can be shut out of a foreign market, other markets can be sought and one at least retains the investment itself. Keynes long ago made a case of this type (albeit an overstated one) against British investment:

Consider two investments, the one at home and the other abroad, with equal risks of repudiation or confiscation or legislation restricting profit. It is a matter of indifference to the individual investor which he selects. But the nation as a whole retains in the one case the object of the investment and the fruits of it; whilst in the other case both are lost. If a loan to improve a South American capital is repudiated, we have nothing. If a Poplar housing loan is repudiated, we, as a nation, still have the houses. If the Grand Trunk Railway of Canada fails its shareholders by reason of legal restriction of the rates chargeable or for any other cause, we have nothing. If the Underground System of London fails its shareholders, Londoners still have their Underground System. . . .

A state of affairs, arising out of the arrangements of the investment market and disconnected from the equilibria of trade and industry, which causes a bias in favour of, and may overstimulate, foreign investment, is capable of doing us a great deal of injury in the terms on which we conduct our international trade. It may be that we should do much better to be content with a volume of exports sufficient to pay for our imports, and to divert our surplus resources of capital and labour into the manifold improvements at home waiting to be carried out.[2]

American corporations have become highly dependent upon the income from their foreign subsidiaries and branch plants; the profits of many of America's most important corporations now come largely from their foreign earnings. In 1974, for example, 46 percent of Xerox's and 54 percent of IBM's net income came from foreign earnings; [3] between 25 and 30 percent of total corporate profits came from foreign operations.[4] As Tables 15 and 16 reveal, key American corporations have become extremely dependent on overseas sales and have placed a substantial portion of their total assets abroad. In the opinion of conservative business leadership, the effect would be devastating if American corporations were deprived of their foreign earnings.

The problems associated with this second-best solution of foreign investment are fivefold. In the first place, the society which lives off investment income grows less in productive capacity than would otherwise be the case. It depends on the growth of others. As in the case of Great Britain in the nineteenth century, the export of capital, management, and technology by the United States has accelerated a shift in the global distribution of industrial and political power.

Second (again as with Great Britain), the investor country becomes highly dependent upon the societies in which its investments and the sources of its income are located; it becomes increasingly vulnerable to blackmail, as in the case of the Arab oil boycott, unless it has the means and will to protect its investment against expropriation or, more likely, against discriminatory policies on the part of foreign governments.[5] Moreover, foreign direct investment in certain societies, such as South Africa or post-Allende Chile, creates domestic pressures in the United States for supporting repressive and repugnant regimes. Its foreign policy can become, and too frequently has been, hostage to this foreign control over corporate assets. This situation can also encourage, and has encouraged, the pursuit of an interventionist foreign policy as well as the use of covert intelligence operations and outright bribes to foster governments and policies sympathetic to American investment.

Third, the foreign investment solution, as has been argued, has had profound implications for domestic welfare and particularly for the distribution of income and the situation of labor in the United States. Specifically, it benefits the owners of capital and certain groups of white-collar workers more than it benefits blue-collar workers; it is detrimental to the latter group unless appropriate compensatory taxation and redistributive measures are taken. But even if such compensatory policies were pursued, the export abroad of America's comparative advantage would still destroy existing jobs and impose on labor the cost of adjustment. Moreover, as blacks compose a relatively large fraction of American blue-collar labor, one can say

TABLE 15

Sample of American Firms with Overseas Operations, 1972

COMPANY	TOTAL SALES 1967 (THOUSANDS)	COUNTRIES WITH PRODUCTION FACILITIES	TOTAL ASSETS ABROAD (PERCENT)	SALES ABROAD (PERCENT)
Singer	$ 1,137,653	28	58	50
Standard Oil of New Jersey	13,266,015	45	56	68
Heinz	630,863	15	55	47
U.S.M. Corp.	283,528	25	50	54
Pfizer	637,770	32	50	48
Colgate-Palmolive	1,025,351	43	50	55
International Telephone & Telegraph	2,760,572	60	47	47
Corn Products	1,072,940	33	47	46
Mobil Oil	5,771,776	38	46	n.a.
Anaconda	1,047,815	9	44	32
National Cash Register	995,455	10	41	44
Ford Motor	10,515,700	27	40	36
Gulf Oil	4,202,121	48	38	n.a.

about foreign investment what has been said about foreign aid: It transfers income from the disadvantaged of American society to the labor elite in other countries.

Fourth, a foreign economic policy which emphasizes investment abroad means an increased concentration of American economic and industrial power; it benefits the large existing oligopolies. They have the resources and skills required to pursue a

COMPANY	TOTAL SALES 1967 (THOUSANDS)	COUNTRIES WITH PRODUCTION FACILITIES	TOTAL ASSETS ABROAD (PERCENT)	SALES ABROAD (PERCENT)
International Business Machines	5,345,201	14	34	30
Warner Lambert Pharmaceutical	656,822	47	32	33
Chrysler	6,213,383	18	31	21
American Standard	599,807	21	30	28
Minnesota Mining & Manufacture	1,281,866	24	29	30
Abbott Laboratories	303,341	24	27	26
Caterpillar Tractor	1,472,500	14	25	14
Goodyear Tire and Rubber	2,637,710	35	22	30
International Harvester	2,451,897	18	21	17
General Motors	20,026,252	24	15	14
Du Pont	3,102,033	16	12	4

Legend: n.a. = not available
Source: From *Managerial Finance*, Fourth Edition, by J. Fred Weston and Eugene F. Brigham. Copyright © 1962, 1966, 1969, 1972 by Holt, Rhinehart and Winston, Publishers. Reprinted by permission of The Drydem Press.

foreign investment strategy. Insofar as American policy favors investment over trade, it discourages the diversification and decentralization of the American economy.

Fifth, reliance on foreign investment means neglect of domestic investment opportunities and social needs. Resources flow abroad to facilitate corporate growth rather than to improve America's cities, decrease her dependence on foreign

TABLE 16

*Dependence of Multinational Corporations
on Foreign Earnings, 1973*

MNC	PERCENTAGE OF EARNINGS FROM FOREIGN OPERATIONS
Burroughs	41
Coca-Cola	55
Dow Chemical	48
Gillette	51
Hoover	60
IBM	54
International Flavors & Fragrances	52
Merck	44
NCR	53
Pfizer	57
Revlon	38
Richardson-Merrell	43
Rohm & Haas	33
G. D. Searle	40
Sperry Rand	50
Sunbeam	38
Xerox	46

Source: Reprinted from the January 12, 1974 issue of *Business Week* by special permission (p. 53). Data compiled by Smith, Barney & Co.

sources of energy, or seek out other domestic investment opportunities. As in the case of Great Britain in the nineteenth century, the emphasis on foreign investment and the search for new markets for old products tends to abort the reinvigoration of the American domestic economy and its technical infrastructure.

In addition, one must ask whether a foreign investment strategy is politically viable over the long run. In time, foreign investment comes to be greatly resented by its hosts. As we are witnessing today, the forces of economic nationalism are on the offensive against American foreign investment. American multinational corporations are increasingly vulnerable to takeovers and other pressures. This in turn can give rise to the type of behavior exemplified by that of ITT in Chile, with all its undesirable consequences for the national interest. Of equal importance, foreign investment generates political opposition to a liberal international economic regime within the United States itself. And in host countries, contrary to the argument that the multinationals spread the gospel of free enterprise, their penetration of the economy, as witnessed today in Canada, stimulates greater state intervention in the economy as a counterweight.

As C. Fred Bergsten, former assistant for international economic affairs in the Nixon administration, has written, a foreign economic policy which emphasizes investment weakens the forces of free trade in the United States.[6] We have already discussed the increase in protectionist sentiment among labor, due in large part to foreign direct investment by American corporations. But of equal, or even greater, importance is that the corporations themselves lose much of their interest in free trade. They gain access to foreign markets through investment rather than through the lowering of trade barriers. Moreover, foreign direct investment also decreases the incentives of host governments to lower trade barriers. On the contrary, they have an incentive to raise trade barriers and thereby encourage corporations to establish production facilities within their borders. These subsidiaries subsequently became subject to attack by local nationalists and became candidates for eventual nationalization, as observed throughout the world today.

The dangers inherent in America's continuing emphasis on foreign investment were best summarized by one of its most distinguished liberal economists, Paul Samuelson. His remarks echo Keynes's warnings to his fellow Britons a half-century ago and those of Hobson a half-century before that (see Chapter III):

> Economics, alas, cannot be divorced from politics and from trends of ideologies hostile to absentee ownership. Suppose that economic equilibrium did dictate our becoming a service economy, living like any rentier on investment earnings from abroad. Let us

grant that such an equilibrium, *if* permanent, could be optimal for the United States. But would it be safe for us to succumb to this natural pattern of specialization in a world of rising nationalism? Can one really believe that in the last three decades of the twentieth century the rest of the world can be confidently counted on to permit the continuing flow of dividends, repatriation of earnings, and royalties to large corporations owned here?

I do not think I am paranoid to raise a doubt in this matter. There is certainly a danger that, *after* the United States has moved resources out of manufacturing, and into the servicing–headquarter regime, it might then turn out that nationalism impairs the successful collecting of the fruits of our foreign investments. We should then not only find ourselves poorer than we had expected but also facing the costly task of redeploying our resources *back* into the fields earlier abandoned. To be sure, private corporations may in some degree already take into account this danger of expropriation and thereby prevent an unwarranted redeployment of resources from taking place; but it is doubtful that they can be counted on to exercise the proper degree of prevision, particularly since they may well know that they can depend on our government to compensate them when such contingencies arise. Hence, there are rational grounds for some apprenhensions concerning this aspect of spontaneous foreign-trade development.[7]

The *first-best solution* to the challenge posed by increased foreign competition and the relative decline of the American economy would be to reform the American industrial structure, capital market, and taxation system in order to channel new productive capacity and resources into the "underinvested" sectors of the American economy and society. This solution would mean a national industrial strategy which emphasized increased domestic competition and the development of new technologies and industrial processes rather than defensive investment abroad. It would mean a national policy to channel many of the resources that presently go abroad into nonmilitary research and development and such neglected areas as urban renewal, mass transportation, energy development, and environmental protection.

While such a solution might permit foreign direct investment at the discretion of businessmen, capital markets and taxation policies should at least be neutral regarding foreign and domestic investment. There should be no incentives, as there are today, to overinvest abroad.

But one need not stop here. Without accepting labor's hostile attitude, a case can be made for a more flexible and discriminating policy toward foreign direct investment. The United States might well adopt measures, for example, facilitating manufacturing investment in lesser-developed countries and discouraging investment in other advanced countries. In terms of global interests, it is the former which need investment if they are to have the capital and technology necessary to develop. Moreover, as we have already seen, foreign investment in lesser-developed countries tends to be more trade-creating than is the case with investment in other developed countries. American policy might also discourage foreign investment in high-technology areas, which does tend to be trade-destroying, and thereby retard diffusion of America's comparative advantage in high-technology products. American corporations would, as a consequence, be encouraged to export high-technology products rather than her high-technology industries.

Other reforms are conceivable and warrant consideration. The United States might well discourage investment and actually encourage divestment in certain sensitive extractive industries, such as petroleum, or in sensitive political areas, such as South Africa.[8] It might encourage international investment codes that could prevent what C. Fred Bergsten has called the "coming investment wars"—a destructive conflict among nation-states to maximize their own gains at the expense of others and at the expense of a well-functioning international economy.[9] It might limit the export of technology and research and development activities that tend to undermine America's comparative advantage. And it might adopt measures discouraging corporations and host governments from pressuring "beggar thy neighbor" policies, which not only threaten the interests of the United States but could, in the long run, force the collapse of the world economy.

The nature and content of a reformed American policy toward foreign direct investment cannot be spelled out here; doing so would necessitate a separate volume. The direction in which we must head, however, is one in which there is a more careful weighing of the long-term national interest. This does not necessarily mean a sacrifice of global interests. Trade is in the world interest, also; and it may well be that certain types of foreign investment are in both the national and the world interest. What is being proposed is a more varied and discriminate policy toward foreign investment and the multinational corporation, based on a calculation of where the national interest lies in an increasingly nationalistic and mercantilistic world. Indeed, as shall be argued in Chapter VIII, this more mercantilistic world is forcing such a policy reassessment on the United States.

The first-best solution to America's relative industrial decline would necessitate the development of national policies encouraging scientific research and technological innovation. We have already acknowledged the crucial role of technological innovation as a factor in the competitiveness of American industry and in the decision of corporations to invest abroad. It is a technological lead that gives American corporations their competitive edge; the threatened loss of this lead has caused them to produce abroad so as to forestall the rise of foreign competition. One key requirement, therefore, of a national economic strategy deemphasizing foreign investment is to stimulate a higher rate of technological innovation in the American economy. There is an imperative need for a national policy to support and stimulate research and development in commercial and nonmilitary products and productive processes.

Ironically, at a time when other industrial countries have developed industrial strategies, the United States has weakened its support of science and technology. Although the United States has invested great amounts in military and space research and development (80 percent of the approximately $20 billion spent each year by the government on research and development), it has neglected research and development for purposes of agriculture, civilian nuclear technology, civilian industrial technology, and infrastructure (transportation, communications, and public utilities). In the 1960s, expenditures in these areas averaged about 1.1 percent of gross national product, in contrast to the major European countries, which were spending about 2.2 percent of GNP. European nations were also employing more technologically trained people in these areas of the economy.[10]

The argument of this book is well illustrated by the so-called energy crisis. Since the end of World War II, American policies have encouraged the overseas expansion of American oil companies. The resources of these multinationals have been devoted to the development of foreign sources of energy. In the short run, these efforts provided the Western economies with a plentiful supply of relatively cheap energy and the United States with substantial foreign earnings. In the long run, however, as the United States has now come to appreciate to its sorrow, this strategy was a cardinal error. By neglecting the development of alternative domestic sources of energy, the United States and its allies became vulnerable to the Arab oil boycott. In belated response to this danger, the United States launched Project Independence, a massive research and development program to innovate new sources of energy in order to achieve a relatively high self-sufficiency in energy. Undoubtedly, the scale of the required investment will lead to measures inhibiting the export of American capital.

Obviously petroleum constitutes a unique problem. Yet the situation does illustrate the dangers to the United States in its present tendency to rely on foreign investment rather than innovation as the solution to the problems posed by rising costs and foreign competition. The only viable long-term solution to the tendency of industry and economic power to migrate from core to periphery is a strategy of innovation and productivity increase at home.

The alternative strategy to foreign investment, then, is to emphasize the innovation of new products and improvements in industrial technology.[11] Instead of being used to attempt to maintain a competitive position in lines of production in which American industry is no longer competitive, national resources should be shifted to newer areas, or a greater attempt should be made to increase productivity in this country. As the Japanese have complained, American foreign investment too frequently arises out of an inability or unwillingness to make American plants more efficient.

To argue for a greater emphasis on domestic investment and innovation does not preclude foreign investment on the part of American corporations. In rejecting the arguments of the strong proponents of the MNC, one need not accept organized labor's total opposition to foreign direct investment. There is, in fact, one very strong argument for foreign direct investment by American firms.

A fundamental fact in the American situation has been that the cost of innovation has been rising rapidly at the same time that the rate of diffusion has been increasing. Improvements in communication and transportation as well as the increasingly systematic nature of technology and know-how have greatly accelerated the ease with which knowledge and innovations can be diffused to foreign competitors. In a world in which industrial and organizational techniques are based on scientific knowledge, comparative advantage has become increasingly ephemeral.[12] Furthermore, both developed economies and certain underdeveloped ones have greatly improved their capacity to absorb scientific and technological advances. For its part, the United States appears less able to capitalize on the great advantage it has long enjoyed over its foreign competitors—the capacity to turn inventions of whatever origin into profitable innovations.[13] Thus, the United States must work faster, and at an increased cost, to keep ahead of its competitors.

The implications of this transformation in the relative rates of technological innovation and diffusion have been profound for the United States.[14] Despite high wages and an elevated standard of living prior to and during the quarter century following World War II, the United States maintained its competitiveness in world markets largely because of its superior technological position and the availability of skilled labor. However, by the mid-1970s the U.S. had to meet the problem of how to remain competitive in a world where comparative technological advantage had become increasingly transitory. The production of new knowledge and innovation is very expensive for the individual firm. Moreover, once such goods come into existence, they are in effect free goods. Even when the innovation is patented, a domestic or foreign competitor can utilize the new knowledge or innovation at a relatively lost cost to itself. Unless a firm can capture a relatively large fraction of the benefits of its research and development efforts, it has little incentive to undertake this investment in the first place. One can argue, in fact, that unless firms are able to realize the benefits of their own research efforts, total investment in new knowledge and technology will be below what can be considered a socially optimum level.[15]

Applied to the multinational corporation, this argument is essentially the Schumpeterian defense of oligopoly writ large.[16] According to Schumpeter, oligopolies are the principal innovators of new technology. They have the resources and are in a position to capture the benefits of innovation. There is, however, a perpetual disappearance of innovational profit owing to the diffusion of technology and innovations within the economy. As competitors acquire the innovation and profit margins decline, there is a renewed incentive for innovation. Thus, capitalism is an evolutionary process of creation and destruction of industries and productive processes.

Owing to the contemporary revolution in communications and transportation, the relevant capitalistic economy is no longer the domestic economy. We now live in an interdependent *world* economy. New knowledge and innovations rapidly diffuse to foreign as well as domestic competitors. Innovational profit is more quickly dissipated on account of the rapid diffusion of technologies and managerial know-how within the world economy. In order to capture the returns on its investment and thereby maintain a socially optimum level of investment in innovation, the multinational corporation itself follows the product as it spreads abroad. It thus maximizes the return on its investment. Foreign direct investment can be defended in principle, therefore, as providing an incentive for American (or foreign) firms to invest in costly research and development.[17]

There is obvious merit in this argument. But two major caveats must be entered. In the first place, foreign investment is too frequently an alternative to investment in research and development. There is, in fact, a tendency among American firms to go abroad rather than increase productivity at home in order to cut costs. Like Great Britain after 1890 in response to the Law of Industrial Growth, they seek out new markets for old products instead of investing resources in the innovation of cost-reducing technologies and new products. Secondly, the Schumpeterian argument does not justify the magnitude of foreign investment and the rapid international diffusion of technology which is presently taking place. Given the oligopolistic nature of the American economy and the high rate of foreign direct investment, the international diffusion of American technology may, in fact, be more rapid than intracountry diffusion. Furthermore, the Schumpeterian argument does not justify the tax and other policies that give corporations a strong incentive to invest abroad rather than in the United States. The basic problem lies in the fact that the incentives are wrong. With proper incentives the market could redirect the flow of corporate investment. Thus, to say that there is a justification for foreign direct investment is not to argue that this investment is justified on its present scale. Reforms are required, especially in American tax laws and in national policies in the area of research and development. The emphasis of corporate strategy and government policy should shift in the direction of domestic investment and exports rather than foreign investment.

These reservations concerning the scale of American foreign direct investment are not to be construed as constituting total opposition to the export of capital, technology, and know-how. Foreign investment can benefit both the home and the host economy. The argument against overinvestment abroad is at one with Adam Smith's denunciation of those mercantilist regulations whose sole motive was "to extend our own manufactures, not by their own improvement, but by the depression of those of all our neighbors." The point is that in the contemporary world of rapid communications and transport, the emphasis of national policy should be the continual rejuvenation of the domestic economy rather than defensive investment abroad. Unfortunately, in the 1970s the decline of American spending on R and D and other changes suggests a perceptible shift in the direction of defending existing products rather than the innovation of new ones. One must acknowledge that the export of capital, technology, and managerial know-how to Europe and Japan in the 1950s and 1960s can certainly be justified in political terms. It strengthened these allies of the United States and made them less vulnerable to Soviet pressures. But in the light of the profound shift in industrial power which this investment has helped to foster, in the mid-1970s one can now question whether a strategy of foreign investment continues to be the appropriate one for a weakened American economy.

In terms of global economic welfare, trade and investment can have the same beneficial effects.[18] The reason why the

United States or any other economy chooses to invest abroad rather than export is largely a function of industrial organization. The difference between trade and investment lies in their internal effects on home and host economies: direct investment, more than trade, tends to have unfortunate economic and political consequences for both home and host countries. In maintaining, therefore, that the United States emphasize a trade rather than a foreign investment strategy, I am not arguing a narrowly nationalistic case. While I believe that a trade strategy would be more in the national interest of the United States, I also believe that such a strategy would serve a world interest.

In the last analysis, the choice before the United States is not one between a wholly trade-oriented policy and a wholly investment-oriented one. Furthermore, the choice will not be made unilaterally by the United States. There is little doubt that immense and powerful centers of industrial and economic power are emerging which will bargain and compete over issues of trade, investment, resources, and monetary relations. The resulting "mix" of trade, investment, contracting, joint ventures, and licensing will depend on the play of power and interests within the United States and among these major centers of economic power. But the United States has to get its own priorities sorted out before it can meaningfully discuss these issues in negotiations with other industrial powers. The argument of this study is that the American national interest dictates an emphasis on trade and the reinvigoration of the American economy rather than on foreign direct investment.

IX

THREE MODELS OF THE FUTURE

On August 15, 1971, President Richard Nixon announced a new foreign economic policy for the United States. In response to the first trade deficit since 1893 and accelerating attacks on the dollar, the president imposed a surcharge on American imports, suspended the convertibility of the dollar, and took other remedial actions. During the following eighteen months the dollar was devalued twice (December, 1971, and February, 1973), the world moved toward a system of flexible exchange rates, and intense negotiations were initiated to create a new international monetary and trading system.

Behind this new economic policy was the fact that American expenditures abroad for military commitments, foreign direct investment, and goods and services had come to require greater outlays of foreign exchange than the United States could earn or borrow. By the time of President Nixon's actions, the American share of international reserves had plunged from its post–World War II level of 50 percent to 16 percent; the Common Market share had in the same period soared from 6.1 percent to 32.5 percent. The American gold reserve had dwindled by June, 1971 to $10.5 billion. During the twenty-one-month period between January, 1970, and September, 1971, alone, foreign dollar reserves had jumped by nearly $30 billion, or more than the total increase over the previous twenty years. If the United States were to maintain its global economic and political position, it appeared to require a trade surplus as well as substantial earnings on foreign investment.

Although the United States now desired a trade surplus, the emphasis of American foreign economic policy continued to be on foreign direct investment. A major reason, in fact, why the U.S. desired a payments surplus was in order to remove controls on capital outflow and to finance the continued expansion abroad of American corporations.[1] In other words, the United States desired a trade surplus in part to finance foreign investment. Thus, under President Nixon's new economic policy the United States would export both goods and capital in order to generate the foreign exchange required to finance its global economic and political position.

By 1971, the American answer to the financial burden of world hegemony had undergone a four-phase evolution. During the first phase (1945–58), the United States had financed its world position primarily through its vast international reserves and superior trading position. Subsequently, the privileges associated with being the world's banker became more important; the United States printed dollars rather freely to finance its political and economic position overseas. As the American payments position declined in the 1960s and other nations began to resist further accumulations of dollars, the United States began to look toward the earnings of multinational corporations as a means to balance its current accounts. Finally, with its new economic policy, the United States sought to finance its world position and overseas security interests through some combination of all three methods: a trade surplus, the international role of the dollar, and foreign investment earnings.

America's deteriorating balance of payments situation was the immediate cause of the new economic policy. A more fundamental factor, however, was at work. Throughout the 1960s the locus of economic and military power had been shifting to the disadvantage of the United States. The rapid growth of Soviet military power and of the economic power of Western Europe and Japan had narrowed the gap between these rising powers and the United States. Subsequently, in the mid-1970s, the emergence of a tightly knit and powerful cartel of oil-producing states, the Organization of Petroleum Exporting Countries (OPEC), has further weakened the dominant position of the United States and her multinationals in the central area of energy. This diffusion and redistribution of power in the international system has undermined the economic and political order created by the United States at the end of World War II.

Although American economic and military power has also grown immensely in absolute terms throughout the postwar decades and although the United States is still the world's pre-eminent power, the relative position of the United States has dramatically declined. In relationship to other states, to America's former primacy in all aspects of power (military, monetary, and petroleum) and, more particularly, to America's vast global commitments, the United States has suffered a major decline in power. This undermining of American hegemony and its implications are the fundamental facts of international relations in the 1970s.

The primary political significance of the economic expansion of Western Europe and Japan has been its consequences for the distribution of power between the United States and the Soviet Union. Contrary to the expectations of American political leadership, the effect of the economic growth of Western Europe and Japan has been to diminish the relative power position of the United States. Although in the long run a powerful Western Europe and Japan could pose a serious challenge to the Soviet Union, in the short run the consequence has been to undermine American predominance.

This paradox can be explained in the 1970s by the fact that

Western Europe and Japan have not filled the power vacuum they themselves have inadvertently caused by diminishing the relative economic power of the United States. Instead, the main beneficiary of the undermining of American hegemony has been the challenging power, the Soviet Union. Though economically powerful enough to challenge America's former economic dominance in the world economy, Western Europe and Japan have lacked the military means necessary even to defend themselves against the Soviet Union, and they certainly could not balance the Soviet Union in the face of ebbing American power. At the same time that growing Soviet nuclear strength has canceled America's former strategic superiority, the economic development of Western Europe and Japan has weakened America's capacity to project its conventional military power around the periphery of the Soviet Union. In effect, the Russians and OPEC have raised the price to the United States of maintaining its global commitments at the same time that European and Japanese economic competition has decreased America's capacity to pay.

A similar consequence followed the growth of American power in the nineteenth century. Then, the growth of a new center of industrial power weakened Britain's military and economic position in the face of the rising challenge of German power. The United States then, like Western Europe and Japan in the 1970s with respect to the Soviet Union, was not prepared to balance Germany's expanding military capacity and presence in the shifting European balance of power. It took two world wars for the United States to convert its economic power into military power and to fill the vacuum it had helped create. Until, and unless, Western Europe and Japan convert their economic power into military power and political leverage in order to balance the Soviet Union, their economic expansionism will be primarily at the expense of America's power position.

President Nixon's new economic policy, the U.S. rapprochement with China, American moves toward détente with the Soviet Union, and subsequent policy initiatives with respect to energy have signaled the end of the political order which had been guaranteed by American economic and military supremacy; this political order had been the foundation of the post–World War II world economy. All these policy initiatives of the Nixon and Ford administrations, such as those in the areas of energy, trade, and money, have been efforts to adjust to the growing economic power of America's partners, Europe and Japan, and to the growing military power of her primary antagonist, the Soviet Union, and to the shift of economic power to the producers of oil and other resources. In terms of the present study, these economic and political changes have raised the question of whether the American multinational corporation can survive in the changing political environment of the 1970s and beyond.

This concluding chapter will not offer a definitive answer to this question. Rather it will present and evaluate three models of the future drawn from current writings on international relations. These models are really representative of the three prevailing schools of thought on political economy: liberalism, Marxism, and mercantilism. Each model is an amalgam of the ideas of several writers who, in my judgment (or by their own statements), reflect one or another of these three perspectives on the relationship between economic and political affairs.

Each model may be said to constitute an ideal type. Perhaps no one individual would subscribe in full to the arguments made by any one position. Yet, the tendencies and assumptions associated with each perception of the future are real enough; they have a profound influence on popular, academic, and official thinking on the future of the MNC in particular and the world economy in general. One cannot, in fact, really escape being influenced by one position or another.

Following the presentation of the three models, I shall present a critique of the strengths and weaknesses of each model. On the basis of this critique, I shall draw some general conclusions with respect to the future of the multinational corporation and the world economy of which it has been such a prominent feature.

Presentation of the Three Models

The "Sovereignty at Bay" Model

The liberal model we shall label the "sovereignty at bay" thesis, after the title of Raymond Vernon's influential book on the multinational corporation.[2] According to this increasingly challenged yet still very influential view, increasing economic interdependence and technological advances in communications and transportation are making the nation-state an anachronism. These economic and technological developments are said to have undermined the traditional economic rationale for the nation-state. In the interest of world efficiency and domestic economic welfare, the nation-state's control over economic affairs will continuously give way to the multinational corporation, the Eurodollar market, and international institutions better suited to the economic needs of mankind.[3] In the words of Charles Kindleberger, "The nation-state is just about through as an economic unit." [4]

Perhaps the most forceful statement of the "sovereignty at bay" thesis is that of Harry Johnson, the paragon of liberalism. Analyzing the international economic problems of the 1970s, Johnson makes the following prediction:

> In an important sense, the fundamental problem of the future is the conflict between the political forces of nationalism and the economic forces pressing for economic world integration. This conflict currently . . . [is] between the national government and the international corporation, in which the balance of power at least superficially appears to lie on the side of the national government. But in the longer run economic forces are likely to predominate over political, and may indeed come to do so before the end of this decade. Ultimately, a world federal government will appear as the only rational method for coping with the world's economic problems.[5]

Though not all adherents of the "sovereignty at bay" thesis would go as far as Johnson, most do regard the multinational corporation as the embodiment *par excellence* of the liberal ideal of an interdependent world economy. It has taken the integration of national economies beyond a liberalized trading and monetary system to the internationalization of production. For the first time in history, production, marketing, and investment are being organized on a global scale rather than in terms of isolated national economies. The multinational corporations are increasingly indifferent to national boundaries in making decisions with respect to markets, production, and sources of supply.

The case for this "sovereignty at bay" vision of the future is held to have been strengthened by the first fruits of dollar devaluation and other developments of the 1970s. As the cost of American imports rose and American exports increased, the reverse flow of European and Japanese direct investment into the American economy began to accelerate. American assets have become relatively cheap, and exporting into the American economy has become more difficult. In order to maintain market shares, European and Japanese corporations have therefore increased their direct investment in the United States (see Chart 5). Even the Soviet Union has praised multinational corporations and invited them in as partners to develop its rich, untapped natural resources. Thus, the MNC is increasingly coming to characterize other advanced industrial economies.

Behind this accelerating counterflow of direct investment into the American economy were several important developments in addition to the devaluation of the dollar and the effects of the energy crisis. In the first place, other economies had become powerful industrial cores and were beginning to follow the course previously followed by Great Britain and the United States. In particular, Japan and West Germany were responding to their newly regained industrial strength (see Table 17). Furthermore, European and Japanese corporations expanded into the American and other foreign markets in order to restore an oligopolistic balance that had been lost on account of the more

In Billions of Dollars and Percent of Total

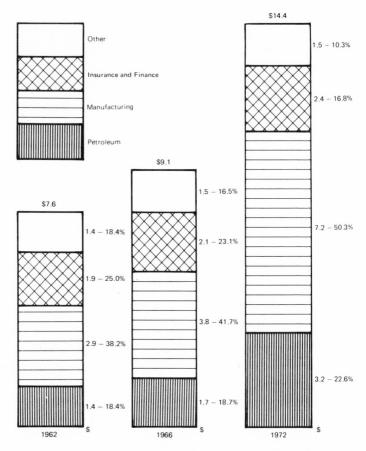

CHART 5. Book Value of Foreign Direct Investment in the United States, at Yearend 1962, 1966, and 1972—by Sector.
Source: U.S. Department of Commerce, Bureau of Economic Analysis, *Survey of Current Business* 53 (February 1973): 29–40 and 53 (August 1973): 50–51. Reproduced from: U.S. Department of State, Bureau of Public Affairs, *The U.S. Role in International Investment* (Washington, D.C.: January 1, 1974).

TABLE 17
Selected Major Countries' Stock of Foreign Direct Investment, 1960–1971
(Million of dollars and percentage)

YEAR	JAPAN	FEDERAL REPUBLIC OF GERMANY	UNITED KINGDOM	UNITED STATES
	BOOK VALUE (MILLIONS OF DOLLARS)			
1960	289.0	758.1	11,988.2	32,765
1961	453.8	968.7 *	12,912.1	34,664
1962	535.2	1,239.6	13,649.1	37,149
1963	679.2	1,527.3	14,646.2	40,686
1964	799.5	1,811.7	16,415.6	44,386
1965	956.2	2,076.1	16,796.5	49,328
1966	1,183.2	2,513.2	17,531.4	54,711
1967	1,458.1	3,015.0	17,521.1 *	59,486
1968	2,015.3	3,587.0	18,478.8	64,983
1969	2,682.9	4,774.5 *	20,043.2	71,016
1970	3,596.3	5,774.5	21,390.5	78,090
1971	4,480.0 *	7,276.9 *	24,019.0 *	86,001
	AVERAGE ANNUAL RATE OF GROWTH (PERCENTAGE)			
1960–65	27.0	22.3	7.0	8.5
1965–71	29.4	23.2	6.1	9.7
1960–71	28.3	22.8	6.5	9.2

* Exchange rate change
Source: United Nations, Department of Economic and Social Affairs, *Multinational Corporations in World Development* (New York, 1973), p. 146.

rapid American corporate expansion in the 1950s and 1960s. Finally, many foreign corporations invested in the United States in order to learn how to operate in a big and fast-moving market. As a consequence, by the early 1970s the world economy appeared to be moving toward a more equitable system of cross-hauling direct investments among non-Communist industrial economies.

The "sovereignty at bay" thesis argues that national economies have become enmeshed in a web of economic inter-dependence from which they cannot easily escape. Through trade, monetary relations, and foreign investment, the destinies of societies have become inextricably interwoven. The costs of the inefficiencies that would ensue if national autonomy or some other nationalistic goal were pursued would be too high; the citizenry, it is contended, would not tolerate the sacrifices of domestic economic well-being that would be entailed if individual nation-states sought to hamper the successful operation of the international economy.

Underlying this development, the liberal position argues, is a revolution in economic needs and expectations: domestic economic goals have been elevated to a predominant position in the hierarchy of national goals. Full employment, regional development, and other economic welfare goals have become the primary concerns of political leadership. More importantly, these goals can be achieved, this position argues, only through participation in the world economy. Governments are reluctant, for example, to shut out the multinational corporations of other countries and thereby forego the employment, regional development, and other benefits which these corporations bring into the country. In short, the rise of the welfare state and the increasing sensitivity of national governments to the rising economic expectations of their societies have made them dependent upon the benefits provided by an open world economic system.

In essence, this argument runs, one must distinguish between the creation of the interdependent world economy and the consequences of its subsequent dynamics.[6] Although the postwar world economy can be said to have been primarily a creation of the United States, the system has now become essentially irreversible; the intermeshing of interests across national boundaries and the recognized benefits of interdependence now cement the system together for the future. Therefore, even though the power of the United States may be in relative decline along with the security concerns of the non-Communist industrial powers, this does not portend a major transformation of the international economy and the international political system.

The multinational corporation is believed to be sufficiently strong now to stand on its own. The flexibility, mobility, and vast resources of the corporations give them an advantage in confrontations with nation-states. A corporation always has the option of moving its production facilities elsewhere. If it does, the nation-state is the loser in terms of employment, corporate resources, and access to world markets. Thus the multinnationals are escaping the control of nation-states, including that of their home governments. They are emerging as sufficient powers in their own right to survive the changing context of international political relations.

On the other hand, the nation-state, it is argued, has been faced with a dilemma which it cannot hope to resolve.[7] It is losing control over domestic and economic affairs to transnational actors like the multinational corporation. It cannot retain its traditional independence and sovereignty and simultaneously meet the expanding economic needs and desires of its populace.[8] The efforts of nation-states to enhance their security and power *relative to* others' are held to be incompatible with an interdependent world economy which generates *absolute* gains for everyone. In response to the growing economic demands of its citizens, the nation-state must adjust to the forces of economic rationality and efficiency.

In the contemporary world, the costs of disrupting economic interdependence, of territorial conquest, and of risking nuclear warfare are believed to be far greater than any conceivable benefits. The calculus of benefits and risks has changed, and "the rational relationship between violence as a means of foreign policy and the ends of foreign policy has been destroyed by the possibility of all-out nuclear war." [9] In contrast to the nineteenth century, the cost of acquiring territory is viewed as having simply become too great. Today there is more to be gained through economic cooperation and an international division of labor than through strife and conflict. Thus, in the opinion of Saburo Okita, president of the Japan Economic Research Center, the exercise of force for economic gain or to defend economic interests is an anachronism:

> We are living in a century when such military action is no longer viable. To build up militarily just to protect overseas private property is rather absurd in terms of cost-benefit calculations. The best course for the Government in case of nationalization or seizure of overseas private Japanese assets is to compensate Japanese investors directly in Japan rather than to spend very large amounts of money to build up military strength.[10]

Just as the nuclear revolution in warfare now inhibits the exercise of military power, the revolution in economic relations by increasing its costs, inhibits the exercise of economic power. Advances in transportation and communications have integrated national economies to the point where it is held to be too costly to threaten the severance of economic relations in order to achieve particular political and econmic goals. Economically as well as militarily, nations today are said to be mutually deterred from actions that would disrupt the interdependent economy. This mutual vulnerability of necessity limits and moderates the economic and political struggle among nation-states. It provides the necessary minimum political order wherein the multinational corporations of all the major industrial powers can flourish and bring benefits to the whole of mankind.

The "sovereignty at bay" view also envisages a major transformation of the relationships between developed and underdeveloped countries.[11] As the economies of developed countries become more service-oriented, as their terms of trade for energy and raw materials continue to deteriorate, and as their labor costs continue to rise, manufacturing will migrate to the lesser-developed periphery. The United States already engages in extensive offshore production in Asia and Latin America. Western Europe has reached the limits of importing Mediterranean labor, which is the functional equivalent of foreign direct investment. Japan's favorable wage structure and undervalued currency have eroded. With the end of the era of cheap energy and of favorable terms of trade for raw materials, the logic of industrial location will favor the underdeveloped periphery. The multinational corporations of all industrial powers will increasingly follow this logic. Manufacturing, particularly of components and semiprocessed goods, will migrate to lesser-developed countries.

This vision of the future has been portrayed most dramatically by Norman Macrae, who foresees a world of spreading affluence energized perhaps by "small transnational companies run in West Africa by London telecommuters who live in Honolulu." [12] New computer-based training methods and information systems will facilitate the rapid diffusion of skills, technologies, and industries to lesser-developed countries. The whole system will be connected by modern telecommunications and computers; the rich will concentrate on the knowledge-creating and knowledge-processing industries. More and more of the old manufacturing industries will move to the underdeveloped world. The entire West and Japan will be a service-oriented island in a labor-intensive global archipelago. Thus, whereas the telephone and the jet aircraft facilitated the internationalization of production in the northern hemisphere, the contemporary revolution in communications and transportation will encompass the whole globe.

"The logical and eventual development of this possibility," according to management consultant John Diebold, "would be the end of nationality and national governments as we know them." [13] This "sovereignty at bay" world, then, is one of voluntary and cooperative relations among interdependent economies, the goal of which is to accelerate the economic growth and welfare of everyone. In this model, development of the poor nations is achieved through the transfer of capital, technology, and managerial know-how from the continuously advancing developed lands to the lesser-developed nations; it is a world in which the tide of economic growth "lifts all boats." In this liberal vision of the future, the multinational corporation, freed from the shackles of the nation-state, is the critical transmission belt of capital, ideas, and growth.

The Dependencia Model

In contrast to the "sovereignty at bay" vision of the future is one which may be characterized as the *dependencia* model.[14] Though the two models have much in common, the *dependencia* model challenges the "partners in development" motif of the "sovereignty at bay" model. Rather, this conception is one of an hierarchical and exploitative world order. Whereas the "sovereignty at bay" model envisages a relatively benevolent system in which growth and wealth spread from the developed core to the lesser-developed periphery, the *dependencia* model sees wealth and benefits as moving from the global, under-developed periphery to the centers of industrial financial power and decision. The international economic system is seen as exploitative, producing affluent development for some but dependent underdevelopment for the majority of mankind. In effect, what is termed transnationalism by the "sovereignty at bay" advocates is considered imperialism by the proponents of the *dependencia* model.

In the interdependent world economy of the *dependencia* model, the multinational corporation still reigns supreme. But the world created by these corporations is held to be far different from that envisaged by the "sovereignty at bay" model. In the *dependencia* model the political and economic consequences of the multinational corporation are seen as resulting from what the Marxist economist Stephen Hymer has called the two laws of development: the "Law of Increasing Firm Size" and the "Law of Uneven Development." [15] The "Law of Increasing Firm Size," Hymer has argued, is the tendency, since the Industrial Revolution, for firms to increase in size "from the *workshop* to the *factory* to the *national* corporation to the *multidivisional* corporation and now to the *multinational* corporation." [16] The "Law of Uneven Development," he continues, is the tendency of the international economy to produce poverty as well as wealth, underdevelopment as well as development. Together, these two economic laws are producing the following consequence:

> . . . a regime of North Atlantic Multinational Corporations would tend to produce a hierarchical division of labor between geographical regions corresponding to the vertical division of labor within the firm. It would tend to centralize high-level decision-making occupations in a few key cities in the advanced countries, surrounded by a number of regional sub-capitals, and confine the rest of the world to lower levels of activity and income, i.e., to the status of towns and villages in a new Imperial system. Income, status, authority, and consumption patterns would radiate out from these centers . . . and the existing pattern of inequality and dependency would be perpetuated. The pattern would be complex, just as the structure of the corporation is complex, but the basic relationship between different countries would be one of superior and subordinate, head office and branch plant. [17]

In this hierarchical and exploitative world system, power and decision would be lodged in the urban financial and industrial cores of New York, London, Tokyo, etc. Here would be located the computers and data banks of the closely integrated global system of production and distribution; the main computer in the core would control subsidiary computers in the periphery. The higher functions of management, research and development, entrepreneurship, and finance would be located in these northern metropolitan centers. Through the operation of the product cycle, branch plants and labor-intensive manufacturing would be continuously diffused to the lesser-developed countries, where cheap, pliable labor, abundant raw materials, and an indifference to industrial pollution exist. This global division of labor between higher and lower economic functions would perpetuate the chasm between the affluent northern one-fifth of the globe and the destitute southern four-fifths of the globe.

The argument of the *dependencia* thesis is that the economic dependence of the underdeveloped periphery on the developed core is responsible for the impoverishment of the former. Development and underdevelopment are simultaneous processes; the developed countries have progressed and grown rich through exploiting the poor and making them poorer. Lacking true autonomy and economically dependent on the developed countries, the underdeveloped countries have suffered because the developed countries have a veto over their development:

> By dependence we mean a situation in which the economy of certain countries is conditioned by the development and expansion of another economy to which the former is subjected. The relation of interdependence between two or more economies, and between these and world trade, assumes the form of dependence when some countries (the dominant ones) can expand and be self-sustaining, while other countries (the dependent ones) can do this only as a reflection of that expansion, which can have either a positive or negative effect on their immediate development.[18]

Though this particular quotation refers to trade relations, much of the *dependencia* literature is addressed to the issue of foreign direct investment. In content, most of this literature is of a piece with traditional Marxist and radical theories of imperialism. Whether because of the falling rate of profit in capitalist economies or because of the attraction of superprofits abroad, multinational corporations are believed to exploit the underdeveloped countries. Thus, Paul Baran and Paul Sweezy see the multinationals as necessarily impelled to invest in lesser developed countries.[19] Constantine Vaitsos has sought to document the superprofits available to American corporations in Latin America.[20] The message conveyed by this literature is that "the imperialism of free investment" has replaced the imperialism of free trade in the contemporary world.

The *dependencia* model as here envisaged is in effect a computerized updating of Karl Kautsky's concept of ultraimperialism. In the intense debates among socialists concerning the responsibility of capitalist imperialism for the outbreak of

World War I, Kautsky was one of Lenin's principal antagonists. According to Lenin, the origin of the war lay in the competition among capitalist states for outlets to absorb their surplus capital and thereby arrest the falling rate of profit. For Kautsky this was too naive a view of capitalism; capitalists were much too rational to destroy themselves in such internecine conflict. Instead, Kautsky asked in 1915

> whether it is possible that the imperialist policy might be supplanted by a new ultra-imperialist policy, which would introduce the joint exploitation of the world by internationally combined finance capital in place of the mutual rivalries of national finance capitals? Such a new phase of capitalism is at any rate conceivable. Is it realizable? Sufficient evidence is not yet available to enable us to answer this question.[21]

Proponents of the *dependencia* model believe that such cooperation among capitalists has in fact been realized. Almost as if he were answering Kautsky, Stephen Hymer writes that

> due to the internationalization of capital, competition between national capitalists is becoming less and less a source of rivalry between nations. Using the instrument of direct investment, large corporations are able to penetrate foreign markets and detach their interests from their home markets. At the same time, capitalists from all nations, including underdeveloped countries, are able to diversify their portfolios internationally through the international capital market. Given these tendencies, an international capitalist class is emerging whose interests lie in the world economy as a whole and a system of international private property which allows free movement of capital between countries.[22]

Though he acknowledges that there are "contradictions" and conflicts among the capitalists and that the system may break down, for the moment, Hymer concluded that the strong tendency is for unity among the capitalists in the exploitation of the underdeveloped periphery.

The Mercantilist Model

A key element missing in both the "sovereignty at bay" and *dependencia* models is the nation-state. Both models envisage a world organized and managed by powerful North American,

European, and Japanese corporations. In the beneficial corporate order of the first model and the imperialist corporate order of the second there is little room for nation-states, save as servants of corporate power and ambition. In opposition to both these models, our third model of the future—the mercantilist model—views the nation-state and the interplay of national interests (as distinct from corporate interests) as the primary determinants of the future world economy.[23]

According to the mercantilist view, the interdependent world economy which has provided such a favorable environment for the multinational corporation is coming to an end. In the wake of the relative decline of American power, the growing conflicts among the capitalist economies, and the new economic power of petroleum and resource-exporting states, a new international political order less favorable to the multinational corporation is coming into existence. Whether there will be a five-power world (the U.S., the U.S.S.R.. China, the EEC, and Japan), a triangular world (the U.S., the U.S.S.R., and China), some form of American–Soviet condominium or whether there will be a more diffused distribution of economic and political influences among industrial and nonindustrial powers, the emergent world order will be characterized by intense international economic competition for markets, investment outlets, and sources of raw materials.

The essence of contemporary mercantilism is the priority of *national* economic and political objectives over considerations of global economic efficiency. The mercantilist impulse can take many forms in the contemporary world: the desire for a balance of payments surplus; the export of unemployment, inflation, or both; the imposition of import or export controls, or both; the expansion of world market shares, and the stimulation of advanced industries. In short, each nation will pursue economic policies that reflect domestic economic needs and external political ambitions.

The mercantilist position in effect reverses the argument of the liberals with respect to the nature and success of the interdependent world economy. In contrast to the liberal view that trade liberalization has fostered economic growth, the mercantilist thesis is that several decades of uninterrupted economic growth permitted interdependence. Growth based in part on relatively cheap energy and other resources as well as on the diffusion of American technology abroad facilitated the reintroduction of Japan into the world economy, the unification of Europe, and the development of a closely linked world economy. Now, both cheap energy and the technological gap, which were sources of rapid economic growth and global interdependence, have ceased to exist.

The mercantilist thesis holds that the end of the era of rapid global economic growth will give rise to an intensification of conflict over issues of distribution. With the slackening of growth and the emergence of resource constraints, nations will increasingly compete over constricting markets and scarce raw materials. They will engage in what Helmut Schmidt, West Germany's prime minister, has characterized as "the struggle for the world product." [24] Underlying this growing conflict, however, is said to be a major transformation of international political and economic relations.

International competition has intensified and has become disruptive precisely because the United States has lost much of its technological lead in products and in industrial processes. Like Britain in the latter part of the nineteenth century, the United States no longer holds the near-monopoly position in advanced technologies that it once held. Its exports must now increasingly compete on the basis of price and a devalued dollar. As was also the case with Great Britain, the United States has lost much of the technological rent associated with its previous industrial superiority. Thus, the loss of industrial supremacy on the part of the dominant industrial power threatens to give rise to economic conflict between the rising and declining centers of industrial power.[25]

From the mercantilist perspective, the fundamental problem of modern international society has been how to organize an industrial world economy. This issue arose with the spread of industrialism from Great Britain and the emergence of several competing capitalist economies in the latter part of the nineteenth century.[26] In the decades prior to World War I, the organization of the world economy, composed of several competing industrial economies, was at the heart of international politics. The resulting commercial and imperial struggle was a major factor in the subsequent outbreak of the war.

The issue was never resolved during the interwar period. During World War II, the organization of the world economy was regarded, at least in the United States, as the central question for the postwar era. Would it be a universal liberal system or a fragmented system of regional blocs and preference arrangements? With the outbreak of the Cold War, however, and the undisputed hegemony of the United States over other capitalist economies, the issue faded into the background. Then, President Nixon's August 15, 1971, speech signaled to mercantilist writers the fact that with the easing of the Cold War the issue has once again moved to the fore.

Mercantilist writers tend to fall into two camps, those of malevolent and of benign mercantilism. Both tend to believe that the world economy is fragmenting into regional and economic blocs. In the wake of the relative decline of American power, nation-states will form regional blocs or economic alliances in order to advance their interests in opposition to other nation-states. International trade, monetary arrangements, and investment will be increasingly interregional. This regionalization of economic relations will replace the present American emphasis on multilateral free trade, the international role of the dollar, and the reign of the American multinational corporation.

Malevolent mercantilism believes that regionalization and economic alliances will intensify international economic con-

flict.[27] Each bloc, centered on one of the large industrial powers
—the United States, Western Europe, Japan, or the Soviet Union
—will clash over markets, resources, currency, and investment
outlets. Economic alliances like the Organization of Petroleum
Exporting Countries (OPEC) and the opposing organization of
oil-consuming industrial states (the International Energy Agency)
as well as bilateral arrangements will also increasingly characterize the world economy. Through the exercise of economic
power and collusive practices, nations in economic alliance will
seek to redistribute the gains from economic interdependence
in their favor. Such an emergence of exclusive blocs and economic alliances would signal a return to the lawlessness and
beggar-thy-neighbor policies of the 1930s.

Benign mercantilism, on the other hand, believes that regional blocs would stabilize world economic relations.[28] It believes that throughout modern history, universalism and regionalism have been at odds. The rationale of regional blocs is
that one can have the benefits of larger scale and interdependence at the same time that it is possible to minimize the
accompanying cost of economic and political interdependence.
Though the material gains from a global division of labor and
free trade could be greater, regionalism is held to provide security and protection against external economic and political forces
over which the nation-state acting alone has little influence or
control. In short, it is argued, the organization of the world economy into regional blocs would reduce national vulnerabilities
to disruptive market forces and could provide the basis for a
secure and peaceful economic order.

Benign mercantilism derives from the view of John Maynard
Keynes and other Englishmen who, during the Great Depression, became highly critical of an increasingly interdependent
world economy.[29] The loss of national self-sufficiency, this
more benign view of mercantilism holds, is a source of economic and political insecurity and conflict.[30] Liberalism, they

believed, is detrimental to national cultural and political development. Today many holders of this position advocate a regionalization of the world economy as the appropriate middle road between a declining American-centered world economy and a global conflict over markets and resources among the capitalist economies. An inevitable clash among industrial economies can thereby be prevented through mutual self-restraint. Thus, whereas malevolent mercantilism believes that pluralism leads to conflict, benign mercantilism believes that it is the only sound basis for international harmony.

In the opinion of benign mercantilism, the thrust of much domestic and international economic policy, especially since the end of World War I, has in fact been away from interdependence. Nations have placed a higher priority on domestic stability and full employment than on the maintenance of international links; they have sought to exert national control over their monetary and other economic policies. This is what the Keynesian Revolution and its emphasis on governmental management of the domestic economy is said to be all about. The same desire for greater latitude in domestic policy underlies the increasing popularity today of flexible over fixed exchange rates and the movement toward regional blocs.

The energy crisis and the vulnerability of consumers to producer boycotts have accentuated these fears; energy self-sufficiency and access to secure supplies have become a goal of state policy. The mercantilists point out that in many industrialized economies there is a renewed questioning of whether the further benefits of trade liberalization and interdependence are worth the accompanying costs. Interdependence accentuates domestic economic problems as economic instabilities in one economy spill over into others. It causes labor dislocations, accentuates inequalities of income distribution, makes national planning more difficult, and increases the society's vulnerability to external political pressures. In short, according to the mercantilists, the erosion of national self-sufficiency has gone too far and the world has surpassed the limits of beneficial interdependence.

A Critique of the Three Models

In the following section I shall evaluate these three models and draw from each what I consider to be important insights into the nature of contemporary international economic relations. This critique is not meant to cover all the points of each model but only those which are most directly relevant.

"Sovereignty at Bay" Model

Fundamentally, the "sovereignty at bay" thesis reduces to a question of interests and power: Who has the power to make the MNCs and the world economy serve its interests? This point may be best illustrated by considering the relationship between the multinational corporation and the nation-state. In the writings I identified with the "sovereignty at bay" thesis, this relationship is held to be most critical. Let us begin by considering the MNC–host economy relationship.

For its part, the host nation-state possesses a primary source of power in its control over access to its territory—that is, access to its internal market, investment opportunities, and sources of raw material. On the other side is the corporation, with its capital, technology, and access to world markets. Each has something the other wants; each seeks to maximize its benefits and minimize its costs. The bargain they strike is dependent upon how much one wants what the other has to offer and how skillfully one or the other can exploit its respective advantages. In most cases, the issue is how the benefits and costs of foreign investment are to be divided between the foreign corporation and the host economy.

The "sovereignty at bay" thesis assumes that the bargaining advantages are primarily on the side of the corporation. Compared with the corporation's vast resources and flexibility, the nation-state has little with which to bargain. Most nation-states lack the economies of scale, indigenous technological capabilities, or native entrepreneurship to free themselves from dependence upon American (or other) MNCs. According to this argument, the extent to which nation-states reassert their sovereignty is dependent upon the economic price they are willing to pay— and, it is assumed that when confronted with this cost, nation-states will retreat from nationalistic policies.

In an age of rising economic expectations, the "sovereignty at bay" thesis rests an important truth: A government is reluctant to assert its sovereignty and drive out the multinational corporations if it means a dramatic lowering of the standard of living, an increase in unemployment, and so forth. But in an age when the petroleum-producing states have, through cooperation, successfully turned the tables on the oil multinational corporations, it becomes obvious that the "sovereignty at bay" thesis neglects the fact that the success of the multinational corporation has been dependent upon a favorable political order. As this order changes, so will the fortunes of the multinationals.

In the two and a half decades following World War II, the political order was characterized by relatively weak or weakened economies and by competition among the economies which have been host to American and other corporations. The differences among and within the host countries themselves and the influence of the American government left the host countries with little leverage for effective bargaining to increase their relative benefits from investments. Thus, in the case of Canada, the competition among the provinces and particularly between English Canada and Quebec greatly weakened Canada's position vis-à-vis American investors. Similarly, nationalistic competition for investment weakened attempts, such as the Andean Pact, to develop a common policy toward foreign corporations. But the importance of political factors in the overseas expansion of American corporations may be best illustrated by the case of Western Europe and Japan.

American corporations coveted both the Japanese and Western European markets; they have been able to establish hundreds of subsidiaries in the latter but only a few in the former. The reason for this difference is largely political. Whereas Japan has one central government controlling access to its internal market of 100 million people, several political centers control access to the European Common Market. By interposing itself between powerful American corporations and intensely competitive Japanese firms which desired American capital and technology, the Japanese government has been able to prevent the latter from making agreements contrary to its wishes. As a consequence, the Japanese home market has been protected as the almost exclusive domain of Japanese industry. American firms, therefore, have had a strong incentive to license their technology to the Japanese or to form corporate arrangements in which they were no more than a minor partner.

The Japanese succeeded in breaking up the "package" of capital, technology, and entrepreneurship which foreign direct investment has most frequently entailed. They didn't need the capital; they got the technology without managerial control by American corporations; and entrepreneurship remained in the hands of Japanese. This Japanese example of untying the "package" and obtaining the technology and, in many cases, capital without loss of control has become an inspiration for economic nationalists in Latin America, Canada, and elsewhere. The Japanese motto, "learn technical knowledge but refrain from depending on foreign capital," will increasingly characterize the policies of these economies.

In Western Europe, on the other hand, an American firm denied the right to establish a subsidiary in one Common Market country has had the option of trying another country and thereby still gaining access to the whole Market. Moreover, the strong desire of individual European countries for American investment has enabled American corporations to invest on very favorable terms. In certain cases, they have followed a "divide and conquer" strategy. Denied permission by President de Gaulle to invest in France, General Motors established in Belgium one of the largest automobile assembly plants in the Common Market. Through this route the corporation gained access to the French as well as other European markets.

In response to this situation, de Gaulle sought to obtain West German cooperation against American investment in EEC countries. Together, these two most powerful of the then six nations of the Common Market could dictate a policy which the others would be forced to accept. Through the instrumentality of the Franco–German Friendship Treaty of 1963, therefore, de Gaulle sought to form a Bonn–Paris axis directed against American hegemony in Western Europe.

Although there was sentiment in West Germany favorable to taking measures to limit the rapidly growing role of American subsidiaries in EEC countries, the West German government refused to take any action which might weaken the American commitment to defend Western Europe. The United States government reminded the West Germans that a continued American military presence there depended on West German support of measures designed to lessen the American balance-of-payments deficit. The United States got West Germany, for example, to increase its military purchases from the United States and to avoid competitive arrangements with France. Largely as a result of these American pressures, the Friendship Treaty was in effect aborted. The first serious counteroffensive of the nation-state against the multinational corporation collapsed. It is clear, however, that the outcome would have been altogether different if West Germany had desired greater military and economic independence from the United States. In short, the American corporate penetration of the European Common

Market has been dependent upon the special security relationship between the United States and West Germany.

One could extend this type of analysis to the whole of American overseas investment. American investment in the Middle East, Africa, Latin America, Canada, and elsewhere has benefited from America's dominant position in the world. This position is now seriously challenged not only by Russia but by Japan, Western Europe, China, and the Arabs and, in Latin America, by Brazil. Throughout these areas economic nationalism is on the rise, threatening American investments and the income they bring to the United States. The thrust of this attack has been to break up the package of capital, technology, and management in order to acquire the first two without the third; the goal is greater local control through joint ventures, nationalization, and other policies. While the host countries are unlikely to "kill off" the American multinational corporations, they will increasingly make them serve local interests. This in turn will undoubtedly make direct investment abroad less attractive to American corporations.

A reversal of fortunes has already been seen in the case of the oil multinationals. The significance of the offensive by the oil-producing states against the large international oil companies is not merely that the price of oil to the United States and the rest of the world has risen dramatically and that the producing states, through the exercise of economic power, forced in a matter of months one of the most massive redistributions of wealth and power in history, but also that the United States has lost one of its most lucrative sources of investment income. The oil crisis and Arab oil boycott which followed the Arab–Israeli war was also a profound learning experience for Europe, Japan, and the United States. The oil boycott and the behavior of the oil multinationals set into motion a series of events which transformed national attitudes and policies toward the oil multinationals. The sudden appreciation of how vulnerable they were to the policies of the oil multinationals and how far their "sovereignty" had been compromised awakened governments to the inherent dangers of overdependence on the corporations and their policies.

The French and, to a lesser extent, the Japanese response to this experience has received the most attention. But perhaps more noteworthy was the reaction of the West German government—after the United States, the nation most committed to a liberal world economy. It was the West German representative at the February, 1974, Washington Conference of oil-consuming nations who demanded that the United States and Western Europe undertake "a joint analysis of the price policies, profits, and taxes of oil multinationals." [31] While the proposal, which became part of the Washington Declaration (which led to the establishment of the International Energy Agency) does not mean the demise of the oil multinationals, it does suggest that the policies of nation-states will increasingly impinge on the freedom of action of these particular MNCs.

The oil crisis and the behavior of the oil multinationals also illustrated another potentially significant development for the future of the multinational corporation. This was the emergence of the "state multinationals." In West Germany, Canada, and the producing countries, nations reacted by creating their own state oil corporations to counterbalance the large private international corporations. This phenomenon is likely to spread to other raw material areas and to manufacturing as well. Its consequences will be to weaken the hold of the MNCs over raw materials and markets.

A change in attitude toward the oil multinationals can also be seen in the United States itself, where the issue of foreign investment became increasingly politicized in the early 1970s. Perceptions first began to change when it appeared that currency speculation by American multinationals was at least partially responsible for the weakening of the dollar in August 1971. But it was the role of the companies as instruments of the

Arab petroleum boycott and the escalation of prices and company profits following the 1973 war that had the greatest impact on American attitudes. Prior to these events, few probing questions about the oil and other multinationals had been raised in the press or in Congress. Other than a few "radicals," few had challenged, for example, the fact that Exxon, Gulf, and other oil multinationals paid virtually no taxes on foreign earnings to the United States government and acted as sovereign entities in their dealings with the oil producing countries. But when the oil companies became the instruments of the Arab boycott against the United States, and could no longer keep the price of petroleum low, even their staunchest defenders began to raise questions about tax evasion. More importantly, the United States government took into its own hands the task of negotiating with the oil-producing states and threatened to participate more fully in the industry. Thus, when the multinationals were perceived as being no longer supportive of the national interests of the United States, there was a reassertion of national sovereignty.

The case of oil and the oil multinationals suggests that nation-states have not lost their power or their will to act when they believe that the multinational corporations are threatening their perceived national interests and sovereignty. The experience of the oil boycott and the role of the multinationals in carrying it out reveal the extent to which the operations and success of these corporations have been dependent upon American power. This case history suggests that the weakening of the *Pax Americana* will affect the condition of other American MNCs throughout the world.

In the future, the situation of the oil multinationals will hold for other types of multinationals as well. Both resource and manufacturing multinationals will increasingly find themselves caught between their home and host governments. In order to maximize their relative gains and to shift the distribution of benefits in their favor, host governments will increase their demands on foreign investors. The MNCs will be forced to export a higher percentage of their local output and to limit the percentage of their profits that they can take out of the host country. They will be pressured to import higher levels of technology and to locate research and development activities in the host country. Corporations will have to accept greater local participation, to guarantee a positive influence on the host's balance of payments, and to incorporate a given percentage of "local content" into their output. In short, the host country will seek to maximize its benefits and to shift the costs associated with foreign direct investment to other economies.

In both developed and developing economies, host governments are undertaking initiatives that are reducing the power and role of the multinationals and are redistributing gains in favor of the host economy. This counterattack by the nation-state takes at least four primary forms. In the first place, as witnessed especially in the case of petroleum and extractive industries, the multinational's role is being reduced to that of contractor or licensee, receiving only a fee for service or for its licensed technology. Secondly, the host governments are exacting higher taxes and are demanding a participatory role in the multinational's subsidiaries or, as in the case of the Canada Development Corporation's purchase of Texas Gulf equities, in the multinational itself. Thirdly, host governments, including the United States in response to the foreign investment offensive of Iran and the Arab petroleum states, are establishing higher barriers to foreign investment and rules of "good" corporate behavior. And, lastly, host governments, particularly in the area of extractive industries, are creating state-owned or sponsored multinationals to counterbalance foreign multinationals. Obviously, it is too soon to know how far the host counteroffensive will go.

In order to meet the escalating demands of host governments, the multinationals will be forced to sacrifice the perceived interests of their home governments; by definition, for example, they cannot improve the balance-of-payments positions of both home and host countries. If they export to third markets from their foreign subsidiaries and meet "local content" rules, they will harm the exports of their home economy. Local participation, especially by officials of the host government, will weaken the MNC's responsiveness to policies of the home government. In short, in adapting to the growing demands of host governments the MNCs will increasingly impinge on the interests of their home governments.

As host governments force the multinationals to serve their interests, the question that will move to the fore is the relationship between the American MNCs and the American government. As we have seen, the general disposition in the United States has been to believe that the interests of American MNCs and the interests of the United States are complementary. In the areas of resources, manufacturing, and balance of payments, American interests have been seen to be served by the overseas expansion of American corporations. American policies have both facilitated this expansion and have made the MNC an instrument of American foreign and economic policy. Will this perception of a complementarity of interests persist into the future if the MNCs increasingly serve the interests of host governments in order to insure their own survival?

At the least, the relative decline of the American economy will have two important implications for the United States and the American MNC. In the first place, the ability of the United States to make the American multinational corporations serve its larger interests will decline as American multinationals become increasingly dependent upon foreign markets and sources of raw materials. As host countries decrease their need for American resources (capital, technology, and management), as more and more European and Japanese multinationals enter the competition, and as the American market recedes in importance in comparison with foreign markets, American corporations will be increasingly constrained to follow the dictates of host governments. Both the inability of the United States government to influence American multinationals and the desire of the latter to satisfy the growing demands of host governments will grow.

The second implication is that as American multinationals conform to the demands of host governments and the terms of investment change to the disadvantage of the American economy, foreign direct investment will become increasingly politicized in the United States. The basic assumption that corporate and national interests are complementary will be increasingly challenged; the gulf between corporate interests and perceived national interests will widen. Taxation and other policies that have encouraged the overseas expansion of American corporations will come increasingly under attack by American labor and other groups. In order to generate greater employment at home and to eliminate the growing shortage of investment capital for projects such as those associated with Project Independence, corporations may well be forced to expatriate a higher percentage of their foreign earnings and will be discouraged from exporting capital and technology. Policies such as those suggested in Chapter VIII and others that go beyond what this book recommends will be adopted to discourage foreign investment or to make such investments serve the perceived national interests of the United States. The multinationals will find themselves caught in a tug-of-war between home and host governments.

In the opinion of certain writers, this new environment will rebound to the advantage of the multinationals and actually strengthen their position in the world economy. According to this thesis, the relative decline of the American economy and the increased importance of other markets will enhance the independence of the MNC. In a world of intensified nationalism and competition among nation-states, the MNCs will be able to play off host and home governments. They will adapt to these cross-pressures in ways which advance their own particularistic interests and insure their continued survival in an increasingly hostile and mercantilistic environment. These global corporations will become truly independent actors with a life of their own.[32]

This sanguine view of the future of the multinational corporation is not shared by the present author. On the contrary, with the passing of the American world order, I believe that the multinational corporation will find itself increasingly constrained by both home and host governments. Blinded by their faith in liberalism, Americans (like the British before them) fail to appreciate the extent to which the overseas expansion of American MNCs has been due to the weakness of host economies and to favorable American policies. As both of these conditions change, the reign of the MNC over the international economy will recede. Yet it would be vain to predict how the reassertion of sovereignty on the part of home and host governments will affect the multinational corporations. That they will somehow survive there can be little doubt. Though they will be increasingly at bay, they are flexible enough and serve sufficiently important needs of an interdependent world economy to insure their survival. But in what form they will survive and whose interests they will serve will become a major factor in the future of world economic relations. The next section will explore this issue further.

The Dependencia *Model*

The weakness of the *dependencia* or ultraimperialism model is that it makes at least three unwarranted assumptions. In the first place, it assumes a much greater degree of common interest among the non-Communist industrial powers—the United States, Western Europe, and Japan—than actually exists. Second, it treats the peripheral states of Asia, Africa, Latin America, Canada, and the Middle East solely as objects of international economic and political relations. Third, it assumes foreign investment is exploitative. As the first assumption will be considered in more detail below, let us consider the second and third for a moment.

After nearly two centuries, the passivity of the periphery is now past. The Soviet challenge to the West and the divisions among the capitalist powers themselves have given the emerging elites in the periphery room for maneuver. These nationalist elites are no longer ignorant and pliable colonials. A new elite, educated at the Harvard Business School and the Colorado School of Mines has emerged to confront the multinationals. Within the periphery there are coalescing centers of economic power which will weigh increasingly in the future world balance of power: China, Indonesia, India, Iran, Nigeria, Brazil, and some form of Arab oil power. Moreover, if properly organized and led, such centers of power, when in control over a vital resource, may, as the experience of the Organization of Petroleum Exporting Countries (OPEC) demonstrates, conceivably turn the tables and make the core dependent upon the periphery. In early 1974, a perceptible transformation appeared to be taking place in the global balance of economic power from the owners of capital to the owners of natural resources.

The third assumption of the *dependencia* model is that a quasi-Marxist theory of capitalist imperialism and exploitation is applicable to the relationship between developed and lesser-developed economies today. Where the *dependencia* theory undoubtedly has a good case is with respect to foreign direct investment in petroleum and other extractive industries. The oil, copper, and other multinationals have provided the non-Communist industrial world with a plentiful and relatively cheap supply of minerals and energy. The dramatic reversal of this situation by the oil-producing countries in 1973–74 and the steady rise in the prices of other commodities support the contention that the producing countries had not been getting a just price for their nonrenewable resources. But what constitutes a "just" price for a natural endowment which was worthless until the multinationals found it is not an easy issue to resolve.

With respect to foreign direct investment in manufacturing, however, the case is far more ambiguous. Even if technological rents are collected, does the foreign corporation bring more into the economy in terms of technology, capital, and access to world markets than it takes out in the form of earnings? The researches, for example, of Canadian, Australian, and other economists suggest that it does. They find, for example, no differences in the corporate behavior of domestic and foreign firms; on the contrary, foreign firms are given higher marks in terms of export performance, industrial research and development, and other economic indicators.[33]

Indeed, one may argue that there is a strong presumption that in terms of economic growth and industrial development foreign direct investment in manufacturing is very much to the advantage of the host economy. Since a major cause of foreign direct investment is the sector-specific nature of knowledge and capital in the home economy,[34] American corporations frequently go abroad to guard against a lower rate of profit at home rather than because of the attractiveness of superprofits abroad. Insofar as this is true—and there is sufficient evidence to warrant its plausibility—foreign direct investment benefits both the corporation and the host economy at a cost to the home economy. Thus, though the Marxists may be right that there is an imperative for capitalism to go abroad, the effect is not to exploit but to develop the recipient economy—a conclusion, by the way, which Marx himself accepted.[35]

Nonetheless, there are three aspects of *dependencia* theory which deserve more serious consideration. The first is that the multinational corporations destroy local entrepreneurship, thereby arresting political and economic development. In part, this thesis parallels the infant-industry argument raised against free trade. It goes beyond this thesis, however, in arguing that foreign direct investment preempts and corrupts the potential indigenous entrepreneurial class; it converts potential local entrepreneurs into a managerial clientele whose interests and consumption patterns commit them to a preservation of the status quo of external dependence. In effect, so this argument goes, *dependencia* involves an implicit alliance between the external corporation and the indigenous managerial elite.

One difficulty with this thesis is that one does not know what is cause and what is effect. Is foreign direct investment a cause of the absence of an indigenous entrepreneurial class, or is it an effect of and response to the absence of such a class? The former position assumes the existence of a potential entrepreneurial class which, if given access to capital and technology by developed countries, could fulfill the entrepreneurial function performed now by the imported entrepreneurial elite. Critics of this position suggest that, on the contrary, the problem lies with the failure of the lesser-developed countries themselves to improve the local capital market, to develop an indigenous entrepreneurial class, and to shop abroad for the technologies they require, as did Japan. Instead, dependence upon foreign direct investment is seen as the easier route to rapid development.

The second aspect of *dependencia* theory which is worth considering is that of technological dependence. Although the multinational corporation provides at least short-term gains through the introduction of new technology and improved productivity, there is an inherent danger of long-term technological dependency. For very sound economic and managerial reasons, the research and development functions of the corporation, i.e., the generation of new technology, remain in the industrial economy. What is exported to the peripheral economy are standardized industrial processes. Herein lies the power of the corporation and the weakness of the host economy. The ultimate source of industrial power—the capacity for innovation and the monopoly of know-how—remains with the corporation and in the core economy. Even nationalization of the corporation's tangible assets may leave intact the real source of the corporation's power.

How is one to weigh the costs and benefits of this situation?

What the underdeveloped country obtains are technology and know-how superior to what it would have in the absence of foreign investment; yet it may not acquire the innovative capacity or the skills which would free it from technological and political dependence on the multinational corporation. It would be a very expensive and difficult undertaking to free itself from this dependence.

While it is true that, in general, lesser-developed countries are economically and technologically dependent upon developed countries, the conclusions to be drawn from this fact are not self-evident. Are they "underdeveloped" because they are dependent, as *dependencia* theorists assume, or are they "dependent" because they are underdeveloped? Japan is certainly dependent upon the United States, but it is hardly underdeveloped. Burma is underdeveloped, but it is not dependent upon any external power. As Benjamin Cohen has pointed out, the critical question is whether the poor are worse off economically because of their dependence than they otherwise would be.[36] Does dependence upon the developed countries entail a net loss or foreclose opportunities of greater benefit to the economy of the undeveloped country? Granted that the opportunity to exploit is there, is it exercised? These are empirical questions to which no general answers can be given. Whether foreign direct investment is exploitative or beneficial depends on the type of investment, its terms, and the policies of the recipient economy itself.

The *dependencia* argument that foreign direct investment by multinational corporations preempts the emergence of an indigenous entrepreneurial middle class and creates a situation of technological dependence provides a clue to the central concern of this theory. Although they are most frequently couched solely in economic terms, the concepts of underdevelopment and dependence are more political than economic in nature. They involve an assessment of the political costs of foreign investment; they refer both to the internal political development of the recipient country and to its external relations. As one of the better dependence theorists has put it, the problem "is not so much growth, i.e., expansion of a given socio-economic system, as it is 'development,' i.e., rapid and fundamental politico-socio-economic transformation." [37]

The third legitimate concern of the *dependencia* model, then, is that although foreign investment stimulates economic growth, it distorts the economic structure of the host country and encourages consumption patterns which will inhibit development in the long run.

This distinction between "growth" and "development" is crucial.[38] Economic growth is defined by most development economists simply as an increase in output or income per capita; it is essentially a positive and quantitative concept. The concepts of "development" and "underdevelopment," as used by dependence theorists, are primarily normative and qualitative; they refer both to internal structural changes in the lesser-developed economy and to its external relations with the developed world. *Dependencia* theory really calls for a domestic social revolution and for a change in the current international division of labor, in which the periphery is a supplier of raw materials and its industries are branch plants of the core's multinational corporations.

But even these aspects of *dependencia* theory are decreasingly true, at least with respect to the coalescing centers of power in the underdeveloped periphery. The American monopoly over technology and entrepreneurship has been undercut by the rise of foreign competitors. While peripheral economies have gained in strength and their bargaining power has been enhanced, technology has been more rapidly diffused through imitation or purchase. American and other multinationals are being forced to export technology and locate research and development facilities in host economies. In short, technology and entrepreneurship are decreasingly a factor in the creation of dependency relations between American core and peripheral economies.

Nonetheless, the fact of dependency and resentment against it are very much a part of the world scene. For this reason, the *dependencia* model is one which will continue to generate opposition against the structure of the contemporary world economy and the multinational corporation throughout the underdeveloped periphery of the world economy. As these peripheral societies grow in power, one can anticipate that they will undertake initiatives to lessen their dependence upon developed countries and to make the MNCs do their bidding.

The Mercantilist Model

Our critique of the mercantilist model will be restricted to only one aspect of contemporary mercantilist thought; namely, the idea that the world economy is fragmenting into economic groupings or regional blocs. Whether they consider this a malevolent or a benign development, mercantilist writers emphasize regionalism and economic alliances as the most likely consequence of contemporary economic developments.

It seems to this writer that mercantilists either ignore or ascribe too little significance to certain primary facts. Although the relative power of the United States has declined, the United States remains the dominant world economy. The scale, diversity, and dynamics of the American economy will continue to place the United States at the center of the international economic system. The universal desire for access to the huge American market, the inherent technological dynamism of the American economy, and America's additional strength in both agriculture and resources—which Europe and Japan do not have—provide a cement which could be sufficient to hold the world economy together and to keep the United States at its center.[39]

Furthermore, the United States can compensate for its loss of strength in one area of negotiations by its continued strength in another. For example, the American economic position has indeed declined relative to that of Europe and Japan. Yet, the continued dependence of Europe and Japan on the United States for their security provides the United States with a strong lever over the economic policies of each.

Thus, a fundamental weakness of the mercantilist model is the absence of a convincing alternative to an American-centered world economy. Western Europe—the primary economic challenger to the United States—remains internally divided; it is as yet unable to develop common policies in such areas as industry and energy or with respect to economic and monetary union. At this point, it is merely a customs union with a common agricultural policy. Moreover, like Japan, it continues to be totally dependent upon the United States for its security. As long as both Europe and Japan lack an alternative to their military and economic dependence on the United States, the mercantilist model of regional blocs lacks credibility.

The so-called energy crisis has affirmed this assessment. In the first place, the Arab oil boycott revealed the fragility of European unity. Theatened with the loss of vital supplies of Middle Eastern oil, every nation began to act for itself. Despite their reluctance, both Europe and Japan participated in the American-sponsored Washington energy conference. The American purpose in calling the conference and in subsequent initiatives with respect to energy conservation and development was in part to reinforce its Middle Eastern diplomacy, but was also to reassert its influence over its allies and to forestall policies, such as competitive currency depreciation and bilateral deals, that would fragment the world economy and weaken ties with the United States. No doubt, too, as the French and others charge, the United States hoped to find a solution to the energy crisis that would not threaten the position of the American oil multinationals.

Calling for cooperation from its European and Japanese allies, the United States reminded them that their security still rested on American goodwill. As Secretary Kissinger told the Europeans, "our military role in Europe depends in part on your willingness to make concessions to us in other areas." Moreover, the United States also reminded them that in the event of a conflict over oil, America's economic weapons were far superior. Thus chastened and reminded where power continued to rest, all but the French among America's allies participated in the conference and joined its counter to the oil cartel —the International Energy Agency.

The shift in the locus of power with respect to energy from Texas and American multinationals to Saudi Arabia and OPEC confronted the United States with a major challenge to its international position and threatened the unity with its European and Japanese allies. This challenge gave rise to policy initiatives that sought to reassert American primacy in the area of energy. The launching of Project Independence, the creation of the International Energy Agency, and the enactment of the Trade Reform Act of 1974 denying trade preference to members of OPEC had for their object not merely a reduction in the cartel-set price of oil; the United States sought also to commit itself, Western Europe, and Japan to a common energy policy and to the cooperative development of new sources of high-cost energy that eliminated the possibilities of bilateral producer-consumer deals and reinstated America's pivotal position with respect to the non-Communist, industrial world's supply of energy.

Despite this effort of the United States to reassert its influence over a fragmenting world economy, the consequences of the redistribution of economic power and the emergence of serious conflicts of interest among non-Communist industrial economies prevent one from dismissing the mercantilist thesis so quickly. Undoubtedly, the conflict that will be the most vexing is the growing demand and competition for raw materials, particularly petroleum. The loss of energy self-sufficiency by the United States and the increase in the demand for petroleum and other raw materials have already shifted the terms of trade against developed economies; commodity prices have become major factors in world inflation. In the long run, these changes put the industrial powers in competition for these limited resources. They are also competing both for the trade surpluses that are required to finance these vital imports and for the capital that the oil-producing states now have to invest. Thus, whereas in the past America's virtual control over the non-Communist world's supply of petroleum was a source of unity, in the mid-1970s, the United States is struggling with other industrial powers to insure its own supply.

In fact, the mid-1970s have witnessed the reemergence of the neo-Malthusian and social Darwinist fears that swept industrial society and were so disruptive in the latter part of the nineteenth century. A common factor in the several imperialisms that burst forth after 1880 and fragmented the world economy then was the growing fear of the potential consequences of exclusion from resources and markets. With expanding populations and productive plants believed to be dependent on foreign sources of food and raw materials, the insecurity of European states was magnified by the loss of their former relative self-sufficiency. Such concern over access to supplies on the part of have-not nations was again voiced in the 1930s and was a major factor in the breakdown of the world economy into rival blocs and imperialisms. The paradox of an interdependent world economy is that it creates sources of insecurity and competition. The very dependence of one state on another and the necessity for access to external markets and sources of raw materials cause anxieties and suspicions which exacerbate international relations.

Another reason for believing that there may be some validity in the mercantilist vision of the future is the weakening of political bonds among the United States, Western Europe, and Japan. During the height of the Cold War, the foreign economic policies of these three countries were complementary. Potential conflicts over economic matters were subordinated to the necessity of political unity against the Soviet Union and China. The United States encouraged export-led growth and anti-American trade discrimination in order to enable Japan and Europe to rebuild their shattered economies, while, through foreign direct investment, American corporations were able to maintain their relative share of world markets. Reciprocally, Japan and Europe supported the international position of the dollar; and neither the Europeans nor the Japanese challenged America's dominant position with respect to the industrial world's access to vital raw materials, particularly Middle Eastern petroleum.

Until the early 1970s, the political benefits of this arrangement were regarded as outweighing the economic costs to each partner. With the movement toward détente and the revival of the European–Japanese economies, however, the political benefits receded in importance, while concern over costs increased. As a consequence, the United States and its industrial partners now desire reforms of the world's trading and monetary systems that would enable each to pursue its own particular set of interests and retard that of the others. For example, the United States desired a reform of the trade and monetary systems that would preserve the privileges associated with its role as world banker and would also limit the right of Europeans and Japanese to run up huge trade surpluses. For their part, Europe and Japan desired to preserve this right and to limit the privileges of the United States as world banker.

Moreover, the relative decline of the American economy and the rise in foreign competition are having an impact on the American political order. The coalition of interests within the American polity which has favored an open and liberal world economy has weakened as foreign imports and domestic unemployment rise. Resentment has increased over alleged "dumping" on the American market as well as over European and Japanese barriers to American exports. While the internal balance of forces remain on the side of liberalism, the Trade Reform Act of 1974 contained new protectionist elements. In short, the evolution of economic forces in the United States and the world has weakened the American domestic political order favoring a liberal world economy.

Regardless of the outcome of negotiations over the future of the international monetary system, one thing is certain. Whatever privilege is retained by the dollar, it will not be sufficient to enable the United States to behave as it has in the past. Gone are the days when the United States could run up an immense balance-of-payments deficit in order to support foreign commitments, buy up foreign assets, and at the same time pursue a full-employment policy at home. It will no longer be able to expand overseas at a relatively low cost to the domestic standard of living. Having already lost much of its technological superiority and technological rents, the United States will have to finance its economic and military position abroad at an even higher cost to the American economy. That is to say, the cost of political and economic hegemony will now descend on the American people themselves. The weight of this cost and how the public perceives it will profoundly alter American attitudes toward its world role and toward America's European and Japanese allies. These changes in political interests and perceptions cannot help but push the world in a mercantilistic direction.

Conclusion

In conclusion, what does this redistribution of world power imply for the future of the multinational corporation and the interdependent world economy? Today, the liberal world economy and the multinational corporation are challenged by powerful groups within the dominant economy; the dominant economy itself is in relative decline and is being challenged by rising centers of economic power. With the decline of the dominant economic power, the world economy may be following the pattern of the latter part of the nineteenth century and of the 1930s: it may be fragmenting into regional trading blocs, exclusive economic alliances, and economic nationalism.

The outbreak of mercantilist conflict at the end of the nineteenth century and today would appear to be correlated with the industrial leader's loss of its industrial superiority. As its technological and comparative advantages diffuse to other economies and imitators cut into its original lead, there ensues a depression of entrepreneurial profits and of the rate of profit on a world level. With the closing of the technological gap, competition becomes increasingly intense. Then as competition intensifies for markets and for resources, the state comes to the defense of its own industries and attempts to cushion the effects of external forces. Growth rates may drop; an accelerating struggle over the world product takes place. In short, international economic relations become increasingly mercantilistic.

As we observed in the case of the transition from a British- to an American-centered world economy, such mercantilistic behavior predominates until a new clustering of Schumpeterian-type innovations advances one economy into new areas of economic and industrial activities, thus establishing the basis for a new international division of labor.[40] Unfortunately, the world had to suffer two world conflicts before an American-centered liberal world economy was substituted for a British-centered one. Is there any basis for hoping that our world might not suffer the same fate and disintegrate into global economic anarchy and eventual war?

There is good reason to believe, as Peter Drucker and others have argued, that the United States and its economic partners have exhausted the innovative possibilities of the industries upon which American economic power, foreign investment, and the immense growth of the last several decades have rested—

such as the internal combustion engine, man-made fibers, electronics, and steel.[41] In accordance with the Law of Industrial Growth, growth curves of these industries, much like those of cotton, coal, and iron in the last century, appear to have flattened out; they appear to have ceased to be major areas of innovation and future industrial expansion, at least in the developed countries. Thus, with the exhaustion of technological opportunities and the closing of the technology gap in commercial (though not military) technology among the industrial and certain industrializing countries, the world appears to be on the brink of an intense mercantilistic struggle.

In the contemporary world, the shortening of the international product cycle due to the more rapid diffusion of technology, the liberalization of trade, and the emergence of many industrial economies have intensified competition. Profit margins have declined; investment and growth have slackened.[42] The industrial world appears to be entering a period of mercantilistic conflict similar to that which characterized the period prior to World War I and the interwar period. As a consequence, though we may not have reached the "limits to growth," as some doomsday prophets hold, or be entering the depression phase of a Kontratieff wave, as others argue, the world is certainly entering an era of major adjustment to new economic and political realities.[43]

From a political perspective, the inherent contradiction of capitalism is that it develops rather than that it exploits the world. A capitalist international economy plants the seeds of its own destruction in that it diffuses economic growth, industry, and technology, and thereby undermines the distribution of power upon which that liberal, interdependent economy has rested. This was the fate of the British-centered world economy of the nineteenth century; it is the challenge that faces the American-centered world economy today. However, there is, I believe, a basis to believe that we can escape the full implications of the intensified mercantilist conflict which followed the decline of the *Pax Britannica.*

In the short run, economic conflict has been intensified by the energy crisis, the global recession, and worldwide inflation. Yet, viewed from a longer perspective, the critical problems of resources, environment, and inflation can have a beneficial effect. They may constitute the "catastrophe" that will stimulate a rejuvenation of the American economy. In the search for solutions to these pressing problems, the United States and her economic partners are being forced to initiate a new order of industrial technology and economic life. If this search leads to technological breakthroughs and the fashioning of a new international division of labor, we may yet escape the mercantilistic conflict that threatens to overtake us.

In the meantime, the decline of American power and the erosion of the political base upon which the liberal world economy has rested suggest that we are entering an era of grave uncertainty. The world economy will undoubtedly be characterized by a confused and complex mixture of the three models we have outlined above. As one astute observer has suggested, it has become a "stalemate" system, since no major economic power appears able to impose its will upon the others in the system, or to provide the leadership required to resolve the complex issues of trade, money, and investment.[44] Yet all, for security and welfare reasons, want an interdependent world economy to survive. It will be a system rife with tensions, strains, and conflict. Whether such a stalemate system marks the transition to something better—or worse—remains to be seen.

In a world economy composed of several major centers of economic power, economic bargaining and coalitions will predominate. Through the exercise of economic power, each center of the world economy will seek to increase the benefits of interdependence and decrease the costs. Trade, monetary, and investment relations will be highly politicized and the subject of intense negotiations. This, in fact, has been the direction of the evolution of the international economy—from a liberal to a negotiated system—since the rise of large rival economic entities in the latter part of the nineteenth century. It will require wise statesmanship and self-restraint to prevent the breakdown of this system into hostile economic nationalisms and antagonistic economic blocs.

It is within this post-*Pax Americana* world of intensified economic conflict that the American multinational corporation must seek its new, albeit reduced, role. In such a world, the American multinationals will have to be nimble and quick indeed if they are to escape suffering the fate of the British East India Company.

NOTES

INTRODUCTION / *The Need for a Political Economy of the Multinational Corporation*

1. Susan Strange, *Sterling and British Policy* (London: Oxford University Press, 1971), pp. 2–3.

2. In classical usage, the term "political economy" referred to the proper management of the national economy. This, however, is not the focus of the current revival of interest in political economy; rather, contemporary writers tend to mean one of two things by the term. One is the application of economic models to an understanding of political phenomena: voting, bureaucracy, the arms race, etc. For an excellent presentation of this conception of political economy, see William Mitchell, "The Shape of Political Theory to Come: From Political Sociology to Political Economy," in *Politics and Social Sciences*, ed. Seymour Lipset (New York: Oxford University Press, 1969).

The other conception of political economy is the interaction of economics and politics. What, for example, is the relationship of the international economic system (including trade, monetary affairs, and investment) to the international political system? The present book falls within this latter meaning of "political economy."

3. For an excellent study which takes the orthodox liberal position, see Raymond Vernon, *Sovereignty at Bay* (New York: Basic Books, 1971). For the Marxist view, see Harry Magdoff, *The Age of Imperialism* (New York: Monthly Review Press, 1969).

4. Mira Wilkins, *The Emergence of Multinational Enterprise: American Business Abroad from the Colonial Era to 1914* (Cambridge: Harvard University Press, 1970), p. 201.

5. U.S. Congress, Senate, Committee on Finance, *Implications of Multinational Firms for World Trade and Investment and for U.S. Trade and Labor*, 93rd Congress, 1st. sess., February 1973, p. 20.

6. Although foreign direct investment and the multinational corporation may be distinguished from one another, I shall use the terms interchangeably, unless otherwise indicated.

7. (Some 40 percent of British foreign investment was in railroads.) A. R. Hall, ed., *The Export of Capital from Britain, 1870–1914* (London: Methuen, 1968), p. vii.

8. In a sense, foreign direct investment by American corporations is partially a response to the cessation of mass migration into the United States and the consequent rise in real wages. The European pattern since World War II has been to import Mediterranean labor, but without conferring the right of citizenship.

9. Kari Levitt, *Silent Surrender: The American Economic Empire in Canada* (New York: Liveright Press, 1970).

10. The history of American overseas investment before the war is treated in Wilkins, *Emergence of the Multinational Enterprise*.

11. Judd Polk, "The Rise of the World Corporations," *Saturday Review*, November 22, 1969, p. 32; see also U.S. Department of Commerce, "Aspects of International Investment, *Survey of Current Business* 54 (August 1974): 5.

12. The source of these statistics is U.S. Congress, *Implications for World Trade*, p. 97.

13. John Fayerweather, "The Internationalization of Business," *Annals of the American Academy of Political and Social Science* 403 (September 1972): 2.

I / *The Nature of Political Economy*

1. Kari Levitt, "The Hinterland Economy," *Canadian Forum* 50 (July–August 1970): 163.

2. George W. Ball, "The Promise of the Multinational Corporation," *Fortune*, June 1, 1967, p. 80.

3. Sidney Rolfe, "Updating Adam Smith," *Interplay* (November 1968): 15.

4. Charles Kindleberger, *Power and Money: The Economics of International Politics and the Politics of International Economics* (New York: Basic Books, 1970), p. 5.

5. Robert Keohane and Joseph Nye, "World Politics and the International Economic System," in *The Future of the International Economic Order: An Agenda for Research*, ed. C. Fred Bergsten (Lexington, Mass.: D. C. Heath, 1973), p. 116.

6. Ibid.

7. Ibid., p. 117.

8. Paul Samuelson, *Economics: An Introductory Analysis* (New York: McGraw-Hill, 1967), p. 5.

9. Harold Lasswell and Abraham Kaplan, *Power and Society: A Framework for Political Inquiry* (New Haven: Yale University Press, 1950), p. 75.

10. Hans Morgenthau, *Politics Among Nations* (New York: Alfred A. Knopf), p. 26. For a more complex but essentially identical view, see Robert Dahl, *Modern Political Analysis* (Englewood Cliffs, N.J.: Prentice-Hall, 1963).

11. Kindleberger, *Power and Money*, p. 227.

12. For Johnson's critique of economic nationalism, see Harry Johnson, ed., *Economic Nationalism in Old and New States* (Chicago: University of Chicago Press, 1967).

13. Adam Smith, *The Wealth of Nations* (New York: Modern Library, 1937).

14. J. B. Condliffe, *The Commerce of Nations* (New York: W. W. Norton, 1950), p. 136.

15. Amitai Etzioni, "The Dialectics of Supernational Unification" in *International Political Communities* (New York: Doubleday, 1966), p. 147.

16. The relevant sections appear in Ernst Wangerman, ed., *The Role of Force in History: A Study of Bismarck's Policy of Blood and Iron*, trans. Jack Cohen (New York: International Publishers, 1968).

17. Ibid., p. 12.

18. Ibid., p. 13.

19. Ibid., p. 14.

20. Gustav Stopler, *The German Economy* (New York: Harcourt, Brace and World, 1967), p. 11.

21. Jacob Viner, *The Customs Union Issue*, Studies in the Administration of International Law and Organization, no. 10 (New York: Carnegie Endowment for International Peace, 1950), pp. 98–99.

22. Ibid., p. 101.

23. Richard Cooper, "Eurodollars, Reserve Dollars, and Asymmetrics in the International Monetary System," *Journal of International Economics* 2 (September 1972): 325–44.

24. Oskar Morgenstern, "Thirteen Critical Points in Contemporary Economic Theory: An Interpretation," *Journal of Economic Literature* 10 (December 1972): 1169.

25. Quoted in F. H. Hinsley, *Power and the Pursuit of Peace* (Cambridge: Cambridge University Press, 1963), pp. 50–51.

26. Jacob Viner, "Power versus Plenty as Objectives of Foreign Policy in the Seventeenth and Eighteenth Centuries," in *The Long View and the Short: Studies in Economic Theory and Practice* (Glencoe, Ill.: The Free Press, 1958), p. 286.

27. R. G. Hawtrey, *Economic Aspects of Sovereignty* (London: Longmans, Green, 1952), p. 120.

28. Albert Hirschman, *National Power and the Structure of Foreign Trade* (Berkeley: University of California Press, 1969), p. 16.

29. John A. Hobson, *Imperialism: A Study* (1902; 3d ed., rev., London: G. Allen and Unwin, 1938), p. 57.

30. Charles Kindleberger, *The World in Depression 1929–1939* (Berkeley: University of California Press, 1973), p. 293.

31. François Perroux, "The Domination Effect and Modern Economic Theory," in *Power in Economics*, ed. K. W. Rothschild (London: Penguin, 1971), p. 67.

32. E. H. Carr, *The Twenty Years' Crisis, 1919–1939* (New York: Macmillan, 1951), p. 117.

33. Quoted in Kari Levitt, *Silent Surrender: The American Economic Empire in Canada* (New York: Liveright Press, 1970), p. 100.

34. Eugene Staley, *World Economy in Transition: Technology vs. Politics, Laissez Faire vs. Planning, Power vs. Welfare* (New York: Council on Foreign Relations [under the auspices of the American Coordinating Committee for International Studies], 1939), pp. 51–52.

35. Ibid., p. 52.

II / The Political Economy of Foreign Investment

1. R. W. Walbank, *The Awful Revolution: The Decline of the Roman Empire in the West* (Liverpool: Liverpool University Press, 1969), p. 47.

2. The extensive use of the core–periphery model by "radical" writers has given it a pejorative connotation to many more orthodox scholars. This is unfortunate, because the core–periphery distinction has a "respectable" lineage. I believe the first person to use it was the distinguished Canadian economic historian Harold Innis, in his staple theory of growth. See, in particular, his *The Fur Trade in Canada: An Introduction to Canadian Economic History* (New Haven: Yale University Press, 1930). The core–periphery model is also the central organizing concept in Gerald Meier and Robert Baldwin's standard text on economic development. See their *Economic Development* (New York: John Wiley, 1963).

3. See François Perroux, *L'économie du XXeme siècle* (Paris: Presses Universitaires de France, 1969), part 2.

4. Meier and Baldwin, *Economic Development*.

5. Mancur Olson, Jr., "Rapid Growth as a Destabilizing Force," *Journal of Economic History* 23 (December 1963): 529–52.

6. François Perroux, "Note sur la notion de 'pole de croissance': Matériaux pour une analyse de la croissance économique," *Cahiers de l'Institut de Science Economique Appliquée*, Series D 8 (1955): 309.

7. Albert Hirschman, *The Strategy of Economic Development* (New Haven: Yale University Press, 1959), pp. 183–87; Gunnar Myrdal, *Economic Theory and Underdeveloped Regions* (New York: Harper & Row; 1971), pp. 23–39.

8. Paul Baran, *The Political Economy of Growth* (New York: Monthly Review Press, 1957).

9. Douglass C. North and Robert Thomas, *The Rise of the Western World: A New Economic History* (Cambridge: Cambridge University Press, 1973).

10. W. Arthur Lewis, *Theory of Economic Growth* (New York: Harper & Row, 1965), p. 353.

11. Hirschman, *Strategy of Economic Development*, p. 187.

12. John Friedman, *Regional Development Policy: A Case Study of Venezuela* (Cambridge: Massachusetts Institute of Technology Press, 1966), pp. 12–13.

13. R. G. Hawtrey, *Economic Aspects of Sovereignty* (London: Longmans, Green, 1952), p. 70.

14. See Harry Johnson, *Economic Policies Toward Less Developed Countries* (Washington: The Brookings Institution, 1967).

15. Charles Kindleberger, *International Economics,* 3d ed. (Homewood, Ill.: Richard D. Irwin), pp. 458–59.

16. For an excellent analysis of the concept and the relevant literature, see Benjamin Cohen, *The Question of Imperialism: The Political Economy of Dominance and Dependence* (New York: Basic Books, 1973), chap. 6.

17. Michael Polanyi, *Primitive, Archaic, and Modern Economics—Essays of Karl Polanyi,* ed. George Dalton (New York: Doubleday, 1968), p. xxc.

18. For the classical statement of the nationalist argument, see Frederich List, *National System of Political Economy,* trans. G. A. Matile (New York: W. B. Lippincott, 1856).

19. Alexander Gerschenkron, "Economic Backwardness in Historical Perspective," in *The Progress of Underdeveloped Areas,* ed. Bert Hoselitz (Chicago: University of Chicago Press, 1952), pp. 27–29.

20. Ibid.

21. Thorstein Veblen, *Imperial Germany and the Industrial Revolution* (New York: Macmillan, 1915).

22. *Capitalism, Socialism, and Democracy* (New York: Harper & Row, 1962), pp. 81–87. For a systemic analysis of Schumpeter's thesis, see Richard Clemence and Francis Doody, *The Schumpeterian System* (Cambridge: Addison-Wesley Press, 1950), chap. 8. The Schumpeterian model is used by Alvin Hansen in *Business Cycles and National Income* (New York: W. W. Norton, 1951), esp. chap. 5.

23. For an analysis of this law, see Jacob Schmookler, *Patents, Invention, and Economic Change,* ed. Zvi Griliches and Leonid Hurwitz (Cambridge: Harvard University Press, 1972), pp. 77–78.

24. See, for example, S. C. Gilfillan, *The Sociology of Invention* (Chicago: Follett, 1935), and A. P. Usher, *A History of Mechanical Investment* (Boston: Beacon Press, 1954).

25. See Thomas Kuhn *The Structure of Scientific Revolutions* (Chicago: University of Chicago Press, 1970).

26. This process has been analyzed historically by Sir John Hicks in

A *Theory of Economic History* (London: Oxford University Press, 1969).

27. Lenin, *Imperialism: The Highest Stage of Capitalism*, in *Selected Works*, vol. 1 (Moscow: Progress Publishers, 1967), p. 770.

28. For a detailed critique, see Cohen, *The Question of Imperialism*, pp. 48–57.

29. *Essay on the Production of Wealth* (London: Longmans, Hurst, Rees, Orme, and Brown, 1821), p. 288.

30. Albert Hirschman, "Effects of Industrialism on the Markets of Industrial Countries," in *The Progress of Underdeveloped Areas*, ed. Bert Hoselitz (Chicago: University of Chicago Press, 1952), pp. 270–71.

31. Meier and Baldwin, *Economic Development*, p. 260.

32. Ibid., pp. 260–62.

33. For a more detailed development of this argument, see Cohen, *The Question of Imperialism*, 75–80 and chap. 7.

III / The British Strategy of Portfolio Investment

1. John Seeley, *Expansion of England* (1883; reprint ed., London: Macmillan, 1925).

2. Eli Heckscher, *The Continental System: An Economic Interpretation* (Oxford: Clarendon Press, 1922), chap. 2.

3. Quoted in Harold and Margaret Sprout, *Toward a New Order of Sea Power* (Princeton: Princeton University Press, 1946), p. 15.

4. Harold and Margaret Sprout, "The Dilemma of Rising Demands and Insufficient Resources," *World Politics* 20 (July 1968): 660–93.

5. Susan Strange, *Sterling and British Power* (London: Oxford University Press, 1971), p. 46.

6. Stanley Jevons, *The Coal Question* (London: Macmillan, 1906), p. 411.

7. John Gallagher and Ronald Robinson, "The Imperialism of Free Trade," *The Economic History Review*, 2d series 6 (August 1953): 1–15.

8. Simon Kuznets *Modern Economic Growth* (New Haven: Yale University Press, 1966), p. 335.

9. J. B. Condliffe, *The Commerce of Nations* (New York: W. W. Norton, 1950), p. 219.

10. Gerald Meier and Robert Baldwin, *Economic Development: Theory, History, Policy* (New York: John Wiley, 1957), p. 207.

11. Ibid.

12. For the character of this investment, see, C. K. Hobson, *The Export of Capital* (London: Constable, 1914).

13. For details, see A. K. Cairncross, *Home and Foreign Investment, 1870–1913* (Cambridge: Cambridge University Press, 1953), p. 2.

14. Ibid., pp. 3, 23.

15. Ibid., pp. 226–30.

16. John Stuart Mill, *Principles of Political Economy* (1848; reprint ed., London: Penguin, 1970), p. 88. Subsequent economists postulated that the

final stage in the evolution of an economy was that of "mature creditor." See, for example, F. W. Taussig, *International Trade* (New York: Macmillan, 1929).

17. For an excellent treatment of this subject, see, Benjamin J. Cohen, *The Question of Imperialism: The Political Economy of Dominance and Dependence* (New York: Basic Books, 1973), pp. 36–39.

18. Ibid.

19. See E. H. Phelps Brown, S. J. Handfield-Jones, and D. J. Coppock, "The 'Climacteric' in the British Economy of the Late Nineteenth Century: Two Interpretations," in *The Experience of Economic Growth*, ed. Barry E. Supple (New York: Random House, 1963), pp. 203–25.

20. Ibid. See also Walther Hoffmann, *British Industry, 1700–1950* (Oxford: Basil Blackwell, 1955).

21. R. C. K. Ensor, *England, 1870–1914* (Oxford: Clarendon Press, 1936), p. 503.

22. Meier and Baldwin, *Economic Development*, p. 259.

23. Ibid., p. 258.

24. E. J. Hobsbawm, *Industry and Empire* (London: Penguin, 1969), pp. 146–47.

25. Hobson, *The Export of Capital*, p. 7.

26. Meier and Baldwin, *Economic Development*, p. 259.

27. Ibid., p. 258.

28. W. H. B. Court, *A Concise Economic History of Great Britain: From 1750 to Recent Times* (Cambridge: Cambridge University Press, 1954), pp. 218–23.

29. *The Stages of Economic Growth* (Cambridge: Cambridge University Press, 1961), pp. 68–76.

30. Richard Pares, "The Economic Factors in the History of Empires," *The Economic History Review* 7 (May 1937): p. 143.

31. Sidney Pollard and David Crossley, *The Wealth of Britain, 1085–1966* (London: B. T. Batsford, 1968), p. 233.

32. Harold and Margaret Sprout, *Toward a New Order*, pp. 660–93.

33. See Colin Clark, *The Conditions of Economic Progress* (London: Macmillan, 1957).

34. Pollard and Crossley, *The Wealth of Britain*, p. 230.

35. Ibid., p. 226.

36. Ibid., p. 228.

37. For a more detailed treatment, see Brown, Handfield-Jones, and Coppock, "The 'Climacteric' in the British Economy."

38. G. R. Searle, *The Quest for National Efficiency: A Study in British Policy and Political Thought, 1899–1914* (Berkeley: University of California Press, 1971).

39. See Michael B. Brown, *After Imperialism* (New York: Humanities Press, 1963); and Bernard Semmel, *Imperialism and Social Reform* (Cambridge: Harvard University Press, 1960).

40. Pollard and Crossley, *The Wealth of Britain,* p. 228.

41. Cairncross, *Home and Foreign Investment.*

42. For the development of this thesis, see Correlli Barnett, *The Collapse of British Power* (London: Eyre Methuen, 1972).

43. This was certainly the opinion of England's great economist of the time, Alfred Marshall, in his penetrating analysis of Britain's relative decline. Sec. L of *Memorandum on Fiscal Policy of International Trade,* completed August 1903, published as House of Commons no. 321, November 1908.

44. John Strachey, *The End of Empire* (New York: Praeger, 1964). See also Louis Zimmerman and F. Grumbach, "Saving, Investment, and Imperialism," *Weltwirtschafliche Archiv* 71 (1953): 1–19.

45. Herbert Feis, *Europe: The World's Banker, 1870–1914* (New York: A. M. Kelley, 1964), p. 87.

46. John Hobson, *Imperialism: A Study* (1902; reprint ed., Ann Arbor: University of Michigan Press, 1965), p. 308.

IV / *The Political Order of American Direct Investment*

1. This is the thesis of Charles Kindleberger, as presented in *The World in Depression, 1929–1939* (Berkeley: University of California Press, 1973).

2. Heinz Arndt, *The Economic Lessons of the Nineteen-Thirties* (London: Oxford University Press, 1944). See also J. B. Condliffe, *The Commerce of Nations* (New York: W. W. Norton, 1950), pp. 699–700.

3. The best statement of this argument is in Joyce and Gabriel Kolko, *The Limits of Power: The World and United States Foreign Policy, 1945–1954* (New York: Harper & Row, 1972).

4. For this history, see Richard Gardner, *Sterling–Dollar Diplomacy: Anglo–American Collaboration in the Reconstruction of Multilateral Trade* (Oxford: Clarendon Press, 1956). Gardner might more appropriately have referred to "conflict" rather than "collaboration."

5. For the development of this theme, see Robert Tucker, *The Radical Left and American Foreign Policy* (Baltimore: Johns Hopkins University Press, 1971).

6. For an excellent analysis of America's liberal ideology, see Felix Gilbert, *To the Farewell Address: Ideas of Early American Foreign Policy* (Princeton: Princeton University Press, 1961).

7. This was foreseen by Nicholas Spykman in *The Geography of the Peace* (New York: Harcourt, Brace, 1944).

8. The consequences of the failure to reintegrate Germany into the world economy after World War I provided, of course, the theme of J. M. Keynes' *The Economic Consequences of the Peace* (New York: Harcourt, Brace and Howe, 1920).

9. See Jacob Viner, *The Customs Union Issue* (New York: The Carnegie Endowment for International Peace, 1950).

10. These contrasting views are analyzed by Gardner Patterson in *Discrimination in International Trade: The Policy Issues, 1945–1965* (Princeton: Princeton University Press, 1966).

11. Ibid., pp. 82–97.

12. Robert Triffin, "Economic Integration," *World Politics* 6 (July 1954): 526–37. See also Fredrick Dunn, *Peacemaking and the Settlement With Japan* (Princeton: Princeton University Press, 1963).

13. For a Japanese view of this relationship, see Morinosuke Kojima, *Modern Japan's Foreign Policy* (Brattleboro, Vt.: Charles Tuttle Co., 1969).

V / The American Strategy of Direct Investment: Why the Multinational Corporation?

1. For a nearly forgotten but excellent study of this struggle, see Benjamin Williams, *Foreign Economic Policy of the United States* (New York: McGraw-Hill, 1929).

2. The President's Materials Policy Commission, *Resources for Freedom* (Washington, D.C.: Government Printing Office, June 1952), 5 vols.

3. Hymer's first and most comprehensive statement of this thesis was his doctoral dissertation in economics at the Massachusetts Institute of Technology, "The International Operations of National Firms: A Study of Direct Foreign Investment" (mimeographed, 1960). For Kindleberger's view, see *American Business Abroad: Six Lectures on Direct Investment* (New Haven: Yale University Press, 1969).

4. The best statement of Vernon's thinking is *Sovereignty at Bay* (New York: Basic Books, 1971).

5. William Gruber, Dileep Mehta, and Raymond Vernon, "The R and D Factor in International Trade and International Investment of United States Industries," *The Journal of Political Economy* 75 (February 1967): 30–31.

6. Harry Johnson, "The Efficiency and Welfare Implications of the International Corporation," in *The International Corporation*, ed. Charles Kindleberger (Cambridge: Massachusetts Institute of Technology Press, 1970), pp. 35–56.

7. For the example of food processing, see Thomas Horst, *At Home Abroad* (Cambridge, Mass.: Ballinger, 1974).

8. Judd Polk et al., *U.S. Production Abroad and the Balance of Payments* (New York: National Industrial Conference Board, 1966).

9. "International Investment and International Trade in the Product Cycle," *Quarterly Journal of Economics* 80 (May 1966): 200.

10. Kindleberger, *American Business Abroad*, p. 9.

11. Robert Aliber, "A Theory of Direct Investment," in *The International Corporation*, C. Kindleberger, p. 20.

12. *The International Money Game* (New York: Basic Books, 1973), pp. 187–88.

13. Ibid.

14. See, for example, Peter Kenen, "Economic Aspects of Private Direct Investment," in *Taxation and Operations Abroad* (Princeton: Tax Institute of America, 1960), pp. 102–115; and Peggy Musgrave, *United States Taxation of Foreign Investment Income* (Cambridge: The Law School of Harvard University, 1969).

15. Musgrave, *United States Taxation*, p. 109. For a more detailed examination of the tax issue, see Robert Gilpin *The Multinational Corporation and the National Interest*, U.S. Congress, Senate, Committee on Labor and Public Welfare, 93d Cong., 1st sess., October 1973.

16. For the development of this argument, see National Foreign Trade Council, "The Implications of Proposed Changes in the Taxation of U.S. Investments Abroad" (Washington, D.C., 1972).

17. Musgrave, *United States Taxation*, pp. 83–86.

18. Edith Penrose, *The Large International Firm in Developing Countries* (London: G. Allen and Unwin, 1969), p. 29.

19. Musgrave, *United States Taxation*, pp. 71–96.

20. "International Corporations: The Industrial Economics of Foreign Investment," *Economica*, new series, 38 (February 1971). See also Theodore Moran, "Foreign Expansion as an Institutional Necessity for U.S. Corporate Capitalism: The Search for a Radical Model," *World Politics* 25 (April 1973): 369–86.

21. See H. Igor Ansoff, *Corporate Strategy* (New York: McGraw-Hill, 1965).

22. Peter Drucker, *The Age of Discontinuity* (New York: Harper & Row, 1969), p. 63.

23. For a similar analysis, see David Calleo and Benjamin Rowland, *America and the World Political Economy: Atlantic Dreams and National Realities* (Bloomington: Indiana University Press, 1973), chap. 7.

24. Quoted in Richard Barnet and Ronald Müller, *Global Reach: The Power of the Multinational Corporations* (New York: Simon and Schuster, 1974), p. 16.

25. This is essentially the argument of Barnet and Müller, ibid.

VI / *Corporate Expansionism and American Hegemony*

1. An excellent discussion of this change is provided by J. B. Condliffe in *The Commerce of Nations* (New York: W. W. Norton, 1950), pp. 687–93.

2. For a detailed account of U.S. policy measures designed to encourage foreign investment, see Commission on International Trade and Investment,

U.S. International Economic Policy in an Interdependent World (Washington, D.C.: Government Printing Office, July 1971).

3. This, of course, is the thesis of Raymond Vernon, as articulated in *Sovereignty at Bay* (New York: Basic Books, 1971), especially pp. 213–17.

4. Harry Magdoff, *The Age of Imperialism* (New York: Monthly Review Press, 1969); Paul Baran and Paul Sweezy, *Monopoly Capitalism* (Baltimore: Penguin, 1966). For a non-Marxist but related thesis, see Richard Barnet, *Roots of War* (Baltimore: Penguin, 1972), chap. 6.

5. Theodore Moran, "Foreign Expansion as an 'Institutional Necessity' for U.S. Corporate Capitalism: The Search for a Radical Model," *World Politics* 25 (April 1973): 369–86.

6. An excellent examination of the relationship between business and foreign economic policy is Raymond A. Bauer, Ithiel de Sola Pool, and Lewis A. Dexter, *American Business and Public Policy: The Politics of Foreign Trade* (New York: Atherton Press, 1963); see also Stephen Krasner, "Business Government Relations: The Case of the International Coffee Agreement," *International Organization* 27 (August 1973): 495–516.

7. Kari Levitt, *Silent Surrender: The American Economic Empire in Canada* (New York: Liveright, 1970), pp. 23–24.

8. Benjamin H. Williams, *Economic Foreign Policy of the United States* (New York: McGraw-Hill, 1929).

9. For the British case, see D. C. M. Platt, *Finance, Trade, and Politics in British Foreign Policy, 1815–1914* (Oxford: Clarendon Press, 1968).

10. For the case of Chile, see Anthony Sampson, *The Sovereign State of ITT* (New York: Stein and Day, 1973).

11. Jacob Viner, "Political Aspects of International Finance," *The Journal of Business of the University of Chicago* 1 (April 1928): 170.

12. Council of the Americas, *Recommendations on U.S. Foreign Economic Policy Toward Latin America* (New York, November 1, 1973), p. 1. For an excellent treatment of this general subject, see Theodore Moran, *Multinational Corporations and the Politics of Dependence: Copper in Chile, 1945–1973* (Princeton: Princeton University Press, 1975); and also C. Fred Bergsten and Theodore Moran, "U.S. National Security and the Impact of Multinational Corporations" (mimeographed, June 1974).

13. Harold and Margaret Sprout, "National Priorities: Demand, Resources, Dilemmas," *World Politics* 24 (January 1972): 311–12.

14. The Soviet Union, on the other hand, has been generally free of this balance-of-payments problem. The bulk of Soviet military forces have remained within the Soviet Union proper, and foreign aid has been in the form of goods or military equipment. But where the Soviet Union has stationed large military contingents outside the country as in Eastern Europe, it has created a monetary and payments system to support this extension of power. By creating the ruble bloc, manipulating the value of the ruble, and keeping the ruble inconvertible, the Russians have forced the East Europeans to finance their military presence in Eastern Europe.

Thus, the extent of Russian influence has been largely determined by the scope of their military rather than their economic power.

15. Benjamin J. Cohen, "U.S. Foreign Economic Policy," *Orbis* 15 (Spring 1971): 235.

16. Benjamin J. Cohen, "The Revolution in Atlantic Economic Relations: A Bargain Comes Unstuck," in *The United States and Western Europe,* ed. W. F. Hanreider (Cambridge, Mass.: Winthrop Publishers, 1974), p. 118. See also Henry Aubrey, "Behind the Veil of International Money," in *Essays in International Finance,* no. 71 (Princeton, Princeton University, 1969).

17. James Ingram, *International Economic Problems* (New York: John Wiley, 1970), p. 158.

18. Christopher Tugendhat, *The Multinationals* (London: Eyre and Spottiswoode, 1971), p. 151.

19. U.S. Council on International Economic Policy, *The United States in the Changing World Economy: A Report to the President,* vol. 1: *A Foreign Economic Perspective* (The Peterson Report) (Washington, D.C.: Government Printing Office, 1971), p. 36.

20. Susan Foster, "Impact of Direct Investment Abroad by United States Multinational Companies on the Balance of Payments," Federal Reserve Bank of New York, *Monthly Review,* July 1972, p. 170.

21. *The Financial Times* (London), March 25, 1970.

22. Quoted in Levitt, *Silent Surrender,* p. 100.

VII / *The Multinational Corporation and the American Economy: Costs and Benefits*

1. Lawrence Krause. "Why Exports are Becoming Irrelevant," *Foreign Policy,* no. 3 (Summer 1971): 62.

2. U. S. Department of Labor, Bureau of Labor Statistics, *The U. S. Economy in 1980,* Bulletin no. 1673 (Washington, D.C.: Government Printing Office, August, 1970).

3. Krause, "Why Exports are Becoming Irrelevant," pp. 62–63.

4. U. S. Congress, Senate, Committee on Labor and Public Welfare, *The Multinational Corporation and the National Interest,* 93d Cong., 1st sess., 1973.

5. Peggy Musgrave, *United States Taxation of Foreign Investment Income* (Cambridge: The Law School of Harvard University, 1969); and J. M. Keynes, "Foreign Investment and National Advantages," *The Nation and the Atheneum* 35 (August 9, 1924): 586.

6. For an analysis of these studies, see my Senate report cited in note 4 above.

7. "International Political Theory from Outside," in *Theoretical Aspects of International Relations,* ed. William T. R. Fox (Notre Dame: University of Notre Dame Press, 1959), p. 69.

8. Robert Stobaugh, "How Investment Abroad Creates Jobs at Home," *Harvard Business Review* 50 (September–October 1972): 118–20. Gus Tyler has responded to the argument by pointing out that business figures for growth in MNC employment do not exclude "new" employment due to acquisitions. See "Labor's Multinational Pains," *Foreign Policy*, no. 12 (Fall 1973): 127.

9. National Foreign Trade Council, "The Implications of Proposed Changes in Taxation of U.S. Investments Abroad" (New York, 1972).

10. Ibid., p. 5.

11. For the viewpoint of organized labor, see Nathaniel Goldfinger, "We're Undermining Our Industrial Base," *Congressional Record*, 92d Congress, 2d sess., August 16, 1972, H7774–H7775.

12. Peggy Musgrave, "Tax Preferences to Foreign Investment," U.S., Congress, Joint Economic Committee, *The Economics of Federal Subsidy Programs*, part 2: *International Subsidies* (Washington, D.C.: Government Printing Office, 1972).

13. Raymond Vernon, *Sovereignty at Bay* (New York: Basic Books, 1971), p. 166.

14. Judd Polk, "The Rise of World Corporations," *Saturday Review*, November 22, 1969, p. 32.

15. Thomas Horst, "The Impact of U.S. Investment on U.S. Foreign Trade," mimeographed (Washington, D.C., The Brookings Institution, January, 1974).

16. Christopher Tugendhat, *The Multinationals* (London: Eyre and Spottiswoods, 1971), p. 151.

17. Musgrave, "Tax Preferences to Foreign Investments," p. 177.

18. G. Hufbauer and F. Adler, *Overseas Manufacturing Investment and the Balance of Payments*, Tax Policy Research Study no. 1 (Washington, D.C., U.S. Treasury Department, 1968); W. Reddaway et al., *Effects of U.K. Direct Investment Overseas: An Interim Report* (Cambridge: Cambridge University Press, 1967); Musgrave, *United States Taxation*, pp. 44–48.

19. For the Latin American situation, see Vernon, *Sovereignty at Bay*, p. 102; for Europe, see John Dunning, "European and U.S. Trade Patterns: U.S. Foreign Investment and the Technology Gap," in *North American and Western European Economic Policies* (New York: Macmillan, 1971), p. 35.

20. Elinor Yudin, "American Abroad: A Transfer of Capital," in *The Open Economy: Essays on International Trade and Finance*, ed. Peter Kenen and Roger Lawrence (New York: Columbia University Press, 1968).

21. Musgrave, "Tax Preferences to Foreign Investment," p. 177.

22. Ibid., p. 214.

23. Ibid., p. 177.

24. Peggy Musgrave, "Statement to House Ways and Means Committee," (mimeographed), 93d Congress, 1st sess., February 28, 1973.

25. Musgrave, *United States Taxation*, p. 32.

26. Robert Aliber, *The International Money Game* (New York: Basic Books, 1973), p. 183.

27. Robert Keohane and Van Doorn Ooms, "The Multinational Enterprise and World Political Economy," *International Organization* 26 (Winter 1972): 100–101.

28. Vernon, *Sovereignty at Bay*, p. 186.

29. Emergency Committee for American Trade, *The Role of the Multinational Corporation in the United States and World Economies* (Washington, D.C., February 24, 1972).

30. U.S. Tariff Commission, "Implications of Multinational Firms for World Trade and Investment and for U.S. Trade and Labor," report prepared for U.S., Congress, Senate, Committee on Finance, 93d Congress, 1st sess., 1973.

31. Musgrave, "Tax Preferences to Foreign Investment."

32. Marvin Frankel, "Home Versus Foreign Investment: A Case Against Capital Exports," *Kylos* 18 (March 1965): 432.

33. Yudin, "American Abroad."

34. Lawrence Krause and K. W. Dam, *Federal Tax Treatment of Foreign Income* (Washington, D.C.: The Brookings Institution, 1964), p. 57.

35. Murray Kemp, "Foreign Investment and the National Advantage," *Economic Record* 38 (March 1962): 56–62.

36. Charles Kindleberger, "An American Economic Climacteric?" *Challenge* 16 (January/February 1974): 35–44; see also "Making U.S. Technology More Competitive," *Business Week,* January 15, 1972, p. 45.

37. Kindleberger, "An American Economic Climateric?" p. 41; Terutomo Ozawa, *Japan's Technological Challenge to the West, 1950–1974: Motivation and Accomplishment* (Cambridge: Massachusetts Institute of Technology Press, 1974), pp. 111–126.

38. For an analysis of this debate, see Philip Boffey, "Technology and World Trade: Is There Cause for Alarm?" *Science,* April 2, 1971, pp. 37–41.

39. See, for example, William D. Nordhaus, "The Recent Productivity Slowdown," in *Brookings Papers on Economic Activity,* no. 3 (Washington, D.C.: The Brookings Institute, 1972), pp. 493–531.

40. An excellent detailed analysis has been provided by William H. Branson and Helen B. Junz in "Trends in U.S. Trade and Comparative Advantages," in *Brookings Papers on Economic Activity,* 1971, no. 2, pp. 285–345.

VIII / *An Alternative Strategy to Foreign Investment*

1. U.S. Department of Commerce, Bureau of Economic Analysis, *Survey of Current Business* 54 (March 1974): 44.

2. John M. Keynes, "Foreign Investment and National Interest," *The Nation and the Atheneum* 35 (August 9, 1924): 586.

3. *New York Times*, March 5, 1972.

4. Peggy Musgrave, "Tax Preferences to Foreign Investment," U.S. Congress, Joint Economic Committee, *The Economics of Federal Subsidy Programs*, part 2: *International Subsidies* (Washington, D.C.: Government Printing Office, 1972).

5. This is the conclusion of Eugene Staley, based on an examination of the historical record. See his *War and the Private Investor* (New York: Doubleday, Doran, 1935).

6. C. Fred Bergsten, "Crisis in U.S. Trade," *Foreign Affairs* 49 (July 1971): 625.

7. Paul Samuelson, "International Trade for a Rich Country," *The Morgan Guarantee Survey*, July 1972, pp. 10–11.

8. See Albert O. Hirschman, "How to Divest Latin America, and Why," in *Essays in International Finance*, no. 76 (Princeton: Princeton University, November, 1969).

9. C. Fred Bergsten, "Coming Investment Wars?" *Foreign Affairs* 53 (October 1974): 135–52.

10. For a critical examination of this subject, see Amitai Etzioni, *The Moon-Doggle: Domestic and International Implications of the Space Race* (Garden City, N.Y.: Doubleday, 1964), esp. pp. 73–74.

11. For a relevant discussion, see Robert Gilpin, "Technological Strategies and National Purposes" in *Science*, July 31, 1970, pp. 441–48.

12. E. Denison and J. P. Poulier, *Why Growth Rates Differ* (Washington, D.C.: The Brookings Institution, 1967), pp. 17–19. See also Keith Pavitt, " 'International' Technology and the U.S. Economy," in National Science Foundation, *The Effects of International Technology Transfers on the U.S. Economy* (mimeographed, October, 1973).

13. George Eads and Richard Nelson, "Government Support of Advanced Civilian Technology: Power Reactors and the Supersonic Transport," *Public Policy* 19 (Summer 1971): 405–427.

14. See Philip Boffrey, "Technology and World Trade: Is There Cause for Alarm?" *Science*, April 2, 1971, pp. 37–41.

15. Harry Johnson, "The Efficiency and Welfare Implications of the International Corporation," in *The International Corporation*, ed. Charles Kindleberger (Cambridge: Massachusetts Institute of Technology Press, 1970).

16. Joseph Schumpeter, *Capitalism, Socialism, and Democracy* (New York: Harper & Row, 1947), chap. 8.

17. Johnson, "Efficiency and Welfare Implications of the International Corporation."

18. Bertil Ohlin, *Interregional and International Trade* (Cambridge: Harvard University Press, 1933).

IX / *Three Models of the Future*

1. All capital controls were lifted on January 29, 1974.

2. Raymond Vernon, *Sovereignty at Bay* (New York: Basic Books, 1971).

3. For a discussion of these issues, see Robert O. Keohane and Joseph Nye, eds., *Transnational Relations and World Politics* (Cambridge: Harvard University Press, 1972).

4. Charles Kindleberger, *American Buisness Abroad: Six Lectures on Direct Investment* (New Haven: Yale University Press, 1969), p. 207.

5. Harry Johnson, *International Economic Questions Facing Britain, the United States, and Canada in the Seventies*, (London: British–North American Research Association, June 1970), p. 24.

6. Samuel Huntington, "Transnational Organizations in World Politics," *World Politics* 25 (April 1973): 361.

7. This dilemma is examined in Keohane and Nye, eds., *Transnational Relations and World Politics*.

8. For an excellent discussion of this subject, see Richard Cooper, *The Economics of Interdependence* (New York: McGraw-Hill, 1968).

9. Hans Morgenthau, "Western Values and Total War," *Commentary* 32 (October 1961): 280.

10. Quoted in John Sterba, "Japanese Buisnessmen: The Yen is Mightier than the Sword," *New York Times Magazine,* October 29, 1972, p. 58.

11. John Diebold, "Multinational Corporations—Why Be Scared of Them?" *Foreign Policy*, no. 12 (Fall 1973), pp. 79–95.

12. Norman Macrae, "The Future of International Business," *The Economist* 36 (January 22, 1972): v–xxxvi.

13. Diebold, "Multinational Corporations," p. 87.

14. The literature on *dependencia* or underdevelopment has now become legend, with many Marxist and non-Marxist versions. One of the better statements of the thesis is that of Osvaldo Sunkel, "Big Business and Dependencia: A Latin American View," *Foreign Affairs* 50 (April 1972): 517–31. Another is Richard Barnett and Ronald Müller, *Global Reach: The Power of the Multinational Corporations* (New York: Simon and Schuster, 1974). For an excellent critical view of the *dependencia* thesis, see Benjamin J. Cohen, *The Question of Imperialism: The Political Economy of Dominance and Dependence* (New York: Basic Books, 1973), chap. 6.

15. Stephen Hymer, "The Multinational Corporation and the Law of Uneven Development," in *Economics and World Order—From the Nineteen Seventies to the Nineteen Nineties*, ed. Jagdish Bhagwati (New York: Macmillan, 1972), p. 113.

16. Ibid.

17. Ibid., p. 114.

18. Quoted in Cohen, *The Question of Imperialism*, pp. 190–91.

19. Paul Baran and Paul Sweezy, *Monopoly Capital: An Essay on the American Economic and Social Order* (New York: Monthly Review Press, 1966).

20. Constantine Vaitsos, "Transfer of Resources and Preservation of Monopoly Rents," Economic Development Report no. 168, mimeographed (Cambridge: Development Advisory Service, Harvard University, 1970).

21. Quoted in E. M. Winslow, *The Pattern of Imperialism* (New York: Columbia University Press, 1948), p. 158.

22. Stephen Hymer, "International Politics and International Economics: A Radical Approach" (mimeographed, 1974), p. 10.

23. See, for example, David Calleo and Benjamin Rowland, *America and the World Political Economy* (Bloomington: Indiana University Press, 1973). Although he is a Marxist, Ernest Mandel's theme is really mercantilism. See his *Europe vs. America: Contradictions of Imperialism* (New York: Monthly Review Press, 1970).

24. Helmut Schmidt, "Struggle for the World Product," *Foreign Affairs* 52 (April 1974): 437–51.

25. See Chapter II for an analysis of this subject.

26. The writer has benefited considerably from the as yet unpublished writings of Kendall Myers on this subject. Myer's manuscript entitled "Appeasement and Nazi Germany: Regional Blocs on Universalism" has been the basis of a seminar held at the Lehrman Institute (New York). See also the reflections of Simon Kuznets in *Modern Economy Growth* (New Haven: Yale University Press, 1966). The issue, of course, is fundamental to the radical and Marxist critique of capitalism.

27. Mandel, *Europe vs. America,* pp. 80–92.

28. Calleo and Rowland, *America and the World Political Economy,* pp. 251–59.

29. See the analysis of Keynes in Hymer, "International Politics and International Economics."

30. This paradox is analyzed by Eugene Staley in *World Economy in Transition* (New York: Council on Foreign Relations, 1939), chap. 6, esp. p. 15.

31. See, *The Economist* (London), February 16, 1974, p. 74.

32. For this thesis, see Huntington, "Transnational Organizations in World Politics"; and C. Fred Bergsten and Theodore H. Moran, "U.S. National Security and the Impact of Multinational Corporations" (mimeographed, July, 1974); see also Barnett and Müller, *Global Reach.*

33. See, for example, A. E. Safarian, *Foreign Ownership of Canadian Industry* (Toronto: University of Toronto Press, 1973).

34. This point is developed in my report, U.S. Congress, Senate Committee on Labor and Public Welfare, *The Multinational Corporation and the National Interest,* 93d Cong., 1st sess., 1973.

35. Karl Marx, "The Future Results of British Rule in India," in *Karl*

Marx on Colonialism and Modernization, ed. Shlomo Avineri (New York: Doubleday, 1969), p. 136.

36. Cohen, *The Question of Imperialism,* chap. 6.

37. This distinction is developed by Keith Griffin in *Underdevelopment in Spanish America* (Cambridge: Massachusetts Institute of Technology Press, 1969).

38. For a more detailed analysis of the distinction, see J. D. Gould, *Economic Growth in History* (London: Methuen, 1972), chap. 1.

39. A forceful statement of this position is Raymond Vernon's "Rogue Elephant in the Forest: An Appraisal of Transatlantic Relations," *Foreign Affairs* 52 (April 1973): 573–87.

40. See Sir John Hicks, *A Theory of Economic History* (London: Oxford University Press, 1969).

41. This is the theme of Peter Drucker's *The Age of Discontinuity* (New York: Harper & Row, 1969).

42. For an analysis of these trends, see William Branson, "International Competition and National Economic Policy" (mimeographed, March 7, 1973).

43. See, for example, Donella H. Meadows et al., *The Limits to Growth* (New York: Universe Books, 1972); and James Shuman and David Rosenau, *The Kondratieff Wave* (New York: World Publishing, 1972).

44. Harold van Buren Cleveland, "Modes of International Economic Order: A Stalemate System," mimeographed (New York: Lehrman Institute, April 29, 1975).

INDEX